HARPOON

HARPOON

INTO THE HEART OF WHALING

ANDREW DARBY

A MERLOYD LAWRENCE BOOK
LIFELONG BOOKS • DA CAPO PRESS
A Member of the Perseus Books Group

Cataloging-in-Publication data for this book is available from the Library of Congress.

First Da Capo Press edition 2008
Reprinted by arrangement with Allen & Unwin
ISBN: 978-0-306-81629-1

Published by Da Capo Press
A Member of the Perseus Books Group
www.dacapopress.com

Da Capo Press books are available at special discounts for bulk purchases in the U.S. by corporations, institutions, and other organizations. For more information, please contact the Special Markets Department at the Perseus Books Group, 2300 Chestnut Street, Suite 200, Philadelphia, PA 19103, or call (800) 255-1514, or e-mail special.markets@perseusbooks.com.

Whale illustrations by Uko Gorter
Harpoon illustrations by Guy Holt
Internal photograph by Frank Hurley, A blue whale and whaling men on the flensing or cutting up plan at the Grytviken whaling station, Prince Edward Cove, South Georgia, Schakleton expedition, 1914–1917, National Library of Australia, nla.pic-an23478495.

10 9 8 7 6 5 4 3 2 1

For Sally,
Heather and Geoff

CONTENTS

FIN

(Balaenoptera physalus)

PROLOGUE

This much we know. The first Fin whale to be harpooned in the Antarctic for 30 years was a 19-metre long male.

It was of a species facing a very high risk of extinction and it was killed to the north of Prydz Bay, eastern Antarctica, in a whale sanctuary. It was just big enough to be sexually mature, and close to the upper limit for handling on a factory ship where it was processed in the name of science.

Some of the death we can piece together. We can see the gunner standing in a slight crouch high on the open bow of the grey chaser. The deck is a-tilt on the Southern Ocean and his feet are apart for balance. His face is hidden from freezing wind blast beneath an earmuffed cap as he stares along a gunsight above the barrel of his cannon. Tracking the whale, he shifts across the deck lightly, like a boxer, swinging the cannon by its handle as he does.

The fast-moving Fin breaks the surface and the gunner squeezes a trigger that looks as harmless as a bicycle handbrake. A grenade-tipped harpoon weighing 45 kilograms blasts out of the cannon's muzzle at 113 metres per second and hits an animal that has the mass of a laden semi-trailer. As the blunt-headed weapon drives in, four steel claws are released, a fuse trips, and milliseconds later the grenade's high intensity penthrite explodes. The line trailing back from the harpoon to the ship strains, and the barbed claws pull open inside the whale, holding it fast.

We do not know why this particular Fin was chosen. We do not know how long it took to chase the whale down, nor whether it was hit with the first shot. We don't know how many harpoons were needed to kill the whale, nor how long it remained alive. Neither do we know who the gunner was, nor the name of the chaser; how difficult it was to process; where its meat was sold, when, nor for what value.

None of this information went to the organisation that rules on the life and death of whales, the International Whaling Commission (IWC). We do know this was the moment, on 3 February 2006, when the only factory fleet afloat began again to collect the whale meat favoured by some Japanese.

Most things about the Fin whale are unknown to us. They are the secrets of an open ocean whale, rarely seen off populated coasts, which lives in the shadow of the Blue as the second largest animal ever to breathe. It grows up to 27 metres long, can weigh 120 tonnes, and outpace normal ships. We don't see a Fin so much as we see where it has been. The rise and dip of its passage is marked by slick pools that linger on the surface after a high blow puffs in the distance. There went a Fin.

This scale and speed make it a hemisphere cruiser. In the north a radio-tagged Fin cantered 2095 kilometres in less than ten days. Fuel for the giant is an overriding need. A 48-tonne Fin, about the size of the 3 February animal, must eat nearly three times its weight in krill over a four-month south polar season to build up enough fat reserves for the remainder of its year.

Organising this banquet needs special skills and Fins have been observed at depth lunge-feeding, taking in tonnes of water and fish at a time. The species also has a unique physical aid: it is asymmetrical. A Fin's right side is whiter than the left, and may flash as a contrasting barrier in the water, helping to concentrate swarming prey, ready for the gulp.

In the twentieth century, the era of industrial whaling, more Fins were killed in their Southern Hemisphere stronghold than any other whale species. Nearly three quarters of a million were routed out of the far south, and the last Fins whaled were taken by Soviets in the Pacific off southern Chile in 1975–76. This is what the adventure of whaling became. Any sense of human daring was fake nostalgia. There was no equality, only the arithmetic of overwhelming mechanical force. The great hunt became the great hurt.

Attempts to heal this deep injury included enactment of the 1986 global moratorium on commercial whaling, and creation of the Southern Ocean Sanctuary for whales, where this Fin swam. Despite these changes, around 28 500 whales since 1986 had been harpooned for sale before this Fin. Whaling was not over, it was growing. Norway and Iceland were raising the number of their kills in the North Atlantic, and Japan was operating at an industrial scale in the Antarctic and North Pacific.

The Fin was Red-listed as endangered by the World Conservation Union, IUCN, but was shot under a scientific permit issued by the Japanese

Government, which fabricated a 'shift in baleen whale dominance' in the Antarctic. In the Japanese world, Humpbacks began to outrank Minkes in 1997–98, and the Fin's habitat was expanding. Minkes were thinner and maturing younger under this pressure, according to its fisheries scientists. These changes might even block recovery of Blues. To find out about this phenomenon, whalers had to begin killing Humpbacks and Fins, and oddly, many more Minkes.

Other scientists said between the lines of their critiques that this was shallow artifice, not logical method. Overall whale numbers were a small and threatened fraction of their pre-industrial whaling size. It was plain wrong just to assume that whales competed directly with each other, or that killing Minkes would help Blues. Among other things, seals and seabirds chased the same food. The implacable Japanese whalers set out to kill as many whales every two years as the rest of the world had done in 50 years of scientific whaling. The new kills would move on to Humpbacks, but their techniques would be tried out with Fins.

To reconstruct the fate of these giants it helps to look to Greenland where a few Fins are still taken in an indigenous hunt. From the Greenlanders' experience we can see how hard it might be to kill the second largest whale ever. In a recent season their exploding harpoons rendered only five of their quota of ten senseless within five minutes. One killing was a harrowing two-hour saga. The initial grenade did not explode. The large, strong, maddened animal broke the line, was chased down and harpooned again with a grenade that blew but failed to kill. Finally the Fin succumbed to a third, grenadeless, harpoon.

At least the Greenlanders *were* prepared to disclose what had happened. Japan said data on whale killing methods was used only to criticise whaling, so it would not be provided.

We do know a little about the Japanese record on Fins. When they last hunted them in the 1973–74 season it took an average of nearly six minutes to kill a Fin using a less efficient grenade. Though none of the current generation had shot one, we should expect they were trained thoroughly. Their trainer, Shogo Tanaka, was an Antarctic veteran who wrote his own little red book setting out the geometry of whale killing, with logarithmic tables and precise drawings.

To him the art of harpooning lay in adjusting for movement of the chaser ship and whale. The challenge was to anticipate where all this movement would lead in the half second it took for the harpoon to travel from cannon to target. If the gunner got it wrong, the point of aim and the point where the harpoon landed would be strangers. 'So, biggest problem is to narrow the differences between these two points,' Tanaka said. His best students memorised the tables and drawings and turned them into an instinctive response to a moving whale. He considered his protégés to be strong, adaptable, diligent and calm men. 'Most gunners are dedicated to their work,' he said. 'Once you become a gunner, you are a gunner for a very long time.'

Their weapon was a 75-millimetre calibre cannon made by Miroku Manufacturing of Kochi in southern Japan. Miroku makes shotguns and rifles for the US brands, Browning and Winchester. Its own .22 rifle was favoured by rabbit shooters in Australia, and it started making whaling cannons in 1934. Drilled and cut from a solid piece of chromium nickel steel, the 124-centimetre-long barrel of the current model was good for 10 000 shots.

The steel harpoons were also made by Miroku, I was told by Hiroshisa Shigemune, a manager of the Kyodo Senpaku whaling company, as he showed me the real thing. I was surprised to see that it did not have a sharp point but a blunt, conical head, that was cupped at the tip. This stopped the harpoon from skipping on the water's surface, Shigemune explained. I had trouble contemplating whether a conical head would be more, or less, painful as it punched into a whale. The harpoon, a big, clanking contraption, took a strong man to lift, or more likely several. Shigemune asked me to try raising one off the floor—a trap for a young player. He gave a friendly chuckle when I could barely raise the shaft, which is loosely coupled to the head.

The same yellow-painted harpoon was stacked in crates on the low foredeck of the 700-tonne chasers that were an emphatic manifestation of Japan's passion for whaling. The whalers' little navy of grey ships were of a design basically unchanged in a century, intended for wet oceanic work, and the latest would be launched only in 2007.

Rails needed to be low to the sea, where kills were lashed alongside before transfer to the factory ship using a line trailed out of its stern ramp.

The chaser also had to be watertight against some of the worst ocean swells in the world. In the centre of the hull was a long steel island of enclosed living and working space, and surmounting this was a main bridge deck below an open-air flying bridge, with a lookout 'barrel' even higher up. A catwalk ran from the main bridge to the bow for the gunner and his assistants.

An historic hierarchy remained intact. The crew took their cue from the gunner. His shot triggered a dash to the bow by others to reload and handle lines, and his hand signals were watched from the flying bridge to determine whether to pay out more line or winch it in. He was also the rifleman to finish a still-living Minke brought close to the ship.

When the time came to kill Fins, the same cannon and harpoon were used on whales at least six times bigger than Minkes. To pull off this kill an extra 20 grams of penthrite was added to the 30 grams already in the grenade, and the gunners needed all of Tanaka's accuracy, otherwise they would have to use the cannon again to complete the kill. And then, possibly, again.

A Norwegian vet who specialises in whale killing methods, Egil Ole Øen, assured me he had seen a 22.4-metre Fin killed instantly with 22 grams of penthrite. 'He was hit here,' Øen said, holding a finger up to his neck and pointing at his brain. 'He did not move any more. It was a very good shot. It's not the body mass itself. It's the placement of the detonation.'

Before Japan stopped disclosing them, its records showed that in the Antarctic in 2004–05, its whalers killed fewer than half of their Minkes instantly, and the record was worse in the North Pacific for the larger Sei whales, also an endangered species. Most took several minutes to die. In the Southern Ocean the whalers were more likely to encounter difficult seas, and Tanaka's protégés were dealing with a whale species they had never killed before.

We may never know, but on balance the death of the first Fin taken in a generation was likely to have been prolonged. It was followed up the stern ramp of the factory ship *Nisshin Maru* by nine more, harpooned close to the ice edge south-west of Australia during February and March of 2006. The largest of these was a 61.5-tonne female; two others were pregnant.

They made a total of 268.9 tonnes of meat for a Japanese market where Fin was once a favoured food.

Shogo Tanaka was not the kind of man to rave about food, but he did believe Fin tasted best. 'I like it because I like it,' he said. 'The tail resembles high class beef, with a high proportion of fat. It has the finest meat texture, followed by the Blue or Humpback.' He asked me to understand that the Japanese vitally depended on marine resources for food.

Hiroshisa Shigemune, the whaling company manager, also had a question: 'Do Australians see us as merciless?'

I said they did.

There was quiet, and then Tanaka sighed.

INTRODUCTION

We have an insistent need to take our measure in the world from other living things. Whales seem to me as good a way as any to do this. They have always been out there. At first regarded as monstrous—until they became useable. Then exploited and nearly annihilated. Now argued over, reappraised, even loved. Still and always larger than us. No matter how much we exceed them mechanically, they remain the greatest physical expressions of individual animal scale and power that we know. Our lives with them tell us much about the role we have chosen for ourselves on earth and its consequences, intended or not.

This book was written on the island of Tasmania, Australia, at the edge of whales' most successful domain: the Southern Ocean. There, in its vastness, the ancestors of modern Cetaceans flourished in the absence of predatory marine reptiles and the presence of abundant food. Through evolutionary epochs they divided into two great lineages—the toothed and the baleen filter feeders—and spread through all the oceans.

They were long hunted in the far north for food, then from the sixteenth century for European and Japanese industry. Whales swam unmolested in most oceans until their riches were realized by the steely fortune hunters exemplified by nineteenth-century American whalers. No attention was paid to them in the Antarctic until an evolutionary minute ago.

In the twentieth century, this domain for millions of whales was reduced to a hiding place for frightened fractions of them. There was often no good purpose to their slaughter. The harpoon did not guarantee a quick or painless death. The indispensable uses of whale oil for lighting a family home, or oiling the industrial revolution, rapidly passed. Useable parts of whales were repeatedly exceeded by wasted parts.

The control of whaling became what it remains today: a struggle between the best and worst of human nature. Great hopes, held out when the International Whaling Commission was founded, were gradually crushed. Rules offered in optimism, in practice, encouraged cheating. The abuse was most flagrant in the far south. Poor regulations at first encouraged excessive kills and, when tightened, were treacherously ignored by illegal

Soviet whaling concerns. A lineal descendant of that treachery today is the disguise of Japanese scientific whaling.

Earlier than other wildlife exploitation, the consequences of whaling gave us a clear lesson about the planet's limits. Very soon after the birth of environmental protest it was apparent that the whale issue was a standard for change. The movement to save the whales was a pioneer of green politics, from the button seller to the international deal maker. This wild ride is thirty-four years old, and it's not over. The whalers are still being chased through the Southern Ocean.

The reader will come to know the great variety among *Harpoon's* central characters. While all breathe through blowholes, some are ugly and infested, others graceful and sleek. All, in their own way. inspire. In the early twenty-first century we are at a privileged time to understand them. The wealth of good science done on whales in recent decades offers a much clearer prism through which to look at the past, to understand the value of what was lost, and to chart a future for what remains.

Some of the great whale species readily stand as metaphors for change, and in this book each of those are described: The lugubrious right whale once batted around most temperate coastlines of the world. Its near extermination by the end of the nineteenth century robbed the New England coast, Bay of Biscay, and Tasmania of a familiar giant, providing a daily caution against the hubris of man. No larger single life has existed than the blue. How worryingly apposite it is that we almost cleared the oceans of them in the era of industrial whaling. In the Antarctic they remain perilously few. Yet they are still there, still mysterious. What do they say when they call across ocean basins?

The sperm is, of course, the universal whale, symbolic nemesis of man the hunter, and a cosmopolitan species. We have had a more complex relationship with the sperm than any other. It was targeted by colonial oceanic adventurers, and then again when the larger baleen whales were exhausted. It was the first that whale savers looked in the eye, and the only whale still being taken in large numbers at the time of a watershed achievement in global species conservation, the IWC's moratorium on commercial whaling.

The smallest, the quick and boisterous minke, became the continuing victim and is the illustration of all that is bad about whaling now. The sustained killing of this species showed the feeble logic of whaling and the determination of those who would keep the remnant industry alive. Other players swim onto this cetacean stage: the environmentally harried gray, and the largest whale that it is possible to "tame," the orca. But to me it is the humpback that illuminates our future with whales. As we look out from the coast, it is the most familiar, the whale whose population and culture we are learning most about. Many people have closely encountered this confiding exhibitionist. The excitement of whale watching embodies a complete reversal in popular thinking over a human lifetime. Yet the humpback population's conspicuous recovery has made it a target, too.

Whaling continues. The targeting again of the humpback and the fin in the Southern Ocean is proof of Japanese determination to revive industrial whaling. The sustenance of nostalgia feeds these whalers, as it does the Norse fishers who go whaling in summer. Of the weapons we have used against other species, the harpoon remains cruelly uncertain. The weight of scientific analysis stands accusingly against the silence of whalers on the question of humane killing.

The IWC today is colored by the cold calculations of international politics among nations with little or no knowledge of whales. Considering the chronic rule bending and manipulation that is crippling this organization, and the lack, so far, of wider political will to stop whaling, it might seem that this book is about failure. Not so. The measure many people take from the great whales is that they keep inspiring us to succeed for them..

PART I · RIGHT

(Eubalaena australis)

1

BONES OF THE PAST

Instead he lapsed into that common failing of naturalists;
to marvel at the intricate perfection of other creatures, and
recoil from the squalor of man.

Bruce Chatwin, *In Patagonia*, 1977

It's about the sixth rib. I feel my own chest for the end of the sternum and
the ribs that don't join. It's down there. This rib tapers away rather than
ending squarely to interlock with a breastbone, and it is 322 centimetres
long. The straight-line distance from end to end is 186 centimetres. The
great length and degree of arc coincide with the larger middle ribs I can see
in a museum photograph. A suspended skeleton hangs from rafters and the
dozen rib pairs cage together like claws grasping at the air. The space they
enclose looks big enough for me to stand inside. Room for organs like my
own, in super size. A half-tonne heart, cavernous lungs, all the anatomy of
an air breather living among fish.

The surface of the rib is smooth and grey, blackened at each end from
resting on wet ground in a garden where it has picked up a fuzz of moss. The
bone is as solid to the touch as a piece of carved stone that has been worked
hard to feel good under a running hand. In cross-section, an elongated oval
rounds towards the tapered lower end. At the top where the vertebrae
locked in, the bone straightens out. I can imagine the broad back it held,
the mammalian engine pumping inside, and the thick oily blubber that
encased it and cost this Right whale its life.

Around 200 years ago this rib was part of the skeleton of a full grown
animal that lived in the Southern Ocean. Its life cycle took it south in

summer where the bone grew tremendous on microscopic oceanic creatures that the whale sieved near the surface. In winter the whale headed for the coasts of southern Australia where it socialised and bred.

For much of its life it would not have known people and their hazards. Perhaps the sand where the bone came to rest was the floor of its ancestral home. Maybe it was just passing; in the wrong place at the wrong time. What can be said with certainty is that this rib washed up at Adventure Bay, Bruny Island, Tasmania, and such giant remnants are all that place really has of Right whales now.

At the south-east corner of Adventure Bay's long beach curve, lines of houses rise above the sand and fade into the sheltering forest. A landing ocean swell rumbles across from the bay's north, but this is a quiet cove. Tall gums overhang the water; their leaves and bark are strewn in the tide lines. Most of the houses are summer homes, facing over the water to catch the sun, simply built and cheerily named.

Among them the Right whale bones are ghostly strange. Lining a front fence in the main street and framing an orderly dahlia bed is a row of big ribs decayed at the edges. Next door's fence has a lower jawbone the size of a kayak wired to it. The jaunty name Anchors Aweigh is freshly painted in black on another jaw, whitewashed and mounted over a porch. Up the road, Bora Bora has a miniature nautical tableau: a lighthouse behind an old ship's anchor, arched over by the curve of a rib, all of them grounded in a concrete plinth. At road's end a caravan-park amenities building has a bone museum—ribs ranked inside each other, another jawbone and an enormous skull, an immense brain case. The Right's distinctive twin blow-holes stare out like empty eye sockets. All of these bones have come out of the bay, tossed ashore in storms or retrieved by divers from skeletal piles that can be mistaken for rock reefs.

By itself one bone is a silent curio: hefty, slightly ghastly, enough to give pause for thought. Together they speak of a past. This bay was a home to whalers and, long before them, to many whales. The whalers are gone. Southern Rights are seen in the bay, as in, 'Someone saw a whale last week', but Adventure Bay is their home no longer, nor is the entire coast of Tasmania. So thoroughly were thousands hunted out from these waters that no individuals regularly return.

infested. Up to 18 metres from mouth to tail, it can weigh around 90 tonnes. So slow is it that an ecosystem has no trouble riding on its head. Adorning the black skin are white skin calluses whalers called the bonnet. On these, barnacles grow and whale lice thrive. Its jaws curve in a giant gape filled with a long curtain of baleen—the springy whalebone that made it 'right' commercially.

The *Caroline*'s Mr Kelly drove his hand-held harpoon into the bull. 'Then the other boat shoved off to his assistance after a little trouble they succeeded in killing him,' Copping wrote. All seemed normal. A reliable target, quickly taken. But the dead whale then sank into the deep of the Tasman Sea. Rights were not supposed to do that.

These hills of blubber were the least complicated whales to take because they floated after death. Copping wrote: 'Unfortunately (though to the joy of many) he sunk like a stone so that it was impossible to keep him afloat.' The crew—preferring to end the voyage than to process a big whale—watched the potential yield sink without regret.

Captain Tregurtha, in his own journal, explained the problem: the bull was seasonally emptied of blubber. 'It being a dry skin on dying he sank so fast that both the boats were compelled to cut their lines to prevent being pulled under.'

Fed up with 'ungrateful rascals' in his crew, and with losing gear to whales, Tregurtha set course for Tasmania. He brought the *Caroline* into Storm Bay to the north of Bruny Island in light winds. 'After dark several fires sprang up in different places which, I could plainly see, were whaling parties trying out their fish.'

The night-time fires of Adventure Bay were boiling Right whale blubber down into oil. Calling them 'fish' was common. After all, they came from the sea, and Charles Darwin's *The Origin of Species* would not reshape natural science for another 25 years. Maybe it was a useful separation too, a nod to sensibilities, the way cattle graziers call their animals beasts.

The Southern Ocean has worked deep into the south-east coast of Tasmania. Drowned valleys are now bays and coves, passages and islands, a network of marine refuges. The worst of the swell is met by high walls of columnar basalt. One of the first to offer calm to voyagers up the Australian eastern seaboard is Adventure Bay. Its safest cove hides behind an abrupt summer where the bone grew tremendous on microscopic oceanic creatures that the whale sieved near the surface. In winter the whale headed for the coasts of southern Australia where it socialised and bred.

For much of its life it would not have known people and their hazards. Perhaps the sand where the bone came to rest was the floor of its ancestral home. Maybe it was just passing; in the wrong place at the wrong time. What can be said with certainty is that this rib washed up at Adventure Bay, Bruny Island, Tasmania, and such giant remnants are all that place really has of Right whales now.

At the south-east corner of Adventure Bay's long beach curve, lines of houses rise above the sand and fade into the sheltering forest. A landing ocean swell rumbles across from the bay's north, but this is a quiet cove. Tall gums overhang the water; their leaves and bark are strewn in the tide lines. Most of the houses are summer homes, facing over the water to catch the sun, simply built and cheerily named.

Among them the Right whale bones are ghostly strange. Lining a front fence in the main street and framing an orderly dahlia bed is a row of big ribs decayed at the edges. Next door's fence has a lower jawbone the size of a kayak wired to it. The jaunty name Anchors Aweigh is freshly painted in black on another jaw, whitewashed and mounted over a porch. Up the road, Bora Bora has a miniature nautical tableau: a lighthouse behind an old ship's anchor, arched over by the curve of a rib, all of them grounded in a concrete plinth. At road's end a caravan-park amenities building has a bone museum—ribs ranked inside each other, another jawbone and an enormous skull, an immense brain case. The Right's distinctive twin blowholes stare out like empty eye sockets. All of these bones have come out of the bay, tossed ashore in storms or retrieved by divers from skeletal piles that can be mistaken for rock reefs.

By itself one bone is a silent curio: hefty, slightly ghastly, enough to give pause for thought. Together they speak of a past. This bay was a home to whalers and, long before them, to many whales. The whalers are gone. Southern Rights are seen in the bay, as in, 'Someone saw a whale last week', but Adventure Bay is their home no longer, nor is the entire coast of Tasmania. So thoroughly were thousands hunted out from these waters that no individuals regularly return.

The bones remain though, and like other whale bones set in towns around the world they are a memorial of a kind. On the coast of northern England a giant jaw arch rises on a hill overlooking Whitby harbour. At Port Stanley in the Falkland Islands, two sets of interlocking jaws link in a portico over a path into a church. Others open the way to a Shinto shrine at Arikawa in Japan. At Bequia in the Caribbean they guard the home of a local harpooner. Shack owners at Adventure Bay are more informal: their bones are more like beachcombing trophies.

To fill the gaps between these few bones, we need to reconstruct the shape of the Right whale's life in these cool, lapping waters. How it almost disappeared from Australian waters. Who those people were who, in just 50 years, removed the largest animal ever known to have lived here—one that was around for eons before they came. What did they think of the Right whale? When did they realise there were limits to their number? And what were the habits and character of these missing giants? How did they live together in these seas? What is this black mystery, this hole in our seascape, the Right whale?

I started my search with the flourish of copperplate writing in whaling ships' log books, where brisk daily entries about wind and wave were punctuated with the drama of a whale's flukes, scratched with a quill and ink beside the name of the victorious harpooner. I flipped through the whalers' and explorers' journals with their tales of hardship and amazement at the new world around them, and read the prim diaries of local colonial worthies, standing beady-eyed and judgmental on the shore. I wanted to see if the bones of the Right whales could be assembled.

Richard Copping was a young whaling new chum who was drawing bad portrait profiles and writing breathless entries in a notepad when his captain, Edward Primrose Tregurtha, saw a whale of 'hidieous size' spout close by their ship. The mate on the Tasmanian Sperm whaler *Caroline* identified it as a Right whale, and boats were lowered for an open-water pursuit in the Tasman Sea north-east of Flinders Island. As the whalers rowed off, another very large Right whale appeared, and swam in close under the ship's stern. Copping, still aboard the *Caroline*, watched it hang there in mid-ocean, apparently peering at the ship, eerily unafraid.

> Raising his head now and then out of the water nor did he seem the least bit gallied he being the first of the kind that ever I saw I could not help looking at his monstrous ugly head covered all over with barnicles applied like a black rock covered (with) osters they were very numerous about his rib ends however we could not take him as we had not boat fit to lowering.

The *Caroline's* day was turning out wrong. Its 1833 voyage into the South Pacific was nearly over, and the crew had to unstow and re-rig two boats to chase the first animal. Right whales were best for the taking partly because they were slow swimmers; faster whales would have left the crew watching a spout in the distance before they could even launch.

Only a couple of weeks earlier in the voyage, Copping had been in just such a boat off Cape Byron, New South Wales. Repeatedly the harpooners plunged their hand-held irons into the animal—a Sperm or possibly a Humpback—but they couldn't draw close enough to drive in the long lance that would find a vital. Instead the whale towed them through the day 'as if Hell kicked him'. Eventually they had to cut free at sundown rather than risk being lost at sea at night.

Copping had watched the whale charge off, 'spouting clear water never giving a chance for a lance—the whole time never hove to one minute during the day—so we returned to the ship after dark with the loss of four irons and about 70 fathoms of line, tired, half drowned and hungery this was the second time I cursed Whaling'.

A Right whale chase might also take hours, but it was a slower animal than a Sperm, easier to harpoon and then play in to the killing lance. Other whales might outrun pursuers or dive deep to escape. Rights were generally taken inshore in shallower waters when they came to breed.

They are not the least bit pretty. No proud nose of the Sperm whale; no grace of the wing-flippered Humpback. The Right whale is big, lumpish and infested. Up to 18 metres from mouth to tail, it can weigh around 90 tonnes. So slow is it that an ecosystem has no trouble riding on its head. Adorning the black skin are white skin calluses whalers called the bonnet. On these, barnacles grow and whale lice thrive. Its jaws curve in a giant gape filled with a long curtain of baleen—the springy whalebone that made it 'right' commercially.

The *Caroline*'s Mr Kelly drove his hand-held harpoon into the bull. 'Then the other boat shoved off to his assistance after a little trouble they succeeded in killing him,' Copping wrote. All seemed normal. A reliable target, quickly taken. But the dead whale then sank into the deep of the Tasman Sea. Rights were not supposed to do that.

These hills of blubber were the least complicated whales to take because they floated after death. Copping wrote: 'Unfortunately (though to the joy of many) he sunk like a stone so that it was impossible to keep him afloat.' The crew—preferring to end the voyage than to process a big whale—watched the potential yield sink without regret.

Captain Tregurtha, in his own journal, explained the problem: the bull was seasonally emptied of blubber. 'It being a dry skin on dying he sank so fast that both the boats were compelled to cut their lines to prevent being pulled under.'

Fed up with 'ungrateful rascals' in his crew, and with losing gear to whales, Tregurtha set course for Tasmania. He brought the *Caroline* into Storm Bay to the north of Bruny Island in light winds. 'After dark several fires sprang up in different places which, I could plainly see, were whaling parties trying out their fish.'

The night-time fires of Adventure Bay were boiling Right whale blubber down into oil. Calling them 'fish' was common. After all, they came from the sea, and Charles Darwin's *The Origin of Species* would not reshape natural science for another 25 years. Maybe it was a useful separation too, a nod to sensibilities, the way cattle graziers call their animals beasts.

The Southern Ocean has worked deep into the south-east coast of Tasmania. Drowned valleys are now bays and coves, passages and islands, a network of marine refuges. The worst of the swell is met by high walls of columnar basalt. One of the first to offer calm to voyagers up the Australian eastern seaboard is Adventure Bay. Its safest cove hides behind an abrupt

274-metre headland called Fluted Cape. Early sailors, wary of the unknown coast of Terra Australis, had an easy mark in this cape.

The Nuenone Aboriginal people had lived on Bruny Island for perhaps 6000 years before the first white sails furled in the bay. They gathered food on the shore, but made no known use of whale, nor were their thoughts on the animal recorded. Their world changed for the worse, as it did for the Right, when British explorer Tobias Furneaux turned *Adventure* into the bay in early 1773. He was following a hint on a map by the Dutch explorer Abel Jansz Tasman 130 years earlier that the bay could be a good anchorage.

The location was well scouted by Furneaux, and the navigator James Cook swung in accompanied by his sailing master William Bligh four summers later. The temperamental perfectionist Bligh came back twice, in 1788 on the *Bounty*, and again four years after that. Of all these voyages, only the ignominious *Bounty* arrived during winter, with the Right whales.

Bligh stopped to take on wood, water and food. He recorded the natural world around the bay in detail, marvelled at the size of the trees and the beauty of the birds, tested seafood, planted a small orchard, and hoped to see the Nuenone. Fletcher Christian, who eight months later would throw Bligh off the ship and into a small boat in mid-Pacific, shot a pair of oyster catchers on Adventure Bay beach where the bird still pipes alarm calls today. Bligh wrote up a careful description of them, just after whining that the Bounty's carpenter had behaved in 'a most insolent and reprehensible manner' towards him.

It was six days later, on 30 August 1788, that Bligh noted, almost as an afterthought to his daily entry:

> We have had these two days past many Whales in the Bay of a consider-
> able size. They were all of one kind having two blowholes at the back
> part of the head. I often regret we had no proper Harpoons for them, a
> thing which in these voyages any ship may easily get supplied with.

It's hard to imagine Bligh as a harpooner, up at the sharp end of a whale boat. And then what on earth would he have done with them? Strip off the blubber along the side of the *Bounty* and salt down the meat for later? Try out the oil in cooking pots? What seems even stranger is that in a log so rich in detail about the surroundings, he made so little of the Right whales which must have been a real commercial discovery.

He seemed already bored with them two days later: 'A few whales were seen in the Bay, as hath been the case these some days, all of the kind already described.' Bligh spent more time wondering why the Aborigines did not come closer, and when they did, in resolving the vexing question of whether they had hair on their heads or wool. It took another sixteen years for Adventure Bay's Rights to figure commercially, when the local extermination of the species began.

The British eventually did invade Tasmania, then called Van Diemen's Land, in 1803. They came to build a convict colony, but with the prospect of whaling in mind. Most first settlers were carried into the Derwent River estuary, 40 kilometres north of Adventure Bay, in Nantucket-born Eber Bunker's whaling ship *Albion*. On the way from Sydney, Bunker found Sperm whales off Van Diemen's Land, killed three and then delivered the settlers. Such feats made him a legend in song among nineteenth-century whalers. 'Lay me on, Captain Bunker,' rolled the words, 'I'm hell on a long dart.' Hire me, the boast was, I can throw a harpoon further than anyone.

Bunker was essentially a Sperm whaler, a hunter of more valuable oil than the Right's. When he arrived in the Derwent with the human cargo to set up Hobart it was late in the Right season, and he quickly left to look for more Sperms elsewhere. It was the next winter before the whaler *Alexander* began poking around the south-east. Perhaps following Bligh, its crew went to Adventure Bay, then to the Derwent and the colonists' camp for the first recorded kill.

On 12 August 1804, just offshore from the pole and canvas outpost, the *Alexander*'s crew harpooned a pair. Taken together at that time of year, it's likely they were a cow and calf. Whalers had the habit of killing the calf first, in the hope of keeping a distressed cow within range. The calf would have been a month or two old.

Aboard the *Alexander* was a Danish adventurer, Jorgen Jorgensen. Later to proclaim himself King of Iceland, and after that to return to Van Diemen's Land a convict, Jorgensen staked his name to the first kill in his memoirs. Then he paused to reflect on what it meant.

Had its brothers and sisters been warned by the violent death to which their near relative was thus subjected, and avoided the fatal spot, the grateful remembrance of further whalers might not have been my due: but the contrary is the case, and the destruction of one has attracted many hundred others to crowd in and incur the same fate, and the rising city of Hobart Town is yearly and rapidly enriching itself on their oleaginous remains.

These are the giddy words of a gold prospector at the head of a rush. If that was the belief of the times, then whalers really did think there was no limit to their riches. An endless Right whale parade was queuing up to fill the vacuum left by earlier deaths, on to infinity.

An editor of Jorgensen's chronicles, Rhys Richards, calculated that in three months in the Derwent, the *Alexander* doubled the whale oil it had taken over the previous 30 months, and covered its voyage costs five times over. Richards figured the seven tonnes of baleen they took was disproportionately large, and meant they probably killed many more whales than they could try out for oil. Instead they went for the Right's richest pickings—whalebone.

The *Alexander* was being watched though, as they killed those first whales, by a colonial busybody onshore called Robert Knopwood. Chaplain to the colony, magistrate, compulsive shooter of birds, Knopwood was Van Diemen's Land's nervous and complaining Samuel Pepys. Like London's diarist of the seventeenth century, Knopwood's daily entries measured the colony's temperature over nearly 40 years, and his notes became a yardstick for the destruction of the Right whale.

He saw the *Alexander* come and go in 1804, and marked the whales' arrival again at the end of May 1805. This is a time of short, cold days in the Derwent, of winds slicing off mountain snow over the wide river estuary. Knopwood noticed 'a great many whales'. Not only were there spouts to be counted, he heard them day and night. Their blows and snores disturbed the colonists' sleep.

Much of the travel in the new colony was by boat, and the settlers anxiously picked their way around the sea monsters. They knew stories like military officer Watkin Tench's 1790 report of a whale that had chased down a small boat on Sydney Harbour. According to the lone survivor, no matter how hard they tried to row, the whale reappeared, eventually rising beneath and capsizing them. 'The midshipman and one of the marines were sucked into the vortex which the whale had made, and disappeared at once,' Tench wrote.

To the British running the Van Diemen's Land convict colony it was already a dangerous world. When Knopwood's ship had left Cape Town two years earlier, he mournfully said: 'The land behind us was the abode of a civilized people, that before us the residence of savages.' Aborigines did fight the invaders; convicts were ruled by capital punishment, and escapers became bushrangers. Even wild beasts threatened them, at least in their imaginations.

Months after Knopwood arrived, absconding prisoners who had spent a few weeks in the bush told him they saw a tiger. 'I make no doubt but here are many wild animals which we have not seen yet,' Knopwood warned his diary. It would have been the marsupial Thylacine, stiff-tailed and stripe-backed, the size of a labrador dog. It was in more strife from the Europeans than the Right whale. Why is it that Tasmanians mourn the Thylacine, and almost forget their largest native animal? Perhaps because the Right was absent longer. No one is alive today to tell tall Right whale stories.

There is no doubt these were the Rights' home shores. The seas were cool enough in winter for their colossal, heat-generating bulk. Inside the bays there was a labyrinth of refuges from the strain of open ocean swimming, clear of oceanic sharks and killer whales when the Rights were at vulnerable stages of calving and suckling. For months before weaning, adults and calves could footle around rocky shorelines or rub along sandy bottoms. There was space for socialising, as well as their tumultuous mating.

Knopwood had a chance to watch all of that. His notes hint at the end of the Rights' peace, at the mayhem whalers flung at the species.

> July 1805. Friday, 19 am—At 11 a large whale opposite my house, and two boats from the 'King George' whaler, after her. They killed the calf but she went down immediately. They did not kill the cow. August 1805. Friday 2—At 2 pm Mr Lucas's men caught a large whale near Hobart Town and while they were towing it to the ship a whale was aground

opposite my house upon the shore, but got off again. September 1805.
Wednesday 4—At 3 pm See Capt. Lucas's boats from the Richd. and
Mary after whales. They killd three opposite Hobart Town this day.

And those were just some of the kills that Knopwood saw. Down in
Adventure Bay the hunters were making their fortunes. The chaplain
farewelled the whaler *Ocean*, sailing with 70 tuns (about 80 000 litres) of
'black' or Right whale oil taken in Adventure Bay in a single month from
perhaps ten large whales.

There was a human cost to this unfolding destruction. They might have
been slow, but so were the whalers, and the Right had great bulk on its side.
Knopwood was soon recounting casualties.

When the *Ocean* came back to the Derwent in 1806, two military
officers borrowed the chaplain's boat to row out and meet the ship. They
set out for shore again after nightfall. Imagine them warmed by the
Captain's rum, in the little cockleshell pulling for the light of the settlement's whale oil lamps. Out of the dark a Right whale suddenly surged at
them. It must have been terrifying. Maybe they blundered between cow and
calf. 'She struck at the boat, but fortunately . . . did not hit it with her fins.'

A year later Knopwood was agog at the *Aurora* tragedy. The ship's
Captain Merrick risked going after a Right whale with a single boat. This
was not a good thing to do. Few whalers could swim and a second boat was
a normal back-up. Perhaps in a river estuary Merrick thought he was safer.

> He struck her and when she rose again he put another iron into her; she
> then turned and struck the boat and stove it, that they were obliged
> to cut the ropes which held the whale. The boat filld so fast that they
> were obliged to hang on their oars. In that dreadful state they continued
> five hours.

The Derwent in May would have been a good temperature for Right
whales—about 14.4 degrees Celsius at the surface, with a wind chill riffling
their black backs soothingly—but too cold for people. One of the *Aurora*'s
men went down with the whale and did not surface; after an hour or so in
the water another crewman died in the boat, and then a third went, also of

hypothermia. Merrick and two others survived, paddling pathetically with a broken oar in the wreckage until they were picked up by a boat from another whaler, the *Elizabeth*.

'They were five hours in the water, expecting every moment that the boat would part with them, and had not the boat fortunately arrived every soul must have perished as they were so deep in the water and they began to be stiff with cold'. Next day Knopwood describes a rare sight: a whalers' funeral. Usually their bodies were not recovered. At noon, four boats rowed up the river, towing two bodies in a fifth. The crew of *Aurora* and *Elizabeth* stood guard while Knopwood conducted the burial.

With their rituals, the European colonists also brought their prejudices. The Right whale bonanza unfolded in front of them, but they did not see all that animal flesh as others might. Whales were not the sort of food that one would admit to eating, even if one was starving as this new colony was. The lieutenant governor, William Collins, had his pigs fed on discarded whale scraps and later complained that the pork tasted like lamp oil.

Knopwood recorded a series of big Right whale kills, and in the same month catalogued the outrageous prices he had to pay for grain and rations, and the effect of famine on the lower classes. 'No work to be done; the poor people go out a-fishing.'

Some time after this food crisis eased, the chaplain revelled in a meal with his tin-pot ruling class friends, nostalgically enjoying hare soup, and 'fresh' salmon from England. Imported at what can only have been great cost and difficulty, packed in seaweed and ice or perhaps an early tin can. Fresh?

To the British settlers of Australia, a cut of whale was something the savages ate. Soon after settling in Sydney Harbour, Watkin Tench was one of a military party trying to make contact with Aborigines. They landed at Manly Cove where their sensitivities were quickly overloaded by a beach-cast whale.

> On drawing near the shore, a dead whale, in the most disgusting state of putrefaction, was seen lying on the beach, and at least two hundred Indians [Aborigines] surrounding it, broiling the flesh on different fires, and feasting on it with the most extravagant marks of greediness and rapture.

The invaders saw this as a good chance to make contact with the truculent and elusive Aborigines. A barbecue of stinking whale was clearly not on their minds. They liked whale oil and bone though. Along with sealing it was the early commercial making of the colonies.

Trade with Britain opened, tariffs were imposed, and local businesses grew around the Right whale. Shiploads of whalers from the United States and France followed. In a sure indication of where Hobart Town's cash flowed, Knopwood drank at the opening night of the first pub: The Sign of the Whale Fishery.

For years it seemed Jorgensen's prediction of an endless harvest from the sea was being realised. Right whales kept coming, Knopwood counting them in the river each late May or early June. As late as 1818 Knopwood logged out the *Ann* that took 32 large whales and would have filled entirely had its try pots not broken.

After that the diarist's messages shift. He starts to record ships leaving to whale elsewhere. It took around fifteen years before the rush was over in the Derwent. The wide reaches where they'd snorted and puffed at night were silent. Dead whales became a strange sight worth seeing by young ladies.

August 1819. Thurs 5. Mr Kelley killd two large whales, a cow and calf, and brought them into my bay. Friday 6 At 11, Miss Charlotte Bowen, little Betsey and Mary Whitehead went in my boat to see the whales.

As the Rights disappeared from the Derwent and the colony pressed further into the wilderness, whalers began to spread out into winter camps along the coast. Recherche Bay, Adventure Bay, Frederick Henry Bay, Marion Bay, Spring Bay, Great Oyster Bay—59 stations were counted by a maritime archaeologist, Michael Nash. Almost all were in south-east Van Diemen's Land, operating in the first half of the nineteenth century.

The spreading whaling stations employed some of the colony's first locally born generation. Equally the man on the oar in front of them could be a British adventurer, a Pacific Islander or a Norwegian. They seized on bay whaling for its cash, and because it was a change from clearing forests. In a good season an ordinary hand could make £35, a harpooner or headsman perhaps triple that. Their share could buy them more animals, a piece of land, or a very long drink at The Sign of the Whale Fishery.

To earn the money they had to attack the diminishing Rights as hard as possible. Their pay directly depended on the amount of oil and bone they produced, and their competitors were in the boat beside them, rowing after the same whale. Life was grimly competitive. 'The more one researches the whalers, the more one is daunted by the sheer . . . privation and conflict in their place of work,' said Parry Kostoglou, an archaeologist whose work brushed off the shards of bay whaling history.

At the height of the Tasmanian industry in the 1830s, the bidding for whaling station shoreline leases was as frantic as a goldfield's. Being first to the whales was paramount. The government was intent on keeping order in the rush, not on sustaining supply. Near the height of bay whaling in 1835, Governor George Arthur imposed 'an Act for the regulation and protection of the Whale Fisheries', to protect the whalers' rights, not the whales. It was enacted to resolve disputes about whose 'fish' was whose and how whaling crews' employment was regulated—the kind of law you apply to hold back conflict over a finite, disputed resource.

The colonial administration claimed to control all waters within 20 miles of the shore, and of course it was keen to tax whale oil. Duties rose and fell as Britain tried to take a piece of the resource, but no effort was made to use the tax as a lever to control the pillage.

Out in the labyrinth of secluded Tasmanian seaways where Rights were hunted, even these catch-up regulations must have been a joke. Casual kills by local people, and orchestrated raids on out-of-the-way whales could be finished and the oil barrelled, before a lumbering boat of redcoats ever rowed into view. A whaling ship could drift in, load and be off into the Pacific without ever troubling the ledgers kept by Hobart duty collectors. In a colony so preoccupied with convict management, unregulated Right whale kills would have come far down the list.

Adventure Bay, at least, has a known history. Apart from the bones, traces of Right whaling's heyday on Bruny Island were dug up by archaeologists at four separate stations where crews raced from the shore beneath Fluted Cape. Fortuitously, there are also two separate accounts of whaling there in the same winter. A watcher on shore, George Augustus Robinson, could have been looking out to sea at a young English adventurer, John Boultbee, relishing life in a whaleboat.

Boultbee was swept up in the game in 1829 after applying for a storekeeper's job on Bruny Island, and instead joining about 40 others who set off to go whaling in the bays. 'Whalers are, I think, people who are as stout as any in the world,' he decided. 'The continual exercise in boats and the fresh sea air has the effect of strengthening the muscles and clearing the lungs.'

The best place to reach Right whales in Adventure Bay was from a station on a waterside flat almost below the cape, sheltered from the weather by a rocky islet. Directly above was the peak that European explorers like Bligh used as a landmark, then a prime headland for spying Rights. Three other camps were lined up along the same kilometre of shore, each of them operating multiple boats and employing upwards of twenty men.

George Robinson was on the lookout for dissolute whalers when he came to Adventure Bay. On his confused and ultimately futile mission as Protector of Aborigines, he wandered the wilderness of Van Diemen's Land to collect and 'civilise' the Indigenous people. He took on the Adventure Bay whalers over their abuse of Aboriginal women for sex. As he clumped onto the bay shore in August 1829, he saw how competitive whalers' lives had become.

Long before any 'there she blows' from the whalers, his Aboriginal companion Robert pointed to a Right whale far out in the bay. It swam towards Robinson's party, then eased along the shoreline to the southern corner. One whaleboat was out, ready for a head start. Its crew spotted the Right and charged off, rowing into the distance as Robinson went to dinner. Late in the day he went for a stroll and saw the same white boat still rowing. Another six, each painted a different colour by rival owners, joined in. It was quite the little regatta.

> The cerelity with which they passed through the water was astonishing, each emulating to get first . . . The steady pull of the men, the beautiful time they kept, and the backing up of the stroke oar by the coxswain as he stood up steering his boat with his long steer oar, was a grand sight.

Robinson's shoreline barrackers backed the white boat and eventually it came in for them, landing the hand-thrown harpoon, then being dragged out of the bay. They stayed clear of the Right's flukes, which it used as a weapon, 'as if in the act of feeling for its aggressor'.

We glimpse this chase barely. The lone whale cruised for some time around the bay before it was struck. Judging by its spectacular panic, it had energy enough to escape the rowers, so apparently it was not alarmed before the harpoon struck. Why did it take so long to hit? Perhaps the white boat's crew spent hours quietly working closer. Tasmanian whaleboats were built for stealth, their carvel planks joined flat to silence the trickling song that clinker planking made.

Robinson gave the whale a pompously biblical death. 'Through the superior tact of man this huge and powerful fish has been converted into an uncouth mass of inanimate matter.'

Hundreds of whales became uncouth masses in Adventure Bay in the 1830s, the decade or so that bay whaling boomed. And so it went along the coastline. Further south at Recherche Bay, Robinson said upwards of 100 were caught in a season, and 'the shore is strewed with putrid carcases and bones of the whale'. The tales of how many Rights there were, of that endless succession, became fantastic. In 1839 *The Colonial Times* claimed that up the coast around Schouten Island, 100 Rights were taken in a week.

It wasn't until the twentieth century that scientists began a forensic reconstruction of total loss to the species. Scouring colonial ledgers, the Australian Museum's William Dawbin calculated the landed catch of Right whales from the first decent records in 1827 to the turn of the twentieth century. Dawbin went to lists sent back to the Colonial Secretary in London—the 'Blue Books'. Where whale numbers were replaced by oil tonnages, he worked them up to an average representation of a whale.

A neatly typed table compiled by Dawbin and published in 1986 by the International Whaling Commission counts out the toll. A total of 7745 Right whales are known to have been landed and tried out in Tasmania in around 70 years, half of them in just four peak years, from 1837 to 1840. In one glorious year for old whalers to remember, 1839, they killed 1064 Rights in Tasmanian waters.

Think also of those that unhelpfully sank in deep water, or lurched off to die when lines were lost or whalers abandoned their chases. Counted as 'struck and lost', Dawbin says: 'at many locations, this certainly exceeded the common estimate of 20 per cent'. And then think of those that disappeared on foreign whaling ships, never to be counted.

Winters have a grand, steely beauty on the coast of south-east Tasmania. Early morning fogs race downriver. Fast-moving cold fronts pushed by Antarctic air bring fizzy snow clouds one minute, blown away to blue sky in the next. Squalls can whirl the sea surface into the air, but just as often it is flattened to a metallic sheen. Out to sea at an early sunset, light fades into chilled pink and violet. It is a big, wild seascape. Once more than a thousand Right whales—many more—swam out there each winter.

This emptiness spread in the nineteenth century throughout the seas of the south-west Pacific. Dawbin counted 24 755 Rights taken by whalers off eastern Australia and New Zealand in the nineteenth century. In New Zealand the bays were whaled later, but just as completely. Around 5300 were hauled ashore. Offshore, French, American and British ships took away more than 8000.

Sailing ships like the barque *Lady of the Lake* were small, itinerant factories that scoured the south-west Pacific. On a winter 1837 voyage to Wilsons Promontory on the Victorian coast, the barque's log counted the prizes in meticulous ink sketches of whale flukes, and the tremendous loss in whales that sank after death, or were harpooned and lost.

> Monday 31 July . . . at daylight moved ship all boats out—2 boats went to the seals rock and did not come on . . . that night 1st mate [sketch of fluke] killed a whale and she sunk. The latter part light breezes from the westward the Captain [sketch] killed a whale and Philip Beer [sketch] killed a whale and anchored them. Broached a cask of beef.

After a few weeks with little more success and many gales, *Lady of the Lake* sailed north to the southern New South Wales coast, and to more bays where Rights were to be found. In the boom year of 1839, Dawbin counted 539 Rights taken in New South Wales, and more than 2000 over 80 years. The whalers set up small, desolate seasonal camps along the coasts of

Victoria, South Australia, and Western Australia, killing sporadically and for small numbers in the peak years from 1834 to 1847.

This passage into the past is signposted by three paintings. The journey is under way with William Duke's *Whaling at Lady's Bay, Tasmania* (1848), climaxes in Oswald Brierly's *The Death Flurry* (1865) and is lamented in *Old Whaling Station* (1874) by John Skinner Prout.

Lady's Bay is a dent in the high buttressed shore at the southern entrance to D'Entrecasteaux Channel separating mainland Tasmania from Bruny Island. The ocean is around the corner, and Duke's painting is dominated by elements: rock, water and wind-blown cloud. In the foreground a whaleboat crew stare dourly out of the canvas. Behind them in the painting's centre the tail of a Right is flung up: thick, ungraceful and as unmistakeable as those inked into the *Lady of the Lake*'s log book. The tail is frighteningly big beside another whaleboat, whose harpooner draws back his dart. Further down the bay more whalers are at work. Duke was an English immigrant who had arrived in Hobart three years earlier, and his painting tells of busy colonial industry at the edge of the world .

To Oswald Walters Brierly seventeen years later, Right whaling is much darker. His picture shows the animal in full. Its profile has a great, ghastly frown. The cavernous mouth curves grimly down. The baleen curtain inside its gape looks fiercely predatory. This whale is harpooned and dying, throwing its tail and spouting blood, writhing above the surface. It's a hellish painting. The whalers look recklessly piratical. Offshore from Twofold Bay, New South Wales, the world is red sky, dark wave and foam. Birds wheel and dolphins flee. There are two versions of this picture by the Cheshire gentleman who was to become marine painter to Queen Victoria. In one a whaleboat is nearly upended. In the other, the dolphins have been shifted. The whale is just as close to its end in each. Man looks far stronger.

A funereal remembrance of a lawless past is engraved in *Old Whaling Station*, published in a colonial travelogue. 'When a good whaling ground had been discovered, the discoverers were not anxious to invite strangers to partake of their treasures,' it said. This fits the sketch by Skinner Prout of the Freycinet Peninsula on Tasmania's east coast, where it was claimed 100 whales were taken in a week. In the distance a vaguely formed ship sails from behind a small peninsula where derricks, tiny figures, and a slight oil slick assemble the possibilities of a whaling station. Bushfire burns into mountainside. On a foreground beach a handful of shapes could be rocks, or bones. Mid-picture lies the skull of a Right, jawbones still attached, lying like the exposed fossil of a mammoth. All that's left.

Prior to this painting there is little evidence that people looked at what was in store for the Right with any sense of regret. Even a visible twinge of conscience proved hollow. An English navy lieutenant, William Henry Breton, wrote a sort of early Victorian tour guide published in London in 1833. He'd watched bay whalers chase down a Right at the Derwent's mouth. There was the familiar race to be first, a short headlong rush after the harpoon landed, and the bloody finish. Breton thought it a fine but melancholy sight.

> Black whales enter the bays in order to seek some retired spot where they may bring forth their young, and during that season become victims of the cupidity of that arch destroyer, man. At no very distant period few, if any, will be found on these coasts, for the warfare kept up against them is so incessant and destructive, that their numbers are already greatly diminished.

Breton might be thought a greater man of vision were he not glimpsed again a few years later. He came back to Van Diemen's Land to be a police magistrate. At his gentleman's home in the garrison town of Richmond he invited Barlatier Demas, an officer travelling with French explorer Jules Dumont D'Urville, for dinner in 1840. A translation of Demas's diaries shows what the bemused Frenchman found when he walked into Breton's house.

> My host was an enlightened natural history enthusiast; we only got to his door after passing through a row of petrified animals of all shapes and sizes: inside a monster crocodile opening its gaping jaws, monkeys grinned on every side, and herons, penguins, kangaroos, snakes adorned a rather long vestibule that had to be crossed to reach the living quarters.

This dispenser of advice about the Right whale's future followed the strange imperial compulsion to collect stuffed wildlife and display it as the pride of his home. It was more evidence of the belief, from Jorgensen on, through colonial business and even to government, that animals could be killed endlessly. That there were no limits to the natural world, or if there were, those creatures were only there for man's use anyway, and when one thought of their passing it was with just a tinge of regret. That 'arch destroyer', man.

2

COUNTING ABSENCE

The 'control of nature' is a phrase conceived in arrogance,
born of the Neanderthal age of biology and philosophy, when
it was supposed that nature exists for the convenience of man.

Rachel Carson, *Silent Spring*, 1962

Along most cool temperate coasts of the world where once they thrived, Rights are too long gone to be remembered. There are two generally recognised species: *Eubalaena australis* in the Southern Hemisphere and *E. glacialis* of the north. Like most baleen whales, there is no record of them crossing the equator. Each species was calamitously reduced.

As early as the eighth century AD Northern Rights, perhaps beachwashed, were used by one Japanese community, but it's likely that the Basques, the great pioneering ocean fishermen of Europe, first organised commercial whaling of them in the eleventh century. The documentary evidence is government regulation of whale meat, recorded at a Basque market at Bayonne, a port in the south-east corner of the Bay of Biscay.

Over the next five centuries, up to 47 French and Spanish towns were partly sustained by whaling. Spanish scientist Alex Aguilar put the longevity of the hunt down to low numbers taken in this pre-industrial era. The only Rights hunted were those that passed close inshore, and the annual catch was probably dozens, not hundreds. It was still a harmful catch for the stock. A harpooner who hit a calf first was more highly rewarded because that brought the cow into range.

The Bay of Biscay began to decline as a Right fishery in the sixteenth century, and it was all over by the seventeenth century, though they were still being killed in the North Atlantic in the twentieth century, with what IWC scientists say was catastrophic effect. Few sightings of Rights have been made in the Bay of Biscay in the past century, which Aguilar said 'denotes the negligible size of the eastern North Atlantic population (if it still exists)'. The last seen was offshore in 1981. He wonders whether some recent claims off the Iberian peninsula and Canary Islands mean remnants of the original stock survive, or stragglers are crossing from the western North Atlantic.

When the Basques sailed to North America, they were chasing Rights as well as cod. Archaeologists in Canada found the remains of a summer station at Red Bay, Labrador, run by the Basques for 80 years from the 1530s, hunting the Right and its near relative, the Bowhead. North American colonists began at Long Island, New York. Towns that are today full of urbane and moneyed people—the Hamptons, Wainscott and Amagansett—were founded on coastal whaling in the mid-seventeenth century when the Right migration came inshore.

At first all able-bodied colonists were required to take a watch for passing whales, and native Americans were hired to go whaling. As colonists took this work over, Rights were the main target for nearly 300 years. By 1900, US scientists estimate the western North Atlantic stock may have been reduced from an original population of 1000 to as few as 50. The last known deliberate kill from the stock was of a calf, grotesquely taken by a 'sportfisherman' off Pompano, Florida, in 1935. Around 300 Western North Atlantic Rights survive today as one of the most seriously threatened whales.

The Japanese were organising their own coastal whaling at the same time as Basque fishermen crossed the Atlantic. Japanese historian Hideo Omura says they began with Gray whales, and chased Humpbacks as well. More prized was the Right whale (or Sebikujira, 'beautiful back', in Japanese). Some thought the Right had the best tasting meat, and it certainly held the most oil.

The traditional hunt was hair-raising. Small navies of flimsy boats carrying dozens of men headed out to sea from a few fishing villages to drive the whale into nets designed to entangle and slow it to exhaustion at the surface. A succession of harpoons weakened it to a point where the whalers could actually clamber aboard the giant. Omura says these men would cut through the dying whale's nasal septum and tail, tie it off, then finish it with long swords. Or wooden plugs were driven into blowholes so that the whale suffocated.

No more than 100 Rights a year are thought to have been taken around Japan before they disappeared from its waters in the mid-nineteenth century. Offshore the pelagic whaling ships were taking them instead. American whalers are known to have caught about 14 500 Rights in the North Pacific, most between 1840 and 1859. British, French and other nations' ships took them uncounted.

Another big hunt in the South Atlantic and Indian Ocean followed the same pattern: first local shore whaling targeted females and calves in Brazil in the seventeenth century and southern Africa in the eighteenth century. Then the whaling fleets arrived offshore and coasts were emptied.

The Right whale disappeared as a casualty of the industrial revolution. Whale oil lit homes and the headlamps of miners; it lubricated machines and made jute pliable to weave; it helped to temper steel and cut screws. It was used in soap and for paint. Sperm whale oil was of a finer grade— used by lighthouses and the wealthy. The lesser 'brown' oil, mainly from the Right, was the everyday oil before petroleum.

The long, elastic baleen from the Right found uses both practical and frivolous in a world before plastics. At an average length of around 2.6 metres, with 266 pairs mounted in each mouth, Right baleen was only exceeded in size and quantity by the rarer Bowhead. Whaling historians counted the uses in sofa springs, chimney brushes and umbrella ribs. The bizarre crinoline fashion, when women competed for the ballooning size of whalebone frames under dresses, coincided with the peak of Right whaling.

In 1998, IWC scientists reconstructed past kills to make sense of what had happened to Rights. Using mathematical models they worked back from today's populations to estimate the original abundance. Known figures such as recent growth helped them deduce that Southern Rights had a population somewhere between 70 000 and 160 000 before whaling. In the next hundred years, nearly 133 000 were counted as killed. Many more were struck and lost, or just uncounted. By 1920 there were perhaps 300 of the 'hidieous creatures' left across the Southern Hemisphere—about 60 breeding females between extinction and a future.

If they had gone, we would have lost the tail-sailor. We would have lost the skim-feeder of the wildest oceans, the great beach snorer, the frenzied sexual competitor with the one tonne testicles, the powerfully diligent mother. We wouldn't have learnt where the Right whale goes.

Some wilder coasts were too hard for the whalers. Places like Peninsula Valdez, which juts into the South Atlantic from Patagonia, Argentina, like an axe-head. Its friable stone cliffs and ocean rollers are strikingly like another refuge where the Southern Ocean chews into the walls of the Great Australian Bight. In these out of the way places, flesh was sculpted onto the human memory of Rights.

The habit of dwelling close inshore that had cost the Rights their lives in coastal whaling allowed these scientists to observe and explain the animal close-up. Its skin callosity clumps turned out to be as singular as fingerprints and, when matched with distinctive white blazes on the belly, unmistake-able. Watchers began to understand individual animals, and fill the spaces of our coasts.

Foremost among Right whale scientists, the American Roger Payne has been observing Peninsula Valdez animals with subtle understanding since 1970. Seeing a herd sleep, he viewed them as beads on a chain, moving back and forth along a 'home beat' with the currents.

But tail sailing? 'The whale holds its tail smartly up in a strong breeze for as long as 20 minutes at a time, so that the whale's body is pushed by the wind through the water,' Payne writes in a memoir. It's unexpected ingenuity on the part of the Right, the kind of behaviour that implies calm familiarity with the wind, as well as the sea. There is the whale, sailing its way from breeze to breeze. How easy life can be.

Payne's many years of Patagonian work were shared in scientific papers: one showed Rights living as a loose-knit group, roughly clustered around females with calves. The 'beat' used by generations of females was perhaps 30 to 40 kilometres long, bookended by a specific geographic feature such as a headland. They stayed within hearing of each other, and used a loose 'whale road', the five-metre depth contour in the coastline, which meant as they moved in, and between, these beats, they met each other. 'Five metres is just enough water for a large mother to be clear of the bottom, but not enough to allow attacks on her calf from below by killer whales and sharks,' Payne said.

Should attack threaten, the Rights could use the defensive powers that brought a whalers' funeral to the Derwent in 1807. 'When approached by anything . . . they often flex their bodies laterally, holding the tail cocked for several seconds. It is an obvious threat display—readiness for a fight—like a person assuming a karate stance.' The scything sweep of such a tail through the water made it a frightening weapon.

Rights emerge as great talkers. Calls do not travel long distances, but close up they make complex use of sound. Breathing blows can be threats to others, or the moans of a snoring whale. Flipper slaps indicate arousal, or are a precursor to a physical strike. The vocal range covers an upsweeping whistle to make contact, a high-pitched call of excitement, pulsive warning sounds, and many subtler shades of conversation in between.

Much talk takes place during sex which is highly competitive, even orgiastic, in Rights. With females available for conception about one year in three, several males may be trying at once to penetrate a single female. In the intense competition to pass on genes, male Rights evolved to possess the largest testicles on earth, producing buckets of sperm to wash out competition. One female seen in the Bay of Fundy made no attempt to resist copulating simultaneously with two males, which is anatomically possible. Other males push females, who had been resistantly belly-up, underwater so 'rivals' had a chance to connect.

In his theory of reciprocal altruism, 1970s biologist Robert Trivers says that organisms aid each other in the expectation that their favour will be returned. It is found in species with longstanding social groups including humans and vampire bats. So for a Right whale male, what goes around, comes around.

A colder view of mammalian motives is that the successful male just seizes the moment. The mating male might simply be parasitising other males' efforts to reach the female. For a cow the advantage of all this sex is less clear. Competitive mating may increase chances of conceiving with a larger male, insuring her greater investment of energy in pregnancy. The one-tonne calf is born about a calendar year after its conception. With stately synchronicity, Rights wean their young another year later.

Familiar to our coasts for half the year, Southern Rights disappear for the rest. Their hidden summer lives were a puzzle to whalers, and later to scientists. They were seldom seen eating, their summer feeding grounds and prey a mystery. Early twentieth-century whalers wanted these unknown grounds to be an El Dorado, of course, and their unfulfilled treasure hunts left clues for scientists to follow.

In the bay whaling era, shadowy, speculative ventures would sail from places like Tasmania. The audacious James Kelly of Hobart, who made a pile in the bays, sent his barque *Venus* where few polar explorers had been. Her master, Captain Samuel Hervey, wrote a quiet note to Kelly from Sydney in January 1832 to explain how he had fared in this 'Southern Speck'. He claimed to have sailed to 72 degrees south, putting him in the as-yet-unexplored Ross Sea in Antarctica. Hervey met fogs and bad weather, found no whales and turned north.

With little evidence, late nineteenth-century whalers chose the Antarctic coast as the place to find Rights when they ran out elsewhere. An Australian map 'Shewing Whaling Grounds in portion of Southern Hemisphere' in 1892 had notations along the ice edge: 'Right Whales, November to February' and 'Right Whales seen during summer months', next to a bonanza claim: 'Right Whales and Sperm and Hump Backs in great numbers all the year. South of 63 degrees'.

Industrial age shipping was picking up, and the first Antarctic whaling fleets went south to target Rights. Scottish and Norwegian voyages in 1892–95 were fruitless, catching only one Right, according to whaling historians Johan Tønnessen and Arne Johnsen. Most Antarctic summering Rights had already been killed at the other end of the migration.

Several Right whale hot spots would be found a decade later. In the western mouth of the Straits of Magellan at the tip of South America, 79 were taken, and another 94 off South Georgia, showing they did swim to the sub-Antarctic. Such catches 'had all the effects of the news of a gold strike', the Norwegians said. The seam quickly emptied. The remaining great curtains of baleen had to open somewhere though.

Unlike faster and sleeker whales, Rights graze the ocean. They don't gulp a load like the Blue or Humpback. They spread their jaws and swim forward slowly, letting sea wash in and microscopic life collect on the baleen. The West Australian Museum's John Bannister had a hunch where to look. He checked old ship records, like those of the US whaler *Pacific*, which steered south from Albany in November 1856 and found Rights on 40 degrees south. By then they were so nervous, the skipper William Whitecar said, 'they absquatulated in as secret and shy a manner as a defaulting bank clerk'.

The likelihood of Rights using this sub-Antarctic zone increased when Japanese scientists in the early 1980s reported seeing 75 summering in a similar latitude. A chance for Bannister to confirm this came in a scientific sighting cruise through the Roaring Forties at Christmas, 1995. There they were, midway between Western Australia and Antarctica. The sightings cruise met 35 Rights, watched some feed along surface slicks, and saw the brick red faeces of others, suggesting they were eating crustacea. Using callosity signatures, Bannister made two sure photographic matches, one of a Right that had meandered 875 kilometres south in 96 days.

Rights are also seen at the ice edge, but apparently they prefer to be like Aesop's tortoise—slow and steady. They make the most of open ocean, enduring all it has for them. Low pressure systems constantly wheel around Antarctica, spinning gales and high seas north. Finding food would seem extraordinarily difficult. Further proof that Rights can do this came from mid-twentieth-century Soviet harpoons that again shot the whale closer to extinction.

The species had been protected from 1934. This unmistakeable casualty of man was in the background of the first international ageement on wildlife. At a 1911 conference to settle disputes over Arctic fur seals, there was talk about the disappearing Bowheads and Rights; US President William Howard Taft said the seal treaty showed international law for other sea mammals was feasible. It finally came in the tentative, ultimately failed attempt to globally regulate the exploitation of whales in the 1931 Geneva Convention for the Regulation of Whaling. Article 4 said: 'the taking or killing of Right whales . . . is prohibited.'

Is it cynical faithlessness, wilful ignorance or simple nihilism that leads some covertly to breach what is so clearly the common will? It wasn't desperate hunger; the meat wasn't eaten. Through much of the twentieth century, the international protection of Right whales was ignored by the

Soviet Union. After its fall, scientists corrected false records to publicly disclose to the IWC a systematic, secret and illegal hunt by Soviet whaling factory fleets. This included from 1951 to 1972 a total of 3368 Southern Rights.

A scientific paper led by D.D. Tormosov is a plainly chilling account of what happened out of the world's sight. Tiny numerals on a series of pocket maps in the paper show where and when the Rights were taken. Most were robbed from the South Atlantic and Indian Ocean, but the fleet also hunted off Australia. In a small zone about 200 nautical miles south of Tasmania, the Soviets hauled in 78 fully protected Right whales at the height of the Cold War, killing 43 in a single month: March 1970.

It's hard to see any good in such a toll, but scientific observers aboard these ships did ink in more of the Right's ocean wanderings.

In November–December they were in the sub-Antarctic. A few were hit off the Antarctic coast at summer's end. By early autumn they were again being taken in the north. Measured against other work, this firmed up the belief that Rights spent a good deal of time roaming in the Forties and Fifties rather than the high Antarctic. From animals harpooned near Tasmania, the Soviets also recovered darts fired into them long before. A female killed in March 1970 was 1060 nautical miles east of where she was marked the previous November. A male winched up in March 1972 had made 178 nautical miles south-east from where he was marked a week before.

Evidence was assembled of the Right's preferred waters, and what they were chasing. Krill, the universal polar food, sustained them almost exclusively further south, but among the 43 shot off Tasmania, zooplankton called copepods were the dominant food. Smaller than the moon on a fingernail, about two millimetres long, these are what build and sustain the long bones of the Right.

In this ocean area, the sea floor rises from a 5-kilometre-deep abyssal plain to a mere 1000 metres depth across the South Tasman Rise, a plateau around one third the size of Tasmania. To the east of the rise, extinct volcanic seamounts reach up to the surface as well. Someone sitting in a boat would look around and see . . . more ocean.

Hidden below the surface, currents and layers of the global ocean intersect and mix on the rise, the way clouds form above a mountain. The warm water conveyor from the tropics, the East Australian Current, runs out just to the north of the rise. The oceanic boundary of the subtropical front wavers across it. At summer's end, as in March 1970, waters around the rise could carry the microscopic nutrients needed to feed copepods. The Rights in turn have good times ahead—an annual autumn picnic. The Soviet data indicates they grazed lavishly.

The Rights of the South Tasman Rise were some of the last to die from the harpoon, but the species' troubles from man are not over. A yacht blowing along at 20 knots in the Atlantic showed why, for at least some stocks, the future is still clouded. The 13-metre yacht nearly sliced off a large part of the tail fluke of an eleven-year-old female Right off Cumberland Island, Georgia, on 10 March 2005.

'The whale suffered a serious near amputation of part of its tail, and scientists are concerned that it may not survive,' said the *New England Aquarium*. 'The whale's greatest hope may be for the injured portion of its tail to fall off.' As well as being heavily fished with nets and pots, the seaboard that is the Rights' migratory path has dense ship traffic. The *Aquarium*'s Scott Kraus calls it an urban ocean. 'The worst place to be is within 30 miles of the shore, and that is where the whales are,' he said.

If an initial strike doesn't kill such an accident victim, the injury's resulting infection often will. A week earlier another female was found dead on Ship Shoal Island, Virginia, severely entangled in fishing gear. US researchers along the Atlantic coast were finding Rights killed at the rate of around one a month, in a critically endangered population totalling around 300.

Amy Knowlton and Kraus found that ship strikes caused nearly half the deaths of seventeen Right whales they necropsied in the 1990s, and many live animals bore propeller scars. An unexplained lower birth rate among North Atlantic Rights further complicates their recovery. In the North Pacific, numbers of Rights are so little understood the IWC says there have been no confirmed sightings of calves in a century.

By comparison, the Southern Right is revelling in life. Population estimates exceed 7000 for the animal of South America, Africa and Australasia, and their numbers are thought to be growing at a rate of around seven per cent. Their fidelity has encouraged local tourism on shore from a handful of their winter beats like Warrnambool, Victoria. Other whales are practically out of reach, such as the Rights wintering in bays and fjords of New Zealand's windblown sub-Antarctic Auckland Islands, and the further washes of the Great Australian Bight.

Which makes those of us on quiet coasts wonder: will the Rights come back? I had heard of remnants in Tasmania. Once I joined watchers on a Derwent beach to see the big, spade-like flipper upraised like the waving hand of a passer-by. Finally in the winter of 2005 I was able to believe they could.

I had driven around Hobart's seaward lookouts and headlands chasing phone messages and radio reports. On nothing more than a hunch I walked up through the scrub on Cape Deslacs, a high and wild promontory looking out over Frederick Henry Bay. The sea eagle, there on my last fruitless visit, was soaring off the cliff updrafts again. That small black reef in the water— that wasn't there last time. It blew. A hollow whoosh; a calm, measured breathing out. The Right hovered in a corner cove. Out to sea several more broke the surface.

Rhythmically the closest whale took two or three breaths at the surface, and then subsided for a few minutes, to appear in the same place. The broadness of the back was clear as waves washed it. From above, the callosities stood up like a pale headdress—the whalers were right to call it a bonnet. Another back seemed to be mottled with a light patch where it had rubbed something. For a second I glimpsed a mouth agape at the surface. The rhythm of their breathing fitted the timing of swells rolling through. It was all slow, very slow.

Boys with bodyboards ran past me like goats down a cliff path to ride a rocky inshore break. One shouted to me: 'They've been here for a couple of weeks. At Barney's Point, they came within about 20 metres! Cool!'

A pair of Rights formed and swam slowly around the cape, followed at a distance by another. The boys' shouts increased as one whale passed close by. The pair rolled on into the bay behind the booming shore break of Clifton Beach, and their pace quickened.

Sometimes there was a loud, stronger blow, like the first blast of air through a didgeridoo: bass, tubular song. Small mists from the blows refracted in the low light. Tails were raised and slid under, heads lifted above the water, occasionally one rolled onto its back, holding both pectorals up and showing a big white belly patch. A female avoiding sex? The single whale caught up, tangled with the pair, and then moved away. The lowering sun shone through the spray of the surf as the three lolled inshore, comfortable just behind the break.

The Rights fitted the seascape. They gave scale and dimension. It made more sense with them around.

PART II · BLUE

(Balaenoptera musculus)

3

TO THE BRINK

At length everything is brought to the utmost limit of growth by nature, the creatress and perfectress.

Lucretius, *On the Nature of the Universe*, 50BC

'Blow.' We swing our heads in the little aircraft's cabin. So soon after take-off? Can that be a glimpse of a back sliding under water? Maybe the mist wraith of a whale's breath? Too late. 'That's a Blue,' says Peter Gill with certainty. He pencils it onto a running sheet on his knee, another data point of his research.

Minutes earlier the little high-winged aircraft had been at Portland airport in south-western Victoria on a breezeless high summer day, the scent of eucalyptus carrying across the apron. Now five of us are crammed aboard for a day's flying over 21 000 square kilometres of Southern Ocean, Gill's survey patch. Some of the rarest of whales have been found here, on the back doorstep of Australia. If they are about today the conditions are perfect for seeing Blues. The intense heat seems to have hammered the ocean flat. There are no whitecaps to confuse the eye. It's the right time of year and we are in the right place.

Along the thousands of ragged kilometres of the southern Australian coast, the continental shelf can extend for 200 kilometres. But here, only 20 kilometres offshore, it falls sharply through a series of great canyons to the abyss thousands of metres below. In summer and autumn a deep ocean upwelling of nutrient rich cold water rises up these canyon walls, encouraged by strong easterly winds that sweep away the surface water like a broom on a puddle.

It is named the Bonney Upwelling after a nearby onshore lake. On a satellite image the indigo-coloured water curls westward. 'The cold water forms fronts where things really happen,' Gill says, as someone who's spent hundreds of hours watching. 'From the air you see plumes and jets and tendrils of water writhing through each other, incredibly twisted. But it's not in the colder water itself. It's when things move sideways into the warmer water—that's when things change.' Under this influence the marine food chain links smoothly. Nutrients from the deep bring plankton blooms that feed the krill, *Nyctiphanes australis*. It swarms, and higher predators come for the feast.

In December 1995 an International Whaling Commission (IWC) sightings cruise along the southern Australian coast, supported by the Japanese Government, located the Bonney Blues. 'They were right over the shelf break, slightly deeper than I would normally find them,' says Gill. 'I've learnt since that their distribution can vary according to the intensity of the upwelling.'

Peter Gill has been poking around the whales' world for years. He began as a research assistant on Humpbacks and Rights, sailed in yachts to Antarctica, did science for Greenpeace and the Australian Government. He saw his first Blue off Merimbula, New South Wales, in October 1984. For that, he thanks an old New Zealand whaler, Joseph Perano, who was there to help count Humpbacks.

'He was aged 78 at the time, but he was a great observer,' Gill told me. 'He would sit there with a big pair of binoculars on a stick, and amazing patience. He saw a blow and thought it was a Humpback, about 12 metres or so. Then its mother surfaced next to it. He said: "There's a Blue whale. She'd be a big one too." That was thrilling. They were just legendary.'

In 1998 Gill and colleague Deborah Thiele flew a speculative survey over the Bonney Upwelling that found three Blues. It was enough. 'In effect, I'd found a whale biologist's pot of gold.' There are few places on the planet today where Blues can reliably be seen. We are flying over waters where Gill once saw 31 in a day. So the five sets of eyes in the little cabin blink away the distractions of heat and muscle cramp as the aircraft turns into another leg of a zigzag track, working offshore and moving north-west.

As we scan from 1500 feet, dolphins dash across the surface. Gill spots one tail-walking. Gannets and an occasional albatross skim low, or sit waiting for a lifting breeze. Krill swarms appear as pinky-brown blotches: ink stains on the azure.

The krill are on the move all the time, trying to track down hot spots which have copepods and phytoplankton. At the next trophic level there are pilchards and redbait. 'Blues wouldn't say no to a few pilchards; they have been known to eat small schooling fish. But they concentrate on krill.'

In the digital age, when movies' ever-more convincing images befuddle our real sense of scale, it is a challenge to comprehend the size of the largest creature known to have lived. The mouth is a good place to start.

'Blues disarticulate their lower jaw and power into a swarm of krill,' Gill said. 'They roll onto their side, using their tail to push them along. They relax the muscles of their throat, the jaw swings out wide and this allows the ocean to flood in. It's a bit hard to work out how much they are swallowing. The mouth is almost half the body length; it's perhaps 15 metres by 6 metres by 5 metres, so there could be 100 tonnes of water and krill in there.'

Aboard the plane we have worked our way up 200 kilometres of coast with no more sightings. The heat and stuffiness is taking a toll. Whatever we suck in from a water bottle trickles down our backs in sweat. Gill usually sees most Blues further back. I fall despondent as I contemplate some big open-decked cray fishing boats beneath us. The fishermen gun their engines along potlines, leaving curling white wakes astern.

'Whale!' calls Gill's research assistant, Shannon McKay. After sitting in a silent trance in the rear of the aircraft for hours, she spots a Blue almost below the plane.

I crane across to her side but can't see, so instead quickly scan through my window. All I find is a distant view of the long white wake of another cray boat. No, it isn't. It's the wake of a submarine. No. It's a Blue whale.

Some moments in life, you gasp at what your eyes tell you. This is one.

As the plane swings into a circle I lose the sight, then see another Blue even closer, and it blows. When most whales breathe, they spout in puffs that quickly fade. This cloud seems to hang in the air forever. I see instantly how sailing ship whalers, squinting into the distance, sometimes mistook the vertical fountain for the rigging of another ship.

Beneath the spray, the Blue is amazingly streamlined—a long, hydro-dynamic body with a smooth spade-shaped head; not the blob profile of a storybook illustration comparing it with 25 elephants or 150 large cattle.

Majestic vertical strokes of the tail flukes push out wide pooling swells behind. On the surface it's gunmetal grey. Then it does the thing that Blue whales do: it slides beneath the water, and turns an ethereal, vivid blue. It lights up the sea.

Over a century ago whalers would watch Blues and Fins spout unattainably in southern Australian waters. Ships' logs tallied them as passing hopes or cursed frustrations. The speed and scale of rorquals—the pleat-throated baleen whales—made most unreachable for rowing boats and hand-held harpoons. Unlike the Right, rorquals also sank quickly when killed.

Captain H.E. Swift's crew on the bark *Islander* were having a tough time of it trying to catch Sperm whales, even stooping to low-value Orcas off the Western Australian coast in 1881 when rorquals powered past. The look-outs occasionally saw Blues, noted as Sulphur Bottoms for the seasonal yellowish algal films on their skin. More often Swift saw Fins.

> August 2—at 4 pm raised some spouts we run the ship off for them but maid them out to them bluming fin Backs so ends this Day of our Lord . . . August 13—have seen five bluming fin Back whales today . . . August 17—We are having a good spell of fine weather but there is no Sperm Whales to be seen which makes us all down-hearted.

A hemisphere away, new armaments already in use would have ended Captain Swift's troubles. American whalers, pioneered by a half-mad, one-handed whaling captain, had been killing Blues in the North Atlantic effectively for twenty years.

Thomas Welcome Roys of Long Island tired of the same Southern Ocean waters as Captain Swift by the mid-nineteenth century. Against his shipowners' wishes, Roys made for the other extremity of the Pacific, the

Bering Sea. He overcame pack ice in 1848 to find waters so rich in whales that the next year, his biographers said, 154 ships sailed in his wake.

It was the last unexploited Arctic ground. Roys looked at the scale of the hunt there, and realised the limits of the Rights and their near relatives, the Bowheads. He then spouted the whaler's universal blind optimism that other species would fill the gap, without end. 'It will come to this,' Roys wrote in a pamphlet. 'The Humpback, Gray and Sulphur bottom will supply the place of the destroyed and used up Right whales and give us wealth for centuries to come.'

The problem was to reach them. Hand harpooners physically plunged the weapon into whales from very close range. 'These whales will not generally allow a boat to come nearer than three or four rods [15–20 metres], hence the difficulty of fastening to them.'

Borrowing from war, competing inventors began to make bizarre weapons to bridge the gap. They tried rocket-propelled harpoons, shoulder-fired bomb lances, rifle-fired arrows, even explosive grenades that generated suffocating gas. Using one of these cumbersome and dangerous weapons, Roys was probably the first person to take a Blue whale commercially. A little south of Iceland in the North Atlantic, in the summer of 1855, he picked up the Connecticut whaler Robert Brown's 15-kilogram brass shoulder gun and fired, commencing the attrition that carried the largest-ever species to the brink of extinction.

Encouraged that the shoulder gun worked, though the whale sank, a completely detached Roys really opened up on rorquals the following year in the Barents Sea. 'We shot 22 Leviathans [Blues], killing one, 26 Humpbacks killing four, and four Finbacks killing none. Nine Leviathans were made to spout blood, 12 Humpbacks and two Finbacks, which is proof that our aim was tolerably good and the shells all exploded.' Out of all this carnage, one whale floated to be taken and processed—a 28-metre Blue, longer than Roys's own ship.

It took him seven years to make the system work, at the cost of his left hand—lost in a gun explosion to his mild surprise. He only realised it was gone when he saw his ring finger on the deck, ring intact. Success with killing and retrieval finally came in 1863 aboard the whaler *Reindeer*. His crew fired a killing shot from a rocket harpoon, the rope held, the whale was dragged up from 70 fathoms (128 metres), and oil started to flow from Blues.

At exactly the same time a charismatic Norwegian sealer, who claimed a God-given vocation to take whales for mankind, built a 29-metre ship he christened *Spes et Fides* —Hope and Faith. Svend Foyn bolted seven whale guns onto the bow of the world's first purpose-built steam catcher. The idea was to be able to fire shots at a single whale from several types of weapon as he experimented with the best method.

Proud of an era when Norway was a global leader, the whaling historians Tønnessen and Johnsen proclaimed Foyn a model Puritan capitalist, who fathered industrial whaling. He developed a ship quick enough to reach rorquals, and a grenade-tipped harpoon timed to explode inside the body. 'Svend Foyn's grenade harpoon was such an ingenious invention that to this day, 100 years later, it is still in use, for all practical purposes unaltered.'

Another Norwegian admirer, Henryk Bull, said that before Foyn, the chase was extremely dangerous. 'Commander Foyn's victory in his battle with the Blue whale claims in one respect the interest of the naturalist,' said Bull. 'It forms the last chapter in the struggle of the human intellect against brute force. Every other animal had long previously had to acknowledge the superiority of man.'

Sometimes a Blue raised a question mark over this arrogance. Near Cape Addington, Alaska, in May 1910, things turned very Moby Dickish for the crew of the *Lizzie S. Sorenson*. They struck and wounded a Blue that swung around and repeatedly rammed the gasoline whaling schooner until it sank.

But the great wildlife hunt of twentieth-century industrial whaling had its foundation. The new mechanised whalers routed out Blues from the Aleutians to California in the eastern Pacific, through the sub-Arctic seas of the North Atlantic, and around Japan in the western Pacific. As the twentieth century opened, they were also nosing into Antarctic waters disappointingly short of the easy targets, the Rights. What another Norwegian ex-sealer Carl Anton Larsen did find was rorquals: the Humpbacks, Fins, and Blues which 'frolicked in countless shoals'. It took Larsen twelve years before he could put together the means to efficiently exploit the find, and he set up the first Antarctic whaling station at mountain-ringed Grytviken, South Georgia, in 1904.

Larsen couldn't have picked a better place had he tried. Scientists now know South Georgia to be astride the breadbasket of Antarctica. Streaming north in ocean currents are nutrients that make these waters prime planktonic pastures for the crustacean at the centre of the south polar food web: Antarctic krill, *Euphausia superba*. Almost 45 per cent of known world stocks are found in the South Atlantic. The delicate 40-millimetre shrimp swarms in vast aggregations. As well as whales, krill supports fish and teeming numbers of seals, penguins and flighted seabirds.

Modelling his base on existing northern European stations, Larsen set up a shore factory and sent little whale catchers into the South Atlantic to harpoon whales, then tow them back for rendering into oil. In the absence of Rights, the next easiest target was the Humpback. So slow and confiding was this inquisitive species that a chaser could steam up beside it, and slot a harpoon in from near point blank range.

The first Humpback was shot just a month after Larsen set up his factory. In nine days, 182 whales followed it up the wide wooden flensing ramp called the 'plan', and eleven of them were Blue. Progressively, deep water bays in South Georgia and other South Atlantic islands began to fill up with whaling stations and ships converted to floating factories.

Norwegians negotiated licences with Britain, which moved into modern whaling too. In the first nine years, 29 016 whales were taken, more than two-thirds Humpbacks, and there were seven shore stations swallowing whales at South Georgia. Just off the Antarctic Peninsula at South Shetland, at a peak in the summer of 1915–16, there were nine floating factories and 29 whale catchers darting out among the icebergs to feed their appetite. The kill count was quickly heading into the hundreds of thousands.

On his way south with Ernest Shackleton's failed attempt to cross Antarctica in the 1914 *Endurance* expedition, the Australian photographer Frank Hurley set up his camera on the plan at Grytviken. Many bleak pictures of a Blue have been taken since: fleeing with a ship-sized bow wave and nostrils flaring to suck in another 5000-litre breath; dead in the water and inflated like a pleated zeppelin; or an anonymous, vaguely mammalian mound hauled tail-first up a stern ramp. The elements of this Hurley image say much about the sad poetry of whaling.

The backdrop is South Georgia's snowy mountain slope. The profile of a ship is misted and ghostly in the distance. A rubbish pile of whalebone tumbles down to the water beside steaming factory buildings. Stretching across the photograph is a single Blue on its side. In front ten men loosely line up, hands in pockets and shifting from one cold foot to the other. They look impossibly puny beside the Blue, incapable of its death.

It is clearly very dead, tail flukes cut off and a pile of entrails released. Yet the whale is the only thing of grace in this purgatory. The body rises, then slides away again to the tail with a concise symmetry, despite its size. From rounded snout, the jawline runs perhaps seven metres to the base, where the ventral grooves of the throat pleats etch into the skin. The eye is quietly closed. A pectoral fin folds back, a flipper twice the height of any of the men.

Looking at this photograph I suddenly comprehend Peter Gill's description of watching from a boat as a Blue lunged into a krill swarm at the Bonney Upwelling. Hurley's dead whale lies in the attitude the whale takes as, turning on its side, it takes in a roomful of water. Gill saw the 4-metre pectoral rise above the surface in white foam. Hurley's image gives scale to the enormous whale below. It shows how superbly equipped the Blue was to take advantage of a bountiful sea.

The krill of the far South Atlantic built many of the largest Blues, and this individual looks to be about 28 metres long, nearing the maximum. The great taxonomist Carl Linnaeus may have had his own wry view of the Blue when he classified it in 1758, calling it *Balaenoptera musculus*, the mouse-like (or perhaps the muscular) baleen whale.

Searching for the largest Blue whale measured—the single largest animal ever known—is a pursuit of the fabulous. The IWC only gives an average length for the species, at 25 to 26.2 metres. Fossicking through the internet brings exaggeration, with high bids around 114 to 124 feet, or 34.7 to 37.8 metres. Complicating the task, the largest Blue may have been stripped of blubber at sea and then dumped, never reaching a steady measuring tape.

Some including the writer George Small find the summit at 106 feet, or 32.5 metres, and 160 to 180 tonnes. He believes it was a female taken at the South Shetlands in 1926. The practical Tønnessen and Johnsen choose the greatest yield for one measurement. They say a 30.7-metre female shot in March 1931, fat at the end of the Antarctic summer, yielded 354 barrels of oil, or 56 646 kilograms. They also pick 106 feet and 32.5 metres as the maximum length for a Blue taken in Discovery Inlet of the Ross Sea in 1923–24. As Henryk Bull said, hunting down giants had become a game loaded in favour of the hunter.

Blues were uneasy if approached. Early in the modern era when chaser ships were slower, they had to be stalked. 'Quite small noises scare them,' said a Falkland Islands magistrate, A.G. Bennett, whose patch included South Georgia. It was thought the whale could 'hear' through its nostrils in the split second it opened them to breathe. Bennett was told that a man's shout at that moment was enough to make the whale bolt. 'When this happens it is seldom worthwhile to give chase, for no boat has the slightest chance of overtaking a thoroughly scared whale.'

The magistrate sailed out with the whaling crews in the 1920s, and thought chasing rorquals was rather like a gentleman's shoot in the Scottish heather. 'The excitement of chasing [the Fin] is much greater than any-thing provided by the hum-drum creep after Blues. The latter process may be likened to walking up your bird on a grouse moor, the former to shooting driven grouse.'

Developments in diesel and oil-fired engines made these ships faster and the hunt much less equal. In the early 1930s, a British zoologist, Frances Ommanney, worked at South Georgia, observing and recording the catch. He went to sea with Norwegians on the catcher *Narval*, and watched them chase *Blåhvaler*. There was no stalking. It was a mechanised pursuit to exhaustion. The first Blue of the day was taken after a short stop-start chase, and the next died breathless, run down in a long race with a chaser from a rival station.

These men did have mixed feelings about what they saw. Ommanney described the terrible struggle of a harpooned Blue that surfaced a mile from the chaser, thrashing the sea into a foam. 'Now a ribbed belly showed, now a pointed flipper, raised on high, smacking down upon the water. Then a red fountain burst upward, and another. He was spouting blood.'

Bennett recalled the 'most revolting' sight of the dying throes of Blue whales that took up to seven harpoons to kill. He was shocked at the defilement of 'those wide spaces of pure air, pure ice and pure water' in which the killing took place.

Twinges of animal welfare and ecological consciousness were joined by anxiety about the wasteful rush for oil, and disappearing stocks. Bennett raised the notion of a sustainable yield. 'If means can be found to so limit the yearly catch that an ample margin is allowed for breeding purposes, no term need be put on the future of whaling.'

He was echoing rising British concern about the Norwegians in the Antarctic. As early as 1922, the director of Natural History at the British Museum, Sir Sidney Harmer, called for strict catching regulations and a reduction in the fleet against 'insensate slaughter'. If Norway was left to it, the Australian polar explorer Douglas Mawson said, not a single whale would remain in twenty years.

The Norwegians claimed this was just imperial jealousy from Britons who wanted a slice of their success. Everyone reassured themselves market forces would safely prevail. Long before the whales' extinction, the business would become unprofitable. Bennett said: 'The bankruptcy of the commercial side of things will be the whale's salvation.'

Across Antarctica a young Australian journalist, Alan Villiers, spent a season in 1923–24 poking into the Ross Sea with Carl Anton Larsen in the first licensed pelagic fleet. Villiers was sold on the same crackpot notion that the immensity of factory whaling was actually the whales' best guarantee of a future. 'These giant argosies cannot continue—they would not be profitable—unless they are assured of full cargoes . . . Therefore as soon as the whales thin, these ships will have to leave them alone. They cannot hunt them until the *last whale*. They can only hunt them to the *last full cargo*.'

Lessons from the recent extinctions of whale stocks in the Northern Hemisphere seemed to have eluded these people. Or the financial imperative to pay the debt that owning a whaling fleet imposed. Or the thought that, what was unprofitable for a big fleet might be fine for smaller Japanese whalers who took the big rorquals for meat. There was no knowing that a command economy like the Soviet Union's would keep whaling beyond commercial reason. Certainly there would have been little science needed to calculate critical sustainable yields. They must have known about the last Dodo, which died at the end of the seventeenth century. But after all, it had lived on a single island. What dazzled the hunters was the scale and adventure of Antarctic whaling—the sheer number of whales, the strangeness of their domain, and the money waiting to be made.

4

MAKING MARGARINE

Only in the last moment of human history has the delusion
arisen that people can flourish apart from the rest of the
living world.

Edward O. Wilson, *The Diversity of Life*, 1992

The pack-ice zone of Antarctica is like the grassy plain of temperate land.
The icescape unfolds to the horizon, sometimes as a snow-smoothed table-
cloth, at others ridged chaotically. In the summer melt, leads of water open
and the fertility attracts grazers and predators. If the conditions are right,
the abundance of life is staggering.

Italian marine scientists steamed into the middle of the Ross Sea in
search of *Euphausia superba* in November 1994. They believed earlier
science had wrongly suggested Antarctic krill was largely absent from this
sea, and proved themselves stunningly correct. Working with acoustic
measuring equipment and sampling nets over the Pennell Bank they found
superswarms.

Rarely encountered, these are giant aggregations of the little
crustacean in open water amid melting late spring pack. The Italians
estimated the superswarms' total biomass at around 1.77 million tonnes.
In one small area of a few square kilometres, a single superswarm was
calculated at 51 761 tonnes. It was encircled by a herd of about 250
gorging Minke whales. No other rorquals were recorded. They no longer
existed there.

The Ross Sea's 500 000 square kilometres was once prime habitat
for Blue and Fin whales, and a stronghold against whaling. A persistent
pack ice wall at its northern extreme guarded its internal open waters

against entry, except in high summer. Few had preceded explorer Ernest Shackleton's *Nimrod* when it dodged through a gap in the pack in 1904. He headed south looking for a shore closest to the South Pole and cruised along the front of the Ross Ice Shelf.

The world's largest floating ice mass covers a further 530 000 square kilometres of water at the southern end of the sea. Along the shelf edge, Shackleton found an ice harbour where, the ship's log said, 'whales were spouting all around'. The Bay of Whales later became a base for Roald Amundsen to launch his successful first expedition to reach the pole. It was where Carl Larsen came with his factory ship, *Sir James Clark Ross*, when he pioneered whaling in the high Antarctic.

This ship was built to withstand the ice, but whalers were less able. Alan Villiers recounts how, on this first trip in 1923–24, the *Ross* was moored alongside its eponymous ice shelf, while the flensers went to work on 'fine, fat, big Blues'.

On that ship there was no stern ramp. Carcasses were tied up beside it, and flensed by men who stood in small boats, or on the dead whales. They froze and frostbite was frequent. 'They cannot even wear fingerless mitts, for they must have sure and steady hold of the greasy knives,' said Villiers. It was the twilight of the Heroic Age for polar explorers, and people were determined to give whalers in this last exploited corner of the world a Hollywood limelight too.

'Nothing ever daunts the captains or the hardy crews of the five little frostbitten whalers,' Villiers wrote. 'They are splendid men, whose powers of endurance, patience and courage are peerless. And they are very quiet—very quiet indeed. They never have anything to say of the experiences and the dangers through which they pass.' The season's haul by Larsen was ordinary—17 500 barrels or 2800 tonnes. The following summer in the north-west corner of the Ross Sea, his ship took huge Blues between Coulman and Possession Islands, and business paid.

The invention of the stern ramp eased the task. Whales were dragged aboard whole to be flensed, but the deck of any Ross Sea factory ship was perilous. Personal records of this life were kept by some of the dozens of Australians who shipped aboard the *Nielsen Alonso*, like Henric Brammall who was just eighteen when he signed on and began taking notes.

'Allright Brarmull. Don't just stand there. Haven't you seen a vhale before?'

'No sir, I haven't.'

'Vell you have now. And you'll see plenty more! Jump to it boys!'

Late in life Brammall typed an unpublished manuscript about his adventure. It still drips with vivid memories.

> Slowly the enormous mass rose from the sea, and slid to a standstill, blocking our view to a height of ten to 12 feet—a vast, inanimate, rubbery mountain of blubber, bone and meat, bluish black in colour, crushed shapeless by its own sheer weight . . . There on the deck to be butchered piece by piece, by a swarm of tiny men with knives as long as their own bodies.

Clive Tilley with his box Brownie camera snapped the messy decks and his fellow crew, many of them fixedly smoking pipes. Late in life Tilley looked back sadly at one of the barbaric sights of Antarctic whaling: red snow. In a blizzard, whale blood was caught up in the whirling flakes and pasted over the ship. William 'Old Bill' Stewart catalogued the exceptionally dangerous work in his diaries. On his first voyage he saw a broken wire hawser swirl across the deck to fatally injure a sixteen-year-old mess boy. The ship's doctor, ill himself for weeks, had been evacuated to another vessel. On Stewart's last voyage a gunner's mate lost an eye to an exploding grenade shell and a 'fine, strong young fireman' went crazy. 'Now, poor fellow [he] is awful to look at and closely secured.' Fractures and respiratory diseases were common and the men 'struck work' over bad food.

The factory ships were knocked around in the ice by gales. On 14 November 1930, one storm hit when the ship was boiling down whale at full capacity. A rush to secure the decks failed, and the chief officer who was caught between hatchway and a sliding head bone was seriously injured. 'On deck it is all roar and yelling with tons of water coming on board, including huge lumps of ice coming right over the foredeck and rushing through the alleyways.'

The storm carried away stores and deck equipment, and the ship was listing heavily when it abated. Catchers survived by sheltering in the ice, but had to be gathered up, repaired and refuelled by the factory ship. Another gale endangered *Neilsen Alonso* two months later, but Old Bill had seen it all before. 'Great excitement with the news our ship is leaking badly in the engine room. Some of the boys very windy.'

Throughout his diaries runs the value of contesting the worst of the Ross Sea in a leaky ship. Old Bill tallies rich catches of whales. In the 1930–31 season the crew boiled down 1352 whales to produce 112 000 barrels of oil—nearly 18 000 tonnes. Most would have been Blues. Halfway through the season, *Neilsen Alonso* filled a tanker that also carried away the mad young fireman in a straitjacket.

There were other signs that this pace couldn't last. Brammall was halfway through his first season wheeling barrows of coal from bunker to boiler when a Blue was drawn in by the catcher boat, *Pol 1*.

'He was very old and very tough, and his liver was so rotten that it fell to pieces directly it was hooked,' Brammall pencilled in his diary. 'I think he was the last in the Ross Sea.' With the gunners choosing the best yielding animals, whaling statistics for the years 1923–30 tell of the deadly focus on a single species. Around 95 per cent were Blue.

The peak of Antarctic whaling was reached in 1931, according to the International Whaling Statistics office. Nearly 40 000 whales gave up a total of 3.3 million barrels of oil—over half a million tonnes of the stuff. Factory fleets girdled the frozen continent and most of the whales taken, more than 28 000, were Blue. Adding average losses from broken harpoon lines and storm damage, thousands more were hit but never brought aboard.

The great hunt reached such a height that an oil glut kept most of the whaling fleet home for the following season—not to conserve stocks, but because it didn't pay to go south. Global business was beginning to determine the future of whales, and a brightly optimistic financial prospectus issued in Sydney in 1929 explained why.

The Pacific and Ross Sea Whaling Company Limited, with two knights on its board of directors, proposed a £500 000 share float to fund an expedition using a New Zealand licence and Norwegian ships and expertise. Glowing with figures showing 'astounding' potential profits, the prospectus issued two months before the Wall Street crash appropriated the words of Mawson. 'The Antarctic and sub-Antarctic seas abound in whales,' he was claimed to have said. 'It is possible that at present there is over-killing of whales in certain areas. Properly regulated and controlled, however, whaling is an enduring asset.'

Encouraging pictures showed riches in store. An ice-rimmed chaser was surrounded by inflated Blue carcasses: 'Chaser with Six Whales—a Fine Catch for a Frosty Morning'. The prospectus invited investors to climb onto a company that had already acquired a precious Ross Sea licence from New Zealand. 'It is a matter of common knowledge that serious consideration is being given to the idea of bringing whaling under international control . . . A monopoly will thus be created for existing licensees.'

The directors thought the market for whale oil was practically unlimited. The finer grades went in lubricating oils, the coarser in industrial processes like leather dressing and making soap. Strong interest was coming from the makers of the new European kitchen staple, margarine.

Today the multinational corporation Unilever calls itself on its website one of the world's great consumer goods companies. It says its mission is to add vitality to our lives by meeting everyday needs for nutrition, hygiene and personal care, and its brands are indeed household names. As the company also says, in the early twentieth century it was part of a Whale Oil Pool. A cartel of European manufacturers, the pool regulated the distribution and price of whale oil through annual bouts of corporate arm-wrestling. Unilever often emerged the winner, using the oil for soap. William Lever, the north of England family grocer who became an industrial mogul, refused to put it in his signature soap, Sunlight. An objectionable smell and colour stood against that, he said. There was no problem with its use in lesser soaps like Lifebuoy. 'The carbolic in Lifebuoy would destroy any smell there might be.'

Margarine was just as tricky to manufacture. First made from beef fat and milk, it was an affordable alternative to butter in Europe's newly booming cities. The chemistry had taken a while to unlock and the key was hardening of the oil by hydrogenation. Gradually developed through a series of patents, the process mixed different liquid oils with hydrogen to produce a spreadable butter-like consistency at room temperature.

After animal by-products, vegetable oils were next poured into margarine vats. As methods of refining and deodorising developed, whale oil followed. Its early use after 1910 was covert. Industrialists like the German, Henry van den Bergh, believed the average housewife would be repelled by the thought of whale blubber on their bread. But during World War One, access to fats became strategically important (as was the glycerine by-product used in explosives).

Unilever waited until 1929 before producing a hardened whale oil for margarine. So confident was it of the future of the whale-based soap and margarine that it forward-bought two thirds of the entire whale oil catch for the seasons 1929–30 and 1930–31.

All those Blue whales.

No wonder that in those years, a bunch of Australian capitalists saw a killing to be made in the Ross Sea. No wonder factory ship crews went to work so perilously in the Antarctic's wild heart. And no wonder that 65 years later, when Italian scientists found Ross Sea krill superswarms, the thing missing was Leviathan, turning on her side and surging into the feast.

We can track the Blues' disappearance mainly because of a bullet-headed Norwegian called Sigurd Risting. Gazing unblinking through round spectacles at whaling companies' returns, Risting compiled and published records of catches from 1903 for the Norwegian Whaling Association. As global industrial whaling concentrated heavily on the Antarctic, he created the International Whaling Statistics, and a new measurement called the Blue Whale Unit (BWU). The concept was simple: a unit could be used to compare oil yields from different species. One Blue equalled two Fins, two-and-a-half Humpbacks, and six Sei, or Bryde's whales.

In later years, the BWU became so entrenched in whaling regulation that it worked like a slow-acting poison. When it was introduced, the standard meant whalers could be held to some account for the staggering waste in Antarctica. Blubber was peeled off floating whales and the rest left to drift away, taking half the oil with it, to make space for the next bunch of carcasses dragged in by chasers whose crews were paid by the number of kills. Risting's statistics benchmarked this waste.

Trawling through them, Tønnessen and Johnsen brought to light some bizarre results. Off the African state of Angola in 1926, lightweight wintering Blues yielded seventeen barrels, or a little over 2 tonnes per BWU. Compare that to the single largest yield: 354 barrels, or 56 tonnes. South Georgia's early shore-based whaling averaged just 26 barrels per BWU. In the Ross Sea, Carl Larsen's second expedition hauled a slightly more meaningful 75 barrels up the side of the *Sir James Clark Ross*, and the average global yield peaked at 112 barrels in 1939–40.

The downside of the Blue Whale Unit gradually became clear when it was accepted as an official quota measurement. Any gunner was foolish not to hit the largest whale possible. If he needed at least twice as many successful chases to match a single Blue, then of course he would go for the Blue. And he would want the biggest, which was also the most successful female, the heart of the breeding stock. In 1932–33, 422 Blue cows were killed for every 100 bulls.

Such a rampage couldn't stand logical scrutiny for long. British and US scientists started to lobby for international regulation. The chief culprit, Norway, made the first attempt to rein in high seas whalers, legislating to count catches, impose a barrel tax and inspection system, and put a lower limit on Blues caught at 60 feet (18.2 metres). Sadly for the species, this was 14 feet, or 4 metres, below their length at sexual maturity.

The first serious international effort to protect Rights in the 1931 Geneva Convention to Regulate Whaling also tried to outlaw killing all calves and all females with calves. Several countries including the Soviet Union and Japan refused to sign up. Through the 1930s other attempts were made to restrict pelagic whaling in a series of international meetings, but they largely failed. Regulation was still basically agreement between major companies.

Japan, particularly, refused to bind itself as it attempted to gain a foothold in Antarctic whaling. Already used to the high seas of the North Pacific, the Japanese whaling company Nippon Hogei first appeared in the far south in 1934, immediately raising alarm from Norway. Despite Oslo's own record, its diplomats in Tokyo warned that the Japanese were ruthless and would overfish the resource. Norwegians also sold Japanese whalers their first fleet, and it took them just three seasons to muscle into Antarctic whales. The invention of refrigerated shipping just prior to World War Two meant they could whale for meat.

In an echo of other pre-war Western appeasements, Japan was allowed to brush off conditions many other nations had agreed to. While they waited for Japan's promised adherence to their international agreement, it started whaling earlier than other nations, and ignored a ban on catching Humpbacks. When war broke out, Japan declared its promise void and went south one more time.

Whales did get a respite during the war. The take fell to a fraction of its pre-war size, as the already toughened sailors joined the armed services, catchers were turned into patrol boats, and factory ships into freighters. Many didn't make it to the end of the war, among them *Neilsen Alonso.* Having survived the Ross Sea's dangers, it took the ghosts of polar crews and giant hauls to the bottom of the North Atlantic when it was torpedoed with the loss of three lives in February 1943.

With peace in 1945, the whale's fat and protein could be a quick fix for the war battered. Even if whalers had to sail to the Antarctic, big quantities of meat were obtainable. Think of that illustration: 150 cattle to a single Blue. In one northern hemisphere country the frozen meat arrived in 1946–47. Unrationed when other meat was hard to obtain, it was sold to home cooks through fish shops, and a restaurant chain claimed to be grilling 600 whale steaks a day. Cooking demonstrations exhorted house-wives to try this nutritious food, which looked like liverish beef. But the people didn't like it. They said it smelled of fish and stale oil. Five years after the war, thousands of tonnes were sitting unsold on the docks. Britons didn't take to whale the way they did in Japan.

Given only two days' warning, Australian Kenneth Coonan found himself heaped among the mailbags on a seatless air force courier aeroplane to Tokyo, just in time to catch Japan's first postwar whaling expedition in November 1946.

Coonan had been discharged a petty officer from the Royal Australian Navy at war's end on medical grounds. He reached Tokyo already weary of the assignment. So was Australia. It had argued against Japan being given this chance, and won only the right to watch it happen.

An American was already installed in the captain's own stateroom on the factory ship *Hashidate Maru*. Lieutenant David McCracken was representing the Supreme Commander of Allied Powers (SCAP), General Douglas MacArthur. The cheery McCracken could have been a role model for the legendary navy hard nut of sitcom television, Quinton McHale.

In McCracken's navy, he was lying on his bunk at SCAP headquarters when a room-mate put it to him: '"Dave, how'd you like to take a trip to the South Pole for six months?"

'"I'll be ready by five. When do we leave?" I responded without even looking up.'

McCracken did his best to alleviate the boredom. Pleading a frightful ordeal ahead, he persuaded a service supplier to give him a record player, 45 new records and a box full of trinkets, toys and games. He tried the same ploy on the services library. As the expedition wore on, McCracken took to shooting seabirds with his semi-automatic carbine. He snapped the wingtip of 'the largest and prettiest' bird, probably a Wandering Albatross, leaving it to flounder helpless in the factory ship's wake. As if imagining himself a latter-day explorer of undiscovered waters, he shot more birds for their skins. He was amused by a penguin kept aboard until it died of starvation. And he got to harpoon a whale.

Coonan appears to have been a more subdued companion. McCracken's first impression, recalled in *Four Months on a Jap Whaler*, was: 'He was dressed in a grey business suit, tan shoes and grey hat.' More familiar with ships than McCracken, Coonan was keen to make sure the Japanese stuck to the rules. McCracken claimed no friction ever developed between them, but Coonan's confidential report to the Australian Government on his return bluntly criticised both the American and the supreme command.

Today Japanese officials clutch at the country's revival of Antarctic whaling after the war as a nostalgic touchstone. This, they say with swelling chests, was when many of their own hungry parents could obtain good food.

It was the point when a defeated nation was able to stand up again, go abroad with pride, and fend for itself.

Masayuki Komatsu, the face of Japanese whaling to 2004, thanks MacArthur. 'The general's decision was made after careful consideration based on his humanitarian ideals to save the Japanese from starvation,' Komatsu said. Then he pushed MacArthur's motives a step further: 'It is also believed that advice was given to him that Japanese traditionally had a custom of eating whale meat, and the whaling crews had good skills.'

Faced with costly food shortages, and approached by Japanese fishing companies whose offshore fishing was restricted, MacArthur decided to let two whaling fleets go south in the summer of 1946–47. He unlocked an industry that would shovel whale into the Japanese diet for a generation. It was already on the move out of a handful of coastal communities and into the general population before the war, but after hostilities it became politically vital. The Norwegian analysts Arne Kalland and Brian Moeran claim that 47 per cent of animal protein consumed by the Japanese in 1947 was whale, and it was still 23 per cent in 1964. Even for a culture with a rice-based diet, not high in animal protein, whale meat clearly counted.

The Japanese re-entry to the far south was angrily opposed. New Zealand, Australia and Britain had spent far too many precious lives defeating Japan's barbaric wartime imperialism. They formally protested against the first expedition, opening a book in Tokyo of diplomatic flourishes against whaling that is still being filled today without any noticeable effect.

MacArthur at the time held the power of a feudal shogun, or British viceroy. He overrode the complainers and authorised two converted tankers and their motley catcher fleet to use waters 'hereinafter referred to as the Antarctic Whaling Area'. They were assigned iron-clad rights to seas where, 60 years later, they still go whaling.

Ranging from 90 degrees east to 170 degrees west and about 1000 kilometres offshore, the fleet had access to whales from the Davis Sea to the Ross Sea—around five million square kilometres of ocean. This is prime whale habitat of the high Antarctic; waters marked by giant tabular icebergs and sea ice that floats over subsea rises and the continental shelf, lifting cold waters up and bringing krill swarms to cetaceans. Gifted by the

American, the Antarctic Whaling Area is also the waters off today's Australian, French and New Zealand polar claims.

The fleet had to obey the rules of the new International Convention for the Regulation of Whaling, just agreed in Washington DC. The same convention, with its elastic strengths and truck-sized loopholes, is in place today. In late 1947, what mattered to Coonan and McCracken were the clear instructions about quotas, minimum length and avoiding waste. McCracken, the inspector, and Coonan, the observer, were there to watch the Japanese whalers take meat for themselves and oil for Europe.

The fleet was working through waters about 1000 kilometres south of Macquarie Island, two weeks into the voyage, when a gunner shot an undersized Blue. At 68 feet (20.7 metres) it was just 2 feet under minimum length. McCracken said he told the Japanese captain, Miyata, it was a serious matter and to reprimand the gunner. No such knuckle-rapping about the waste of whales was recorded in his book. Coonan's confidential report said it was clear after the first week's whaling that the factory ship was poorly set up to process whales, and MacArthur's office knew that before the fleet left Japan.

It was the old story. Blues and Fins were reaching the factory deck faster than they could be processed. To Coonan the answer was simple: kill fewer whales. He didn't have the authority though—McCracken did. That became absolutely clear when the American decided to join a catcher for a change of scene, and became part of a bloody debacle in which it took five harpoons to kill a Fin. Registering his own lordly power, McCracken recorded in detail what happened.

The Fin had been harpooned twice by the catcher's crew, and not killed. The harpoon's ropes winched the giant in close to the ship, and the crew reloaded for a third, seemingly easy shot to despatch it. McCracken 'somewhat jokingly said to the skipper: "If this harpoon does not kill whale, I fire number four".' What alternative would a humble Japanese chaser skipper have? To end the agonies of a Fin, or humour the man who occupied the captain's cabin on the factory ship? So number three harpoon duly missed, and the Fin continued to heave and fall.

McCracken stuffed wadding into his ears against the noise of the explosion as the whale was pulled closer. He tried to time its next rise to breathe, fired a harpoon, and saw it strike home at too shallow an angle either to explode the grenade or hold in the flesh. A fifth shot was needed to finish it. McCracken's observation? He was glad that the whaling company directors weren't around to count the cost.

On the factory ship, Coonan was beginning to steam. To clear the deck of a glut of bone, McCracken had already given written permission for whalers to discard 'poor bones'—parts of a whale that had little oil. Late in the season Coonan watched as, with whale kills backing up, whole sides of Blue and Fin ribs were lifted on a deck crane, swung over the side and cut loose.

'A side of ribs is a huge affair,' Coonan said in his report to the Australian Commonwealth Fisheries Office. 'When the factory has been quiet I have watched the workers separate and cut away the meat from them, and the amount of meat thus obtained was astounding . . . The complete backbone was also discarded.'

Coonan complained to McCracken, but the American accepted the Japanese view that the loss of a little oil was outweighed by the gain of much meat. In between the measured words of a government report is Coonan's real anger with the Supreme Command and its man.

> It would appear that SCAP was aware of the deficiencies in the equip-
> ment on board this vessel, and that it was intended to produce as much
> salted meat and salted blubber as possible without regard to international
> whaling agreements. It was also apparent that the SCAP representative,
> Lieut. McCracken, was prepared to allow the infringements of whaling
> regulations in order to increase production.

Coonan's superior, F.F. Anderson, added a note to the file as it headed towards the Department of External Affairs. The US War Department had said this first voyage was not intended to set a precedent for future years, and Anderson saw the waste as clear evidence that the Japanese whalers did not take the regulations seriously—ammunition to use if they tried to go back for a 1947–48 Antarctic season.

That was futile, though. Japan was back whaling. On the *Hashidate Maru*'s first voyage, it took meat from 297 Blues, 189 Fin and four Sperm whales and saved many people from a slow death by starvation, Komatsu said. Together with the *Nisshin Maru*, another converted tanker, the two catcher fleets went south through the years of occupation until in 1951 Japan was allowed to develop its own industry and to join the International Whaling Commission.

5

HEROIC LIARS

A man cannot think deeply and exert his utmost muscular force.

Charles Darwin, *The Expression of the Emotions*, 1872

Hero of Socialist Labour Alexi Solyanik stood in the open air of the flying bridge on his ship *Slava*. A following wind was pushing the flagship of the Soviet Union's first factory whaling fleet along. Its Captain-Director wore a commanding smile for the camera as he lifted a pair of binoculars, eyes focussed on the distance. His deep braided uniform tugged a little at his barrel chest. The gold star of his title was unmistakeable on his right breast.

With Hero status went priority housing, reduced taxes, and free medical benefits. But such special privileges were uncertain even for someone as senior as Solyanik. This was the Soviet Union of 1952, a deeply totalitarian Communist government run by the genocidal Joseph Stalin. The Iron Curtain separated Russia from the West. Secret police watched the people and the unlucky disappeared.

In that year the great writer Alexander Solzhenitsyn was eking out life at a labour camp in Kazakhstan, unknown to the world. Stalin and his henchmen were concocting the Doctors' Plot, in which prominent Jewish doctors, falsely said to be poisoning the leadership, would be killed. US President Harry Truman's State of the Union address warned that the Soviet Union was expanding military production, shadowing humanity with the spectre of another world war.

Solyanik's task as the fleet left Odessa on the Black Sea was to meet the targets of the current Five Year Plan. *The New York Times*'s Moscow correspondent Walter Duranty believed Stalin's Five Year Plans fulfilled a deep need for Russians. 'The whole purpose of the plan is to get the Russians going—that is, to make a nation of eager, conscious workers out of a nation that was a lump of sodden, driven slaves.'

These central commands covered all kinds of production. Many plans failed, but Solyanik would claim that his targets were better than achieved, even though success demanded a 10 per cent increase on the previous year's take.

After this, its seventh voyage, the *Slava* fleet's 2726 whale kill would fulfil its plan by 102.6 per cent. 'There were 15 whaling flotillas from other countries in the Antarctic at the same time, some of them larger than ours, but none of them equalled our record,' Solyanik boasted.

As history would have it, the Captain-Director's words have come back to haunt whalers. In a little English language paperback he wrote about the 1952–53 season, *Cruising in the Antarctic*, Solyanik noted diligently that the hunting of rare species and lactating whales was prohibited, and seasons were fixed 'on the initiative of progressive scientists'. He dismissed as 'reckless extermination' the scale of pre-war whaling.

But we now know why Solyanik's fleet caught more than any other in the season. It killed totally protected species and lactating whales. Seasonal restrictions were a joke. The killing went beyond recklessness into pathological destruction. This Hero of Socialist Labour was a champion liar, and for 25 years other Soviet whalers followed his example. They killed nearly twice as many whales as they reported. They drove already endangered species to within a finger's breadth of the cold clutch of extinction. And when they ran out of the best, the Blues, they even invented them.

The Soviet Union's first Antarctic factory ship was an ageing war prize. Originally built as the *Vikingen* for a British and Norwegian consortium, it was sold to Germany in 1938 with five whale catchers, and after war's end was claimed by the Russians. Norwegians were hired as advisers for the first two years. Then, when the Soviet Union joined the International Whaling Commission in 1948, *Slava* embarked on its fraud.

The first words of the convention signed by the Soviets recognise the interest of the nations of the world in safeguarding the great natural resources of whale stocks for future generations. Years of abject failure finally forced postwar agreement on this founding charter for the IWC, the

International Convention for the Regulation of Whaling (ICRW). The same mood for global cooperation that created the United Nations spread into whaling. Recognising the industry had been out of any sustainable control for the first half of the century, diplomats from nineteen nations saw the ICRW as a means of managing what the US statesman Dean Acheson called 'wards of the entire world'.

Limited regional agreements had tried to resolve disputes over contested animals like fish stocks and Arctic seals. The ICRW brought a greater notion: that any country could jointly agree with others to protect and manage globally the largest members of an order of animals: Cetacea.

This idea was fitted out from the start for stormy progress through the voyage of history. The ICRW's home port is at the US Department of State in Washington DC, but the IWC is run by a small secretariat in a converted home known as the Red House, in Cambridge, UK. The course is charted by the IWC meeting—part science, part diplomacy, and very quarrelsome. Competing observers lobby for their particular direction. The ship is fuelled with resolutions of varying strength. High-octane measures are Amendments to the IRCW's accompanying Schedule, agreed by three quarters of the members. But any member nation can spike this fuel: the recalcitrant only has to object to a Schedule Amendment within 90 days of the annual meeting to nullify its power. Tucked away there is also an outlandish piece of cargo: called Article Eight, it gives each member nation absolute control over its own lethal scientific research.

Early in life the IWC agreed on two measures that made sustainable use of whales impossible.

First, diplomatic haggling settled on an annual overall quota for Antarctic baleen whales of 16 000 Blue Whale Units (BWUs). A similar quota would stay in place for nearly twenty years. Of course so many Blues were nowhere to be found. Among the rorquals, the Fin, at two whales per BWU, was already the mainstay. Almost three times as many Fins were taken in the 1950s. Solyanik called it 'the most important whale in the business'. When Fins ran out, the next smallest Sei whale (six per BWU) followed as the target. Instead of trying to manage each species, the IWC opted to treat these great whales as one lump of oil and meat. Whalers harpooned purely for expedience, shooting down through the sizes successively.

Graphs of kills for each species rose and plummetted like a series of tech. stocks booming, then crashing in the bust.

The IWC's other defining foolishness was to set up a race between fleets to kill the most whales first. Instead of splitting the BWU into national quotas that might be policed, it set an Antarctic season. How to work such a rule for best profit? Kill whales—any whales—quicker than anyone else. Fleets raced to be in place on opening day. They used more and deadlier catcher boats to feed factory ships built bigger to outcompete rivals. They worked through the 24-hour daylight of a high Antarctic summer, and atrocious polar weather where kills were lost and crews endangered. As the annual race unfolded, they radioed their catches progressively to the International Bureau of Whaling Statistics. It rang the bell on the final lap, giving four days' warning when the overall limit would be reached.

Some protections were in place for endangered species. Right whales were still totally off limits, and the Humpback season was very brief. But there were no independent observers on factory fleets to umpire this. It became known as the Whaling Olympics, and it was just as open to deliberate nobbling by unscrupulous nations.

As the *Slava* fleet's 700 crew sailed south with catchers, tugs and factory ship in October 1952, Moscow was drawing breath ahead of the 19th Party Congress. For the first time in thirteen years, Stalin allowed a sham show of representative government. Solyanik faithfully described shipboard party meetings by the good Communists.

'In off hours the sailors equipped a room for political education, with a beautifully made stand showing, in drawings and diagrams, the targets of the new five-year plan.' Somewhere on board the *Slava*, maybe using the same carefully crafted stand, Solyanik explained to his subordinates what to catch and how to fabricate data for the International Bureau of Whaling Statistics.

This is the story that he told the world: 'The seasonal quota and the length of the season are fixed annually. Fin whales and Blue whales, for example, may usually be hunted from January to March; Humpbacks in February, and then only for a few days. No restrictions have been placed on the hunting of Sperm whales, and we were planning to begin our hunt with them. We began to hunt Sperm whales on November 17.'

Actually in November 1952 the *Slava* fleet's gunners shot whatever they found. The factory crew dragged 236 Fins up the stern ramp. They also took 33 Humpbacks and two Blues. The legal catch was five Sperm whales. And that was just the first month of the hunt.

In the flush of Russian Glasnost, open criticism of the party in the early 1990s, the books were opened on illegal Soviet whaling and these lies finally were laid bare. As revelations of scientific falsification, they were deeply scandalous. Their implications for whale stocks were profound. The discovery came about by chance after the South African scientist Peter Best talked to his American colleague, Bob Brownell, about rejection of a paper on pregnancy rates because the data were too limited. Brownell happened to mention this to his friend, Alexey Yablokov, a former whale scientist who rose to become Environmental Adviser to Boris Yeltsin on the Russian National Security Council. Yablokov said that he had a few hundred more samples he could offer.

'I kept talking to Yablokov,' Brownell told me. 'We had a pretty good idea from some sightings off Tristin da Cunha that Rights had been taken illegally in the South Atlantic, for example. The factory ships were seen. Yablokov said: "Well, really, there's a lot more data". And I said, "Well we've got to get it, because we need to understand what happened".'

The first revelations came from Yablokov and Dimitriy Tormosov. In November 1993 they committed what would have been a Soviet treason: they told publicly of the 'criminal and barbaric' deception at a biennial meeting of the Society of Marine Mammalogy in Galveston, Texas. Tormosov said real catches from one fleet, the *Yurii Dolgorukii*, were almost twice as many as reported to the IWC.

Yablokov carried the flag in work that took ex-Soviet whaling observers and scientists, including the fisheries union leader Ernst Cherny, years more to complete. 'They collect the data,' Yablokov told me. 'Falsification happened in VNIRO (the Russian Federal Research Institute of Fishery and Oceanography).' Yablokov blamed a senior VNIRO figure who had represented the country for years. 'Personally, Mikhail Ivashin, who was responsible for preparing the report to the IWC. He carefully calculated false data to make its looking real.'

Ivashin was aided at sea by people like Solyanik, who had not counted on the observers and scientists keeping diaries, and spiriting away copies of individual 'whale passports' or catch documents, hidden in places like a potato cellar. In the new Russian Federation where academics scraped by, the data were a saleable commodity.

One who helped Yablokov blow the whistle, Ivan Golovlev, happened to have been on *Slava* under Solyanik. The Captain-Director recalled by Golovlev was devious and distrustful. Solyanik had learned to whale in the Soviets' first factory whaling ground on the Pacific coast, where in pre-war years the kill was totally unrestricted. He pointed to past walrus and seal hunts as proof that the capitalists would violate any regulation for profit, and needed to be beaten at that game.

Golovlev at the time was low on a career ladder that culminated in 1962 with a job as Chief State Inspector of whaling in the Antarctic. He recalled being issued written orders by an Odessa official for the *Slava*'s whaling captains detailing regulations for the catch. When he tried to distribute them at sea, Golovlev was told by Solyanik to give them to him instead.

'At the same time, A.N. Solyanik instructed captains and harpooners during dispatcher meetings: "A barren desert must remain where the *Slava* has operated. Catch all whales you meet. Follow the example of V.L. Tupikov. He catches small size, sucklings and lactating females alike".'

Solyanik extolled several of his gunners, but in his book Vasily Tupikov was the great Soviet pathfinder. At the cost of many misses, the marksman who had been a soldier in Siberia learned to treble his harpoon range to an unheard-of 70 metres. The Captain-Director backed him, making the point that he did so, even though Tupikov wasn't a party member. 'Naturally, if it were possible to shoot at a longer range, the catch would increase greatly.'

With the pride of a mentor, Solyanik claimed that Tupikov set an individual gunner's world record in 1951–52 with a catch of 372 whales, and in the seventh cruise even started shooting at longer range in gales. How better to win the Whaling Olympics?

When the Soviets began their deception, some lies were elaborate. Solyanik told Golovlev which dates to report baleen whale catches so as to show them in season, and which species to claim were killed instead of protected whales. Others were no better than fishermen's fibs. 'As a rule he misplaced the areas of profitable operation,' Golovlev said. 'Once, instructing me on distorting the co-ordinates, he moved a pencil across the Weddell Sea south of the glacier edge. I noted that this water area was covered by an offshore glacier, and A.N. Solyanik smiled in return, saying: "Let the statistical bureau puzzle about our work".'

Solyanik was raising a middle finger to the rest of the whaling world. It was the arrogance of someone who believed himself to be untouchable. He knew that Moscow stood behind him.

Golovlev said the demands of the Soviet plan—an extra 10 per cent each year—meant it was impossible not to violate quotas and seasonal restrictions. The Ministry of Fisheries had to be aware of the scale of the deception. The whalers had a direct interest in fraud because their pay only rose when the plan was met.

Even when Golovlev was appointed as Chief State Inspector, he was warned not to be too diligent. He finally wrote his account in 2000 in an article that has, in translation, the cryptic title of an old survivor: 'The Echo of Mystery of Whales'.

The true Soviet whaling data is patchy. A good deal has been lost or burned. But to reconstruct the *Slava* fleet's seventh cruise through an IWC paper prepared by the Moscow professor, Vyacheslav Zemsky, is to hear Golovlev's echoes. In years to come *Slava* would take almost double the whales it reported. In 1952–53, Solyanik's real take was only 109 whales greater than the total he later proclaimed to the world. What really mattered was the emerging pattern.

The IWC-approved Humpback season in the Antarctic at the time was three days in February, with the option of a few more days depending on the reported catch. The *Slava*'s 311 Humpbacks were slaughtered throughout five months of the season. On that voyage Solyanik's harpooners also shot nine totally protected Right whales, unmistakeable to any whaler because of their dual blow. Most deviously, 136 Blues were claimed on the *Slava*'s list when the fleet only took 39. Solyanik conjured up the world's largest whales. They were numerical phantoms.

The reason was simple, another of the Soviet whistleblowers, Yuri Mikhalev, told IWC scientists. 'The motivation to inflate catch data was to mask illegal catches of other species, as well as to create the impression that

Blue whale stocks were healthy, and were not in need of lowered quotas, or a catch ban.'

The *Slava*'s imaginary Blues were bigger, more female, and more often pregnant. The real Blues were slightly shorter overall, more often under legal size, sometimes lactating, but less often pregnant. A single real 130-centimetre embryo was found in 22 Blue cows on the seventh cruise. The statistics claimed there were five.

Solyanik, who presided personally over this kill, was not only commander of the Soviet fleet. He was the country's IWC commissioner for eight years through the 1950s, and on its delegation for years after that. It was Solyanik's face that Soviets showed to the world through most of the years of illegal whaling.

The *Slava* flotilla returned to Odessa after its seventh cruise to a welcome of cheering throngs and flowers in May 1953, a contented Solyanik recorded. Days later he went to London for the fifth meeting of the IWC. There with a straight face he put forward proposals for all member nations to release more statistical data on their catches. This should be done, the Soviets said, on the grounds of 'reciprocity'.

Cold War remoteness made it hard to see what the Soviet whalers were up to in the mid-twentieth century. Outside the Iron Curtain, official guesswork was obsessed with nuclear arms and Communist aggression, not the survival of whales. The *Slava* was watched sailing out of Odessa in 1949 by British officials who passed on to Australians their view that the whale catcher crews 'gave the impression of being very much merchant seamen, and no other uniforms or strange-looking equipment were seen'.

A memo from the Australian High Commission in London to the head of the Department of External Affairs in Canberra decided a report that the *Slava* carried helicopters was just speculation. Still, the diplomats worried about Soviets nosing around Antarctica, perhaps snooping after the United States.

Quaintly, the Australian Chargé d'Affaires in Moscow monitored the *Slava* fleet in 1951 by going to the cinema and watching a new propaganda film, *Soviet Whaling*. He wrote a detailed review of the film for Canberra, saying many whales were clearly taken and there was a lot of floating ice, but the film contained 'a great deal of padding' and no reference to Australian interests in the Antarctic. His department head soberly copied the memo to four other chiefs. The *Slava* fleet itself had little to do with the West in the 1950s. Golovlev described how once Solyanik told a whale chaser to shadow the Dutch factory ship *William Barentz* for a week, but it failed to catch them violating the same regulations he had torn up.

Not that the capitalists were entirely innocent. Just as the Soviets were getting into their stride a Greek shipping millionaire decided he would go whaling. Aristotle Onassis puffed the smoke from his big cigar into the face of the IWC. This epitome of a 1960s self-made global jetsetter made part of his fortune by being an enthusiastic pirate whaler.

Onassis's Panama-flagged *Olympic Challenger* used the same general tactics as the Soviets: harpooning any whale that happened by, regardless of whether it was protected or undersize, grossly under-reporting the total catch, and inflating or decreasing the true hauls. Onassis kept this up for five years in the early 1950s. His contribution to whale management was that he did much to exterminate Blues, Fins and Humpbacks from the south-east Pacific, off the coast of Chile and Peru. Famously, he equipped the drinks bar of his motor yacht *Christina* with Sperm whale tooth footrests. In 2005, its charter agents still claimed that the bar stools on board were upholstered with whale foreskins, 'which Onassis used to shock his guests'. Norwegians driven to distraction by *Olympic Challenger* probably paid German crew to pass on the real catch details, which were published in the *Norwegian Whaling Gazette*. Exposed, Onassis sold the fleet to Japan and it kept on whaling for another fifteen years. He shrugged his shoulders as he moved on to something else. After all, he had made millions.

Through the 1950s suspicions trailed in the wake of the Soviets. The *Slava* was known to be running three more whale catchers than the maximum of twelve agreed by other IWC countries. It upped the number to eighteen in 1955, ignored an IWC protest, and a few years later was running 24 catchers—enough to swell the head of any Captain-Director. Other whaling nations noticed the *Slava*'s catch numbers seemed technically impossible.

An unheard of 1600 BWU was claimed to have been processed in a season in 1958–59. Such a total was described cryptically by Tønnessen and Johnsen as 'tactical, rather than actual'. It was 622 BWU greater than the quantity processed by any other floating factory, and more than twice the average.

Actually *Slava*'s report for the season was an understatement. The real figures show its boilers were likely running for 180 days. It killed 5917 whales in 1958–59, or 2120 more than reported, and it was making oil for margarine and dried animal meal out of highly protected Humpbacks. Not only the Blues but now the Fins were starting to run out.

Competition for whales was tightening not just because of illegal whaling, but because the IWC, against repeated pleadings from its scientific advisers, set unsustainable quotas. Through the 1950s, most whales were being taken by non-Soviet whalers. Factory fleets from Norway, Britain, Japan, the Netherlands and Argentina ran in the Whaling Olympics. But the ugliest face of Antarctic factory whaling was Soviet. Then Moscow decreed it should also be the biggest.

Whale stocks were so exhausted it ceased to be a viable business for most countries. Only a command economy could continue beyond commercial reason, or a country that made more profitable use of the animals, such as killing for meat. In the depths of the Arms Race, from 1959 to 1963, the Soviets built and sent to sea a new factory fleet each year. Three of these fleets were the largest ever to operate in the Antarctic: the *Yurii Dolgorukii*, the *Sovetskaya Ukraina*, and the *Sovetskaya Rossiya*. These last two 32 000 tonne factory ships, twice the size of *Slava*, were built on round, capacious lines. They were like 1950s American cars—designed as if there would never be an oil shortage.

Solyanik the Hero was probably an architect of the new order, and certainly rose with it. He left *Slava* to become Commodore of the *Sovetskaya Ukraina* fleet which put to sea in 1959. Soviet whaling became paranoidly secretive, and more damaging. 'All the whaling operations of the Soviet fleets looked like activity of a clandestine military organization,' said Ernst

Chernyi, an early 1960s research worker on the fleet who became leader of the Union of Independent Fishery Managers. Coded warnings of outsiders, KGB minders and secret informers tried to keep the lid on. Outlandish equipment was built to hide the wrongs. Chernyi said systems of pipes were designed to raise a screen of steam across the flensing deck against aerial observers.

Factory whaling with these super fleets meant strip-mining the open ocean and chasing down pockets of animals in under-exploited waters. The ruthless old habit of taking the blubber and discarding much of the meat and bone was revived. Less time was spent in the Antarctic in the early 1960s and Soviet fleets began to close on coasts further north. Solyanik's ship devoured 1200 totally protected Right whales one year, south of Peninsula Valdez in Argentina. Another year, Blues were all but exterminated in the Arabian Sea. The *Yurii Dolgorukii* fleet worked its way east across the southern Indian Ocean in vast loops before vacuuming whales out of the Australian coast in 1964–65. It took 5149 animals that year—almost exactly twice the number officially reported. The whistleblowers' map of catch distribution showed they were hunting equally in the mid-Indian Ocean, and by working close around the coastline from Shark Bay in Western Australia to the Eyre Peninsula of South Australia. Of 507 Blues it processed, 198 were taken in April, probably in waters of the Great Australian Bight.

This happened before 200 nautical mile Exclusive Economic Zones (EEZs) were declared, and before there was much deep sea fishing of any kind. Beyond the 12-mile limit the Soviets were unchecked and, despite the Cold War, apparently little watched. Ink-blotched maps put together by the Russian whistleblowers show that sooner or later all of the Soviet fleets hit temperate waters around Australia and New Zealand. In late summer or early autumn they would steal big catches of Sperm, Sei, and Blue.

There were few times when Soviets tested their charade by poking their heads over the Western horizon while they were in the local whaling grounds. Solyanik did once, strange to say, in Storm Bay, Tasmania. Locals woke to see the 34 ships of the *Slava* and *Sovetskaya Ukraina* fleets anchored together off ragged-toothed Cape Queen Elizabeth on 15 April 1964. The first word that Canberra had of the fleet came in the local newspapers. Archived memos showed the Australian Government caught completely flat-footed. Learning from the press that the fleet was preparing to make a shore visit to Melbourne, bureaucrats briefed ministers on whether a formal protest was possible. No, they decided, the Soviets had a right of innocent passage. And there was no suggestion of any breach of the ICRW.

'The convention established a closed season for the taking of baleen whales which terminated on 7 April. There is no evidence that the Soviet ships took any whales after that date, and in fact Australia has no rights of inspection under the convention.' Australia's total lack of control over what was happening to whales in its waters was then confessed. 'Indeed, there are no Australian whaling laws, either Commonwealth or State, in force in Tasmanian territorial waters.'

The fleet came to Melbourne for four days. Earlier in the same month, the real catch included 34 Blues, five Humpbacks and an extraordinary 695 Sperm whales. Evidence that the Soviets had breached IWC rules was on the ship. Acting as overall Commodore of both fleets, Solyanik blandly told reporters that the voyage had been 'very successful', taking 5139 whales. The fleet actually cut down 7827.

A slightly nervous embrace was offered to the crews in Melbourne, where they were proclaimed as the largest fleet to enter the port in war or peace. It was not as if the Cold War had eased. A few days before they arrived, the morning broadsheet, *The Age*, led with a British–Russian spy exchange at 'a lonely Berlin checkpoint'. It seems the Australians just decided it was easier to waive the politics. Certainly, anti-whaling protests were not heard.

Solyanik split the fleet in two. *Sovetskaya Ukraina* and its chasers came in first, to be besieged by nostalgic Russian emigrants and the curious. *Slava* stayed outside Port Phillip Bay, chipping paint and waiting, officially because there were not enough pilots to bring all of the ships through the dangerous Port Phillip Heads at once.

'All my crews want to do after seven months at sea is walk and walk,' said Solyanik.

The whalers were reported as polite and reserved. They went shopping in the city, leaving their cameras behind on instructions. Invitations to visit homes or go touring were refused. A group of scientists from the *Ukraina* failed to turn up for a pre-arranged meeting with other academics at

Melbourne University. When too many visitors pressed on the gangplank, they raised it. The press was fascinated by the women on board, including Solyanik's pretty young wife, Svetlana, fetching in a tight sweater as she raised binoculars to her eyes. Other women worked as meteorologist, book-keeper and dishwasher. Solyanik appeared reserved and slightly patrician in his braided uniform as a dinner host for Melbourne's Lord Mayor.

There was one other small surprise. A picture in the paper of a modestly smiling, balding, middle-aged man, who could have been mistaken for another of the ship's bookkeepers. It was the former Siberian soldier, Vasily Tupikov, standing beside a harpoon. He was still with Solyanik, teaching the next generation how to shoot everything that breathed out of a blow-hole. 'I haven't given up,' said Tupikov, by now the holder of the Order of Lenin and the gold star of the Hero of Socialist Russia. 'I can't. Whale hunting is an exciting business, and it's habit-forming.'

6

WHALING FOR PYGMIES

Pygmies raised on the shoulders of giants see more than the
giants themselves.

Marcus Annaeus Lucanus, *The Civil War*, c.60AD

The sea floor rises from the Indian Ocean's abyssal plain off Western
Australia through a 200-kilometre-long, hook-shaped canyon. Slowly the
ground angles up from a pitch-black depth of 4 kilometres to a shadow
world 350 metres under the waves. There may be no sunlight in the deep
sea, but places like the Perth Canyon are not hidden to us. We have learned
to do what the whales do: see by sound.

The multiple beams of a swath mapper bounce off the canyon walls and
floor, producing three-dimensional images showing its ridges and gullies in
fine detail. Acoustic instruments plot krill swarming over its flanks. The ear
of an echo sounder captures the dive curve of a single whale, bottoming out
at 470 metres. Arrays of hydrophones anchored to the floor track the movements of whale around the canyon rim by their calls.

The long, low moans of the Blues can travel far. US Navy listeners
found they could routinely detect animals calling from 1800 kilometres
away, and track them effectively over many hundreds of kilometres. Calling
at up to 185 decibels they are, briefly, louder at source than a jet engine,
though they are below our threshold of hearing.

Perth Canyon is a path for nutrients to rise from the deep ocean, fer-
tilising the waters for the krill *Euphausia recurva*. A group of Western
Australian scientists studying Blues counted upwards of 50 in a late summer
day in 2003. They watched hundreds of cycles from depth to surface,
counted their blows, collected sloughed skin fragments, and listened to

them. In the canyon, it seems that Blues converse. The common song is a three-part call with a clear sequence. And up to eight Blues at a time may sing out, strongly enough to carry the call through deep water and along the shelf edge. Now and then, the whales' behaviour will suddenly shift. Discarding their cloak of cool majesty, the Blues rise to the surface and charge through the water at speeds of up to 33 kilometres per hour. Breaking the surface in white spray and crashing back, they chase each other. It's the kind of behaviour you might expect of dolphins one-thousandth their size.

Recognising individual Blues is hard. Rights grow obvious callosity patterns on heads they often poke above the surface. Humpbacks' distinctive tail colouring signatures are helpfully lifted as they dive. Blues have less above the surface to set each apart, though scientist Curt Jenner has photographed one Perth Canyon animal with a piece of its tail stock missing in a bite mark 1.2 metres wide. Starting with small differences in the dorsal fin shape as a marker, and then scrutinising detail of the skin pigmentation pattern, Jenner and his associates built a catalogue of around 190 individual Blues. 'There is a quite subtle but intricate mottling of the skin, often coupled with small cookie-cutter shark bites,' he said.

Just such a fingerprint turned up for Jenner's research associate, Vanessa Sturrock, when she matched a Perth Canyon whale photographed in February 2004, with a Blue image shot fourteen months later, at the Bonney Upwelling off Victoria. The Bonney scientist, Peter Gill, also had a satellite track that showed a Blue suddenly shooting off south, apparently to a new potential feeding area. 'These are not neighbourhood animals,' said Gill. 'These are great, "long-legged" animals who move vast distances quickly. They have a feed and then they decide to check out an area 200 nautical miles away. They might go to Chile or to Kerguelen Island. Who knows?'

Kerguelen in the sub-Antarctic, about 5600 kilometres away from the Bonney, is not such a stretch at all. It was in the waters around Kerguelen that Blues also found off Australia in summer were first identified as a separate sub-species: Pygmy Blues. This name, borrowed from the small people of equatorial Africa and applied to a 22-metre-long animal, serves to emphasise the scale of 'True' Blues. The word also meant a great deal to whalers when it was announced by Japanese scientists in 1961. With stocks dire, a new sub-species appeared in healthier numbers. Was it real, or a convenient invention?

At the time, the name also fitted IWC nations' own stunted thinking. Even the least imaginative had to realise that great whales were crashing towards extinction. The Whaling Olympics ended with no new game agreed, and attempts to carve up a single quota failed. The IWC stumbled on for three years in the early 1960s without even an agreed BWU total. Legal pelagic whaling failed to pay for British whalers, who sailed their last season in 1963. The Norwegians and Dutch left the IWC, though each later returned. The Soviet makers of whale deserts were untrammelled, and Japan's fleet expanded, gathering around 130 000 tonnes of meat at its peak, mainly Fin—the benchmark for the Japanese palate. That year the kill excluded Humpbacks for the first time, as their stocks suddenly disappeared.

The Blue Whale Unit was left to poison other species' future, making the incidental killing of remaining strays all the more likely. 'Modern whaling ceases to be profitable when the supply of whales sinks to a certain level,' warned a British pioneer of whale stock science, Neil Mackintosh. 'But there is a real danger of extinguishing the stocks of Blues while the industry is supported by Fin and Sei whales.'

The True Blues of Antarctica, *Balaenoptera musculus intermedia*, were a dispersed remnant. The roaming *Slava* fleet caught 43 in 1961–62—its last sizeable catch. At South Georgia's shore factories that season no Blues were hauled onto the platform where they had been flensed yearly since 1904. IWC scientific advisers thought there might have been about 1000 to 2000 left. The signs were not good that the animal would survive at all.

Tadayoshi Ichihara, of the Whale Research Institute in Tokyo, sailed into this crisis with *Balaenoptera musculus brevicauda*. He launched an argument over differences between the Pygmy Blue and the True Blue that reverberate today.

Ichihara argued the Pygmy Blue matured smaller than the True Blue and was distinctive for its shorter tail stock and baleen plates, and lighter silver-grey colouring. It appeared to prefer temperate waters, particularly an area labelled the 'Pygmy Box' in the Southern Ocean, with Kerguelen near its centre. The Japanese weren't alone in believing the Pygmy Blue existed. Mackintosh accepted that it belonged to the outer fringes of the Antarctic, or even sub-Antarctic, and probably numbered around 2000 to 3000. To other scientists who were increasingly desperate about the fate of great whales, the Japanese discovery was a ruse to keep on killing undersized animals in the last overlooked stronghold for Blues on the planet.

When in 1963 the IWC tried to ban any Blues catch, Japan refused, insisting on access to the box. The American author George Small called the Japanese 'blatantly rapacious' and thought them willing to kill the very last Blue. He said Remington Kellogg, the US patriarch of the IWC, believed the so-called Pygmies were either just a collection of runts or immature True Blues. It took two more years before the box was closed too, with the catches down to twenty in the last season. Blues were entirely protected in the Antarctic from 1965. Not as if that counted. The next year *Slava* killed 466 Pygmy Blues, the Soviet whistleblowers said. Tupikov's students apparently searched without result for True Blues.

Legal whaling of Blues and Humpbacks denied, the focus in the 1960s turned to the Fin, Sei and Sperm. The greatest toothed whale was thought so abundant that unlimited numbers could still be taken. An eight-month season for the Sperm gave the big fleets a pretext to roam temperate waters, and hit whatever passed along the way. Fin and the Sei were thought to be alive in numbers just strong enough for the IWC to calculate a sustainable yield.

Mackintosh explained the vital importance of this limit in a single sentence. 'There is a world of difference between catching just above and just below the current sustainable yield.' It was clearly too late for Humpbacks and Blues. There was no sensible sustainable yield. For the Fin and the Sei things might be different. Numbers were so low though, that a mistake in calculations of just a few hundred individuals would mean another species sliding towards extinction.

The second-ranked Fin is followed by the Sei, a middling 18 metres at maturity, a grey whale of temperate waters and the fastest of swimmers, measured fleeing from a threat at 60 kilometres per hour. The habits of each work against any easy calculation of sustainable yield. They are open-ocean swimmers and little is known about their breeding grounds. The kind of

0.009 (or nine thousandths) of a Blue for every 100 square nautical miles of the eastern Ross Sea.

Around Antarctica it was figured in 2004 that True Blues may have increased to 1700, or about 0.7 per cent of their pristine level. The finding by University of Washington zoologist, Trevor Branch, had a bleak caveat. 'Their current scarcity makes it difficult to determine whether Antarctic Blue whales have increased since the end of illegal Soviet whaling.'

In the Northern Hemisphere, calculations are more optimistic. US authorities believe some thousands live in the North Pacific; and a small but steadily increasing number inhabit the North Atlantic. The Pygmy Blue of the south is doing alright. The Australian scientist John Bannister suggests as many as 6000, or half the original stock, survive today.

Those who watch Blues now usually do so from a distance, such as in a little high-winged spotter's aircraft. These whales don't like boats too close. Peter Gill and his colleagues have been out in the Southern Ocean off the Bonney Coast in fast inflatables, trying to buzz near enough to launch a biopsy dart or satellite tag. 'If they don't want you around, you'll never catch up to them, even in something as fast as a Zodiac,' said Gill. 'They'll dive, do a turn and pop up behind you.'

When, usually after hours of trying, the researchers manage to time the Blues' breathing sequence well enough to move in quietly from behind and ping a tag onto them, the reaction is different. 'They don't try to retaliate, unlike Right whales or Humpbacks which will use their tails. You've got to watch for them. But you can shoot the tag on a Blue and ten minutes later it's calm again.'

Observing them from a vessel such as a sailing catamaran, Gill notices another difference.

'They're not like Humpbacks, which can be very curious, and will spend ages around a boat checking you out. Blues are more stand-offish. This is something that's quite distinct about them. You get the sense that they don't need us at all.'

PART III · SPERM

(Physeter macrocephalus)

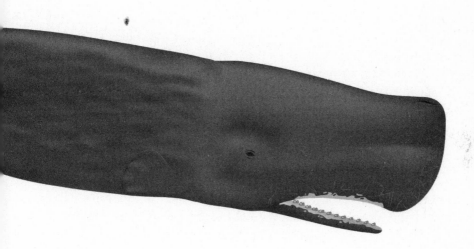

7

MOBY'S CLICK

Enough is known to lead us to believe we are dealing
with special creatures with remarkably developed brains . . .
They could have taught us much if we had only listened.

Peter Morgane, *Mind in the Waters,* **1974**

To the whalers of Albany, sonar was a black art. Like grasping mathematical
formulae or the Romany language. Either you could, or you couldn't. Good
sonar operators were born, seldom made.

Ex-navy men tried for the work, but some who had been smart at tracking the enemy were no good at hunting wild animals. Using a squawking
headset and an ink line on paper to find a submarine was one thing.
Following the clicks of a Sperm whale and sorting its track from the sea
floor or a fish school was something else.

The good operators turned out to be unruffled and imaginative. They
were tradesmen on shore, deckhands on boats: men who could picture the
waterscape below that the signals through the transducer in the ship's hull
only hinted at. Once the ship had the right sonar operator, the odds ran
heavily against the Sperm. Its chance of disappearing into the depths was
all but gone.

Master/gunner Gordon Cruickshank and his crew were working over
the continental shelf break off Albany, in the south-west of Western
Australia, when their sonar lit up the dark-world life of one bull Sperm
whale.

'Gee they're wonderful things,' said Cruickshank. 'They could just go
down.'

Cruickshank's chaser *Cheynes III* was still half a mile away from the bull
on the surface when he flicked his tail straight up in the air and was gone.

'The sonar operator was just coming good,' Cruickshank remembered. 'He was self-taught. He had been a carpenter. He took to it like a duck to water.

'We watched the bull dive. They make a hell of a noise going down, with the tail. The sonar went down to 1100 metres. It went down and down, and out of visual contact. But you could contact it still to 1400 metres by sound—his crick and crack talk—and he sat there.'

Above, the pilot of a spotter plane that had first pinpointed the whale on the surface passed back and forth without a re-sight, and suggested they give it away. The crews of other boats began to tease Cruickshank, who was closest to Albany, that he was stooging around waiting for the day to end.

'They said: "You're near to home, that's what you're bloody doing." I said no, I'm going to give Tom a chance. So an hour and 40 minutes it was down there. Then this little thing comes up the sonar track.'

The bull moved too fast for them to crank the transducer's angle up in time to follow. 'It was down 1400 metres and it came straight up like a train. We had an idea where it would be, and it came up a couple of hundred yards from us. It popped the surface, took two, maybe three quick blows, and down he went again. And I said: "Oh no!" But he levelled off at 400 metres, was running for a while, and he popped up again. And I said: "Poor bugger. You're mine".'

Cruickshank pointed to a pair of large white Sperm whale teeth, mounted among the photographs and newspaper clippings behind his little living room bar. 'They are his. He deserved better than that of course. But you don't think with your heart.'

A long and globe-girdling line of whalers ended with the Albany whalers like Gordon Cruickshank.

It began in the eighteenth century with British fortune hunters who went after whales in the Arctic, then ran through the Americans and other colonials who chased the Right, the Humpback and the Sperm into the Atlantic and Pacific in the nineteenth century. The British factory whalers who took Blues and Fins at South Georgia in the twentieth century; adventurers from Australia and New Zealand who set up shore stations on their own coasts—all were antecedents. After the Albany men there were no more industrial whalers in the English-speaking world.

A picture of Cruickshank on his ship shows a small man balancing on the balls of his feet at the harpoon cannon. His gaze is fixed on the rising whale, his right hand on the gun and his left held up, one finger raised, in a signal to the helmsman: ahead, port, slow. In black-and-white film footage he tenses, fires the gun with a slight grimace and then stands clear, gazing fixedly at the whale below as two crew quickly reload the cannon with a 'killer' harpoon. Too often the second harpoon, and more, were needed to kill the Sperm.

Still a thorough and careful person, Cruickshank brought out his own log book of the last whaling years, recording the sightings and the kills. 'The best day we had was twenty-three or twenty-four,' he said. 'The day the last was taken was November 16, 1978.' Even then Sperm were not exhausted. The species may have been hunted for centuries, but survived in numbers worth the business. Instead, time ran out. The world changed, and it did so with the most romanced, the universal whale.

The Sperm was known to be laden with mistaken history even in the early nineteenth century when ship's surgeon Thomas Beale described the animal's anatomy. 'Notwithstanding that the Sperm whale is the most noiseless of marine animals, yet the Abbé Lecoz, in his account of it, gives it the power of emitting terrible groans when in distress.' Wrongly it was claimed to be ferocious. 'For not only, according to their accounts, does the Cachalot consistently thirst for the blood of every fish in the sea, but actually possess a relish for human flesh.'

More likely, Beale said, it was fearful of approach and when harpooned was momentarily paralysed. 'They rarely turn upon their cruel adversaries, for although men and boats are frequently destroyed in these rencontres, they are more the effect of accident during violent contortions and struggles to escape, than from any wilful attack.'

The look of the Sperm helped its reputation along. It lacks the harmless sleekness of the baleen-mouthed rorquals. Instead a big-toothed lower jaw is slung under a blunt bombshell of a body. Its oversize head scarred by other teeth, skin wrinkled and grey, the whale seems a warrior. It is that, but also much more. The Sperm is a complex, highly specialised predator with an intricate social system and a physical prowess still being revealed.

Hunters needed good reason to go after such an animal. It was bad luck for the Sperm that there were reasons in quantity. There was the fine oil it yielded, its peculiar spermaceti, its dark meat, and occasionally, a mystical intestinal nugget called ambergris.

At least since the mid eighteenth century, European manufacturers wanting smokeless candles and lanterns began paying three to five times more for Sperm oil than for the standard oil rendered from Rights and Bowheads. Paraffin, gas and then electricity made this use obsolete, but Sperm oil's other uses were limited only by inventiveness.

Filtered Sperm oil contains 76 per cent wax esters and 23 per cent triglycerides. The chemistry makes it an organic oddity; an extremely fine and 'slippery' oil, highly resistant to breakdown. Tanners poured it into vats to keep their leather supple. As machinery tolerances tightened, it was dripped in as the high pressure lubricant of choice. Locomotives benefitted. So did the automatic gearboxes of cars, and the mechanics of ballistic missiles.

Spermaceti felt different. 'God that's lovely stuff,' said Gordon Cruickshank, as he remembered the strange contents of the upper chamber of the head. 'It's like honeycomb. Grey. You pick it up in your hand. It melts. Beautiful stuff.' Left unmixed with other oil from the whale's body, spermaceti solidifies as it cools. Greasing the ocean surface when an animal was head-shot, it had a semen-like appearance. Spermaceti found uses in the twentieth century as a non-greasy, odour-free wax used in furniture polishes, children's crayons and food coatings.

Taking Sperm whales for food is a limited tradition. Hand harpooners on Lembata in the far east of the Indonesian archipelago have long seized on its passage through deep waters near shore. They trade its meat between villages. Japanese consumers may have eaten it in quantity until the 1980s, and along with the Blue it was fed to mink and sable in the Soviet Union. To people with a greater choice of animal protein, Sperm is said to look an unappetising purplish-black, and taste most unpleasant.

Oil and meat were the stuff of most whales. Wax made the Sperm different, but it had something very precious as well. Inside intestines that unravel to around 150 metres in length, an alchemy is at work producing ambergris. Literally 'grey amber', after another beach-washed treasure, the waxy impaction occurs sparsely and unreliably in Sperm. When found, it's often worth its weight in gold.

Museum curator Robert Cushman Murphy became the chronicler of ambergris:

> The aroma is as subtly pleasing to the majority of human beings as catnip is to all feline creatures. Its real purpose may be said to be that of hood-winking the olfactory sense of perfume users. After the delicate breath of roses or lilies of the valley has entirely evanesced, the exhalation of ambergris still remains.

Certainly the whalers were tantalised by this get-rich-quick gallstone. Even before inshore Rights were exterminated, the Sperm was a target of choice. It was another relatively slow, commonly distributed whale. It swam in temperate and tropical waters, and occasionally up to the poles.

Around 1.1 million Sperm whales called the world's seas their own before whaling. The hunt became a legend embodied in the colossal novel, *Moby Dick*, and played out by forgotten people like those of the Hobart bark *Fortitude*. South of New Zealand in November 1846, an anonymous log keeper on the *Fortitude* was inking in his book a fearsome grim mouth on every Sperm that passed by. He chronicled an 'axcident' near a tall rock edifice on the way to the sub-Antarctic.

> Saturday December 5: Solander Island NE by N about 10 miles at 2 pm sperm whales in sight at 4 lowered all boats at sunset the captain got fast killed the whale came on dark lost sight of the Ship and was oblight to hang on to the whale all night Midnight fresh gales with heavy seas.

The boat crews were tied to a dead Sperm as a floating life preserver in the Southern Ocean dark. At daylight the weather worsened, but as luck or good seamanship had it, the boats were only 3 miles from the ship. They closed on each other until the captain, Charles Bayley, left the other two boats with the whale, and made to board *Fortitude*.

> Got within about 300 yards of the ship's weather quarters when the boat Capsides—the Captn was the only man picked up off the bottom of the Boat about 4 hours after the axcident happens. The other five men was drowned. At 8 am got the whale alongside at 9 parted the warp and lost the whale at noon heavy gales . . . the captain was quite senceles for about two hours after he was picked up with both legs and right hand greatly bruised—lost the boat and all the gear. names drowned: James Angus, John Stacey, George Roger, Henry Marritt, Ahiou.

These are the bare bones of a marine tragedy, of the deaths of four Europeans and a Pacific islander, and the struggle to find any survivor in the ocean rollers. Bayley made it when the others didn't by jamming a hand between planks of the whaleboat. He had to be prised free by the crew. Not only did they recover him, they initially hung onto the whale. Then the reason for all this chaos was carried off by the sea.

Before the voyage was over another crewman suddenly sickened and died, and lightning knocked out two mastheads and several crew. Still the *Fortitude* sailed on for months in pursuit of the toothed whale. 'July 4th landed at Hobart Town. 12 tons of Sperm Oil. Ended a Bad Voyage and put the ship in the Hospital.'

Surviving the whale itself could be more difficult. In those fragile rowing boats, killing in close with hand harpoons and lances, whalers feared the Sperm as a boat breaker, even a ship sinker. Among the different age and gender groups, Beale said females and young bulls would make 'the most violent' efforts to escape the harpoon, the larger male causing great havoc. In the animals' dying flurry some would revolve in the water, wrapping the line around them and drawing in an off-guard whaleboat. Others convulsively thrashed their tails, or steamed off in a demented circle that brought them back at the boat.

Sperm whales' deaths were seldom instant, and often the stuff of grandly savage nautical paintings: horror shows of their day. The bigger old bulls, which could reach 15 metres and 45 tonnes, were generally a slower, easier target. If they weren't killed outright, that meant trouble.

'These enormous creatures are sometimes known to turn upon their persecutors with unbounded fury, destroying everything that meets them in their course,' Beale said. 'Sometimes by the powerful blows of their flukes, and sometimes attacking with the jaw and head.'

A century later as the Russian scientist Alfred Berzin thought about this, he found it hard to say whether such collisions were random or deliberate. He was inclined to believe it was simple luck. Nevertheless individual Sperms, all big bulls, had names and bad reputations. Timor Jack smashed every whaleboat sent after him. Others had beats around the Pacific: there was New Zealander Jack, and off the South American coast Paita Tom, Don Miguel and, of course, Mocha Dick.

Killing capacity grew with the telling. Over the nineteenth century the story of a white whale named after a Chilean island was embellished until he was longer than a Blue. Executed at last, Mocha Dick was said to have evidence of nineteen old harpoons rusting in him. The historian of Pacific whalers, Granville Allen Mawer, thought all that was missing from this animal was an eye patch, a parrot and a black flag.

Though it seems to be the Sperm's place to be exaggerated in history, there is good evidence of deliberate attacks by apparently enraged old bulls that sank two ships, the *Essex* in 1819, and the *Ann Alexander* 32 years later.

The *Essex* was just south of the equator in the eastern Pacific when it was menaced by a giant bull that had quietly watched the ship after two other whales were harpooned. Its first head butt hit the side of the 238-tonne sailing ship 'as if she had struck a rock'. The whale then swam to leeward where it beat the surface of the water 'distracted with rage and fury'.

It next charged into the ship's bow and stoved in the hull—a copper sheath over a yellow pine outer layer, and 10-centimetre oak planks on 30-centimetre square oak ribs. The *Essex* began to sink bow first, then capsized on its port side. The whale seemed dazed as it swam away.

'"My God! Mr Chase, what is the matter?" I answered, we have been stove by a whale.' The astonishment of the Captain was the least of the problems that first mate Owen Chase was to recount in his later harrowing narrative of survival at sea.

As Melville's book was published in 1851, he had confirmation of Sperm malevolence in the same central Pacific region where he set the *Pequod*'s sinking. The crew of *Ann Alexander* had survived the breaking of two whale boats in a Sperm whale's jaws, before it turned its attention to the ship. Again, it stove in the bows at the second strike.

How useful these killer Sperms were in balancing a whaler's conscience. The notion of a treacherous animal with the power to destroy its pursuer swims as a cold undercurrent through *Moby Dick*. The whalers might have been scouring Sperms from the ocean at the rate of around 6000 annually in the 1830s. Herman Melville's super whale set about squaring the ledger.

An open-mouthed Sperm whale rising from the deep beneath a whale-boat must have been a hair-raising sight. The lower jaw holds around 48 teeth, many as thick as a fist, running along a Y-shaped shaft up to 5 metres long. Above the jaw, the bulbous head forms a third of the whale's body length. This piece of anatomy which gave a Sperm whale ship-battering power is still being deciphered. It may have several roles, including combat. Sperm males, twice as big as females, physically contest the control of cow and calf herds—as do many mammals, from deer to elephant seals.

'There have been numerous descriptions and mentions of fierce fights among large males for females,' said Berzin. '. . . During the encounter Sperms inflict heavy blows on each other with their forehead (like rams), often leaping out of the water at this time.'

Inside the head, two oil-filled sacs sit one above the other, looking much like a cannon barrel and its recoil chamber. Which is almost what they might be. The upper spermaceti organ is sheathed in heavy muscle. Its long, conical shape gradually widens from the blowhole back to the massive shell of whale skull that cradles it. Below the spermaceti 'case' is the second chamber, called the 'junk'. It contains a denser oil held above the broad, usually toothless, upper jaw. In a big bull these two chambers can extend like the underwater bow bulb of a cargo ship. With skin scored by teeth marks and squid sucker discs, the Sperm's head does look a hard-used weapon.

To work as an evolutionary benefit for fighting, University of Utah biologist David Carrier said, it would have to be both battering ram and shock absorber. This is where the head liquid comes in, damping the

impact. He found the momentum of the spermaceti organ in a large swimming Sperm whale could seriously injure a stationary rival. 'Further, and
most importantly, the level of damping necessary to protect the attacking
whale from injury would not necessarily diminish the effectiveness of the
system as a weapon.'

Other scientists see the battering ram as an evolutionary sideshow. After
all there's no evidence that Sperm cows fight. Some thought the oil
chambers could act as a buoyancy regulator, letting the whale cope with its
deep dives. But scientists have spent most time looking at the world's
largest nose for its acoustic powers. The Sperm may have big brown eyes,
but like other whales it sees best underwater by sound.

Working their way through the valves, pipes and sacs inside the heads
of Sperms in the 1970s, Kenneth Norris and George Harvey of the
University of California explained how this complex anatomy produced
sound. Pulses originate near the tip of its nose where air is sucked in past a
tight valve at the Sperm's blowhole. They pass back along the spermaceti
organ to a sac near the skull, then bounce back and down through sheets of
tissue in the junk that act as acoustic lenses, magnifying and directing
them. They emerge as clicks. Long after the whale dives, the clicks continue
as air is recycled through the head.

According to Hal Whitehead, of Dalhousie University, 'Sperm whale
clicks seem to be more powerful and contain substantially more low
frequency energy than those of other [toothed whales]. The sperm whale's
clicks allow it to echolocate and communicate over ranges of hundreds
of metres to tens of kilometres. So in its most fundamental terms, the
spermaceti organ extends the sperm whale's sensory environment far out
into the ocean.'

Bursting out at up to 223 decibels at source, the undersea hunter can
produce the loudest sound of any animal. It likes to click a lot. Streams of
clicks scan the darkness, echo-locating prey. It also produces codas—brief,
distinctive click patterns—to communicate with other Sperm, and clangs,
very resonant sounds that males use like bull bellows to declare their
presence to herds of cows.

To imagine the great toothed whale hunting with its clicks is to see
a dominant animal at home, the way a grizzly bear would appear at ease

sniffing the air of a sub-Arctic forest, or an elephant raising its trunk clear of the dust on an African plain.

Marking its rise with a low bushy blow that spouts forward of the head, a resting Sperm lies 'logging' at the sea surface between dives. Its body looks like a tree trunk, low, flat and curved, as it takes dozens of breaths to re-oxygenate. Then its knuckled back arches, a stubby tail flicks the broad spade of its flukes skyward, and it dives. Powered by regular, slow fluke strokes, the Sperm eases into darkness at a little over one metre a second, to forage among the canyons and seamounts.

As water pressure rises with depth, the whale nears neutral buoyancy. Down 1000 metres, the pressure is 100 kilograms per square centimetre of skin, or 100 times surface atmosphere. It's a world populated by outlandish cousins of the sealife we know at the sunlit surface: fan-like worms, huge-eyed fish, spidery-legged crabs, and black corals.

The Sperm needs to catch around 1000 kilograms of food each day, and an accounting of its diet by Berzin shows broad tastes. Crabs, tuna, Antarctic toothfish and cod are among the many species taken by Russian researchers from Sperm whale stomachs. Mostly though, it likes the cephalopods: squid, cuttlefish and octopus. Fitting the legend of the Sperm, it hunts another monster: *Architeuthis*.

The giant squid is up to 12 metres long from its head to the two longest tentacles that 'zip' into a single shaft with a clawed club tip. Of all the strangers of the deep, this is the nightmare of people above. It's the kraken of the Middle Ages; the writhing sea monster. *Architeuthis* bodies wash up sometimes—flaccid, white and ammoniacal. Until 2004, no one had evidence of it alive. Japanese researchers found what they were hunting on a canyon slope off Ogasawara Island in the North Pacific.

A camera mounted over baited hooks on a longline caught a series of images of an 8-metre *Architeuthis* 900 metres down. The first showed a body as big as a human, hooked to the line by one of two long tentacles. The creature struggled over four hours to free itself while the camera clicked, before the limb finally tore away. 'The recovered section of the tentacle was still functioning, with the large suckers of the tentacle club repeatedly gripping the boat deck and any offered fingers,' said Tsunemi Kubodera and Kyoichi Mori.

They concluded from the images that the giant squid is no sluggard, but uses the long tentacles as active weapons. 'It appears that the tentacles coil into an irregular ball in much the same way that pythons envelop their prey within coils of their body immediately after striking.'

On size alone, such contests must be difficult for the Sperm. Researchers of the Soviet *Slava* fleet found a 12-metre animal in the stomach of a 15.8-metre Sperm killed off the South Orkney Islands of the Atlantic. But as the fights unfold in the deep, it's hard to disentangle drama from reality.

A nineteenth-century adventurer, Frank Bullen, claimed to see by moonlight in the north-east Indian Ocean a 'very large Sperm whale locked in deadly conflict with a cuttlefish or squid almost as large as himself'. Its tentacles seemed to cover the whale's whole body, the head 'as awful an object as one could imagine even in a fevered dream'. Like many fish—and whales—the size of Bullen's *Architeuthis* grew with the telling. Eventually it was 18 metres long, excluding tentacles, with a 6-metre girth.

When whalers saw the Sperm turn on its back to die, as it did, the meals regurgitated were nothing like this size. Much more often it would be the dozens of small squid it needs to catch each time it dives.

Some think the Sperm could pump out a click loud enough to stun prey in close, or hang motionless, white-skinned mouth open, waiting like a deep sea angler-fish for something to be attracted to the light colour. But acoustic tags attached to 23 Sperm in a 2004 study show them actively pursuing prey through the bottom phase of a dive. None were sit-and-wait predators. The Sperm clicked away, prowling the darkness and seeking the echo of prey that may have been hundreds of metres distant.

Sorting and processing this fish-finding data is one use for the world's largest brain. Communication is another. The more time that whalers spent chasing their target, the more they realised it watched them too—and spread the word. Beale saw Sperms up to 7 miles apart somehow signal approaching danger. 'The mode by which this is effected remains a curious secret,' he said.

Scientists who recently cracked the codas did much to unveil the softer nature of the animal Melville libelled as a lone marauder. Sperm generally live together in small pods or larger herds in tropical and temperate oceans. Cow and calf herds may be accompanied by a dominant bull; sub-adults gather by gender in pods. Mature bulls are thought to swim alone, as far as polar waters, and to visit the herds to mate.

The Sperm herds probably have 'home' ranges around 1000 kilometres in radius. When they click in a stream—as distinct from the single clicks of echo-location—they share this coda. It's a snatch of animal music, a common tribal theme. One click assemblage collected by Welsh researcher Luke Rendell brings to mind a rhythmic skip; another, footsteps hurrying along a wet pavement at night. The codas are constants among the whistles and creaks of socialising Sperm whales. The question is, how far is this song sung?

Rendell and Hal Whitehead think the same codas are passed from cow to calf. They chatter through a Sperm whale clan that shares the same ocean with other clans, a single call understood by all those within hearing. 'Clan signatures may give Sperm whales a cultural identity that is of great importance to their individual survival and reproduction.' It could be used to socialise, to care for a calf, or for defence.

Before whalers this must have been very effective. A herd would work the same grounds in loose synchronicity, and danger came in few forms. If a pack of Killer whales skulked along, the call went out and nearby Sperms of the clan bunched up like petals on a daisy with calves at the centre and their powerful tails facing out. A formidable defence.

Of course, whalers picked up on this quickly. As harpooners waded in, the herd would fail to scatter. Group protection instead gave the whalers a chance to surround and devastate. The Sperm's devotion to calves made these an obvious target to keep other whales close by. Pitiful cases were recounted of distressed cows picking up harpooned calves in their jaws, trying to recover them.

Sperm whaling had two great eras: in the nineteenth century, and again from the 1950s when the factory fleets resorted to them. As baleen whale stocks were driven down, the factory ships took the hunt for Sperm out of the Antarctic and into temperate oceans. In the decade to 1974, they were killed around the globe at the rate of more than 24 000 a year.

Then one day in the northern summer of 1975, a belligerent young Canadian climbed out of a rubber dinghy in the North Pacific to stand upon a dead, floating Sperm, the better to measure it. And the world turned.

'That's when the realisation came to me that these whalers weren't interested in rules and regulations,' said Paul Watson. 'That whale was definitely undersized. They were just going to bring it on board and butcher it, and nobody would have been the wiser unless we actually witnessed it.'

For a lineal precedent to Watson's step from a Greenpeace Zodiac onto the wave-washed back of a dead whale, look back six years earlier to Neil Armstrong's awkward hop from the ladder of the lunar lander *Eagle* to the dusty Sea of Tranquillity.

The Greenpeacers clearly differed in approach and scale. They were a bunch of hippies and self-styled eco-guerillas aboard an old fishing boat off California; not global heroes atop costly rocketry to the moon. But behind each was a soaring ambition. The work of many others was needed to get there. And in its own way, the arrival of their carnival boat amid the Soviet Union's grey and rusting *Dalniy Vostok* fleet also marked a moment of change in the way that we see our world.

Through Armstrong and his colleagues we looked back to Spaceship Earth. On it, these activists showed us that humans were still killing the biggest animals ever to live here, out of control. They would make whaling a lightning rod for global species conservation. And they would chase the whalers to the ends of the world.

8

WAKING THE VILLAGE

For one, I gave myself up to the abandonment of the time and place; but while yet all a-rush to encounter the whale, could see naught in that brute but the deadliest ill.

Herman Melville, *Moby Dick*, 1851

Snow white, the Sperm cow was. She had been seen for a few years with a pod, off Albany. 'We used to call her a Judas whale,' said Gordon Cruickshank. The whalers easily followed the underwater glow. Year after year they exploited her unwitting betrayal, sparing her so she would come back again as telltale.

Then another Albany master/gunner, Kase van der Gaag, admitted: 'I shot it. Aagh, I'm not proud of it. It was 32 feet. It was ghostly white. We were chasing cows and I could have shot another one. Oh, and it happened when Greenpeace was here. It was stupid to do.

'It was never mentioned anywhere. But there is a video with the white whale tied up to the station. The other thing is that even if I didn't like killing them, as long as the company paid me I killed as many whale as I could. Or I should move on. And I was paid well too.'

Albany stuck in van der Gaag's mind when its broad, deepwater sound sheltered his ocean tug in the early 1960s. He came back in 1969 to be another of the global strays who became the last Australian whalers.

He was quite the cool captain, with longish hair and whiskers, a striped beanie, wraparound sunglasses and the rigorous training of a Dutch ship's master's ticket to back him up. Cruickshank had grown up on cod trawlers out of Aberdeen, with the iced rain of the North Sea trickling down his back to stiffen him. Another master/gunner, Paddy Hart, had his steel beaten into him in a Dublin Catholic upbringing.

Each of them had status, not just on the boat, but in the town. The whalers were seen as hard men of Albany, the way Australians once looked to a line of sheep shearers in a shed to rank masculinity.

Postwar whaling began there as a tearaway venture in a port town for a farming hinterland, far from anywhere. These whalers bought a war-surplus plywood launch with a makeshift cannon bolted to the bow. They hand-winched carcasses of inshore swimming Humpbacks onto a local beach and learned flensing by trial and error. The muscular struggle evolved into the Cheynes Beach Whaling Company, which slowly cobbled together a small fleet of chasers and a processing factory.

The chasers mainly came from British shipyards and started business in the Antarctic for Norway. By the 1970s, the ships were into a third or fourth change of use, gravitating, like their crew, to a last stronghold as other businesses in South Africa and on Australia's east coast went bust.

'They were beautiful ships to handle, really good sea ships,' said van der Gaag. 'They had a big prop and free-hanging balance, a spade rudder which makes it turn easily.' The chasers had 15 knots of speed, but Sperm whaling still relied on surprise. 'They had steam engines; very quiet. I love steam engines. All the arms and legs go up and down.'

Sheltered by the granite southern arm of King George Sound, the factory was built to make use of a natural rock slope into the water. Sperm were hauled onto wooden flensing decks by oversized winches. Flensers, flabby and tattooed, stalked around the deck in football shorts and gum boots, carrying hockey stick-sized knives. They worried at the carcasses like the big sharks swimming just offshore.

A giant bonesaw clattered into the Sperm's head. Lumps of whale were heaved and pushed into holes on the deck to fill the boiler below. The meat and bone meal was dried and sold as stock feed: Sperm whale for layer hens. Oil gurgled out of a confusion of pipes and was stored in shiny tanks, to be collected in bulk. The final export pipeline had to be tended by a diver, who once came face to smiling face with a Great White shark. They stared equally at each other, unmoving, until the diver realised the shark was dead and lying on the pipe. Van der Gaag had shot it the night before.

The whaling station was a workplace safety nightmare, where broken wire hawsers could whip across the deck, or a flenser might follow the whale chunks into the boiler below. By the seventies it was also a tourist magnet. Crowds lined a chain-link fence above the flensing decks, holding their noses against the stench, appalled and hypnotised by the infernal sight.

The chaser crews lived a separate life from this stink and gore. Each day after leaving their catch moored to a rock islet offshore from the factory, they steamed over the sound to berth miles away at the Town Jetty, and drink at the White Star hotel. More whales were caught in the White Star, they used to say, than anywhere else. And they were bigger. That was where Paddy Hart went when he was breezing through town in 1959, the youngest chief cook in the history of Irish shipping, looking for excitement.

'I thought it was a great adventure,' Hart said. 'At the time I'll be quite honest with you, I never give any consideration to conservation—anything like that. I was caught up in the thrill of it.

'You could have been at sea all your life and have your Able Seaman's ticket, and it would mean nothing when you stepped on a whale catcher. A lot of people that actually came to work on the whale catchers were tradesmen, draftsmen, people like that. They may not stay the distance for the season, they may be there just to say they had been whaling. So you worked with deckhands who didn't know the boat. You asked them to go to the galley and they went to look for a big rowing boat.'

Hart was duly taken on as a cook. Cruickshank started as a deckhand. So did van der Gaag, when his Dutch ticket wasn't recognised. Each of them gradually worked up through the boat to master/gunner. Albany preferred this title. One man was supreme on board.

Each day Town Jetty was deserted two hours before sunrise. The chasers left early to gain most daylight at the whaling ground, their oil-fired engines building a good head of steam as they chugged past the long, round granite bluff of Bald Head, which signposted King George Sound from the ocean like a monolithic Sperm at rest.

They whaled for perhaps 200 days of a ten-month season. There was no point to going out when the weather was too rough to see whales, or too hazardous to tow them back unbroken for processing.

The first ship out always turned to run above the continental shelf, about 20 miles offshore. The others ranked themselves seaward, line abreast a few miles apart. Below them, the shelf was steeply incised by a series of long canyons. Among the broader cuts due south of the town was the 40-kilometre-wide Albany canyon, which runs 3975 metres deep to the abyssal plain below. Sperm hunt these waterways for squid. Other things lived there too.

'The mystery bugger', they called it on Cruickshank's ship. They would pick it up always at the same spot, and follow by sonar as it slowly cruised through the canyon, leaving a larger imprint on the screen than a whale. The creature would almost break the surface and then disappear. It was no air breather. It might have been a giant squid, or a giant shark. They never found out.

The chasers generally steamed east to meet the whales, which invariably swam west above the shelf, heading from the Great Australian Bight to the Indian Ocean. 'Tomorrow's whales' were those that were too far east. Each catcher had a man 'in the barrel'—that is, in the crow's nest up the mast. The sonar operator hunched in a small metal box cabin near the open bridge. The company also flew a spotter plane above, whose pilot radioed sightings to the catchers, or circled and dipped his wings. He would drop homemade oil markers out of his window to dye the surface where a Sperm sounded.

In these waters the Sperm often moved in mixed herds. A bull had his 'harem'. His much greater size, proud head and long log of a back made him easily visible at the surface.

There was no 'there she blows' from the Albany whalers. More likely an oath and a compass bearing would be cast in their direction. 'Somebody would call up,' Cruickshank said. The master/gunner made the grim, adrenaline-lifting walk down the whaler's catwalk to the bow. 'The mate or the deckie took the wheel. He did everything you said, or had hell to pay.

'If it was a big pod, we'd try to take the bull. You would look for the biggest bull. If he was out the front, you had a hell of a job to get through without panicking the cows. Once they started to panic, he was gone.'

Albany whalers saw many a bull Sperm vanish when it twigged to them, and they held a poor opinion of his masculinity in defence of his cows. Flight wasn't a universal reaction though. Van der Gaag was slowly ticking his ship in closer behind one very big bull when it turned around and headed toward the ship. 'The biggest bull I ever . . . well, he's getting bigger all the time. He had his mouth right open, but only the point of his nose out of the water. I could have shot him in the head, but for a start you lose a whole lot of spermaceti out of his head, and you don't kill. So I thought I would let him go.'

The master/gunner watched as the bull slowly turned on its side and looked up at him, then slid under the hull and came up behind the stern. Some Sperm seemed deliberately to do that; resist the urge to panic and instead survive by using the ship itself as a shield.

'The sonar man lost them in the wake,' van der Gaag said. 'By the time you turned the ship around, he was gone. We had it once seven times with the same whale. We just couldn't get him. I think the Sperm whale is very clever.'

Paid a barrel-of-oil bonus, the whalers would always look for the largest animal. Hart said that once they were asked to take 'granny cows'—larger, older cows considered barren. In a Sperm herd, such animals may have a matriarchal place but that wasn't why the whalers didn't want to hunt them.

'Number one you get close on ten tonne of oil from a 50-foot bull,' Hart said. 'Whereas your 35-foot cow, you get two or three tonne. And it's a lot harder to kill a cow than it is a bull.

'Those Sperm whales, you could shoot 'em in the head all day, you could shoot 'em in the bum all day, you will make a difference eventually,' said the Irishman. 'The shot you want is just behind the pectorals. The thing is, you use the same harpoon all the time; the same weight, grenade, powder. With a cow what could happen, even if you get it in the pectorals, is that the grenade would blow outside the whale.

'The right shot works, the wrong shot doesn't. Everybody tries for the right shot. It made life easier. Better for the whale, better for you. But cows were hard to kill. I don't think any of us really liked even the thought of shooting them.'

In truth the Albany chasers, like most, were built to deal as a matter of course with whales that did not die instantly. They were equipped to slowly reel a thrashing whale in, like a trout on a rod. The line rose up the mast toward the crow's nest, and back down into the ship's bows on a web of pulleys and springs, compensators and winches, that played out the forces of a whale hooked by harpoon barbs, trying to flee in pain. Once the animal was drawn in close, the next 'killer' harpoon was fired. This carried no barbs or line. Its task was to sink in and explode.

Multiple harpoons were often needed. The ship was moving, the whale was moving, and a missed shot was not unusual. Working in a storm, van der Gaag remembers chasing whales that were higher up the waves than his gun. 'It was like duck shooting.' Sitting in his comfortably worn captain's cabin of a living room, van der Gaag stared at the floor. Now thinner, he bears life cautiously. 'The notion that there was one shot never happens. I think you will find the average number of shots per animal was at least three, maybe four. It's cruel. There's no doubt about it. But it is exciting. The hunt is exciting. I've killed about 1000 whales. I never counted them. I don't count them. I don't.'

Albany may have been a forgotten place where whalers' work was unquestioned and their daring admired. Out in the world though, Sperm, and all whales, were taking on a different meaning. People's affection for them grew with undersea exploration. As their stocks crashed, scientists were more outspoken over whales' bad treatment. Activists were born in baby-boomer rebellion and the hippie movement who feared for Earth's ecology. Nations began to feel their way toward global agreements on how to run the planet's natural wealth. Enabling all of this, the magic of new technologies like satellite-linked colour television joined distant communities with vivid images.

'"Time" has ceased, "space" has vanished,' wrote the Canadian media mystic, Marshall McLuhan. 'We now live in a global village . . . a simultaneous happening.' The clock was ticking against the master/gunners.

At the edge of change were people with an instinct for mass communication, men like the Austrian Hans Hass and Frenchman Jacques Cousteau. Hass developed a camera that could bring pictures of the undersea to the surface; Cousteau an aqualung that liberated divers below. Running their own sea-going research expeditions, they wrote books and made TV documentaries that brought sea life into the living room.

In the fifties, Hass had the first known underwater encounter between human and Sperm whale, finding it far more timid than reputed. In the sixties, Cousteau sailed to the West Indies to record an underwater 'concert' of singing Humpbacks, following a Gray whale migration from the Bering Sea to Baja California. He tracked Fin, Sperm and Killer whales in the Indian Ocean. Hard-bitten commercial needs of these adventurers sometimes came first. Cousteau harpooned a big Pilot whale in 1948 so he could check its stomach contents, killed scores of dolphins for bait to record shark feeding frenzies, and continued the entanglement in a net of a Humpback calf to gain film footage. Times changed, and he declared: 'We were the first to seek them out in a spirit of friendship and curiosity in the depths of the sea.'

A sugar-coating was brushed over the 'kind and gentle' Bottlenose Dolphin in a sixties US family television series called *Flipper*. As the perpetually smiling animal squeaked on into series repeats, the French writer Robert Merle conferred the power of saviour on cetaceans. Inspired by pioneering work on dolphin intelligence, he combined it with fears for the planet's future at the height of the arms race in *A Sentient Animal*. Later known as *Day of the Dolphin* and transmogrified by Hollywood, it proposed that they could save the world from nuclear destruction.

Shy Sperm, singing Humpback and heroic Bottlenose; these marine air breathers were clearly no longer just useful prey. They were planetary companions for people, with commercial value alive.

Many scientists also worried about the ghastly mismanagement of whales. After the Three Wise Men failed to achieve sustainable yields, the Norwegian biologist Johan Ruud threatened to resign as chairman of the IWC's Scientific Committee if rational quotas were not set, and the Blue and the Humpback protected. They weren't, and he did, after just one year as chair in 1964.

A Princeton University scientist, Scott McVay, rang the alarm publicly in 1966 with an article in *Scientific American*. It was one of the first to take whaling's sins out of the IWC closet and put them before a wide audience who could recognise a crisis when they saw it. McVay drew graph after graph that showed different species' numbers tumbling. 'If essentially unrestricted

whaling continues, the only surviving stock of any economic importance—the Sperm whale, of whose numbers more than 250 000 have been killed in the past 12 years—is doomed to become a monument to international folly.'

McVay soon became absorbed in the new whale science, working with Roger Payne on Humpback songs. He talked about things that made older colleagues uncomfortable, like the intrinsic values of whales beyond the price of oil. 'What happens to the whale . . . will affect the quality of human life and impair the human spirit. Because of the lateness of the hour for the great marine mammals, a touch of futility haunts us.'

Like one of those infernal hippies, not a sensible agnostic scientist, McVay reached back to the woodsman philosopher Henry David Thoreau for guidance.

> Can he who has discovered only some of the values of whalebone and whale oil be said to have discovered the true use of the whale? Can he who slays the elephant for his ivory be said to have 'seen the elephant'? These are petty and accidental uses; just as if a stronger race were to kill us in order to make buttons and flageolets of our bones; for everything may serve a lower as well as a higher use.

Against McVay stood an old guard locked into obscure mathematical arguments among themselves about the correct factors to include in stock management equations. Whatever ideals they had found no room at the IWC's calamitous bargaining table. At the same 1971 conference in Shenandoah, Virginia, where McVay invoked Thoreau, another American, John McHugh, thunderously warned against damaging the commission. Like many IWC scientists, McHugh was trained in fisheries, not on the more complex and fickle marine mammals. He made what now looks like a pompous defence of the right of elite experts to get on with it, and not be interrupted by an ignorant public.

'There have been occasions in the last year when I have been frustrated and irritated by the public furore about whales and whaling,' said McHugh. 'I have seen it as threatening the efforts, now beginning to be felt, that several of us have been making to achieve rational management of world

whaling, and restoration of the whale resources to full biological productivity for utilization by man.'

Could a prestigious American scientist seriously propose a return to 'full biological productivity for utilization by man'? In 1971, after a holocaust of the scale of industrial whaling that had already swept through the world's whales? But there he was, so well regarded that he was about to become chairman of the IWC.

The American strategy was to alert public opinion to what McHugh called the 'slow progress' of the IWC. McHugh was not so sure of the outcome. 'We did what we could—and our magic incantations, like those of the sorcerer's apprentice, appear to have been successful. The problem now is to halt the forces we have set in motion before they destroy the object of our efforts.' Anyone who saw Walt Disney's animation, *Fantasia*, remembers Mickey Mouse as the cocky apprentice who conjures a broom to cart water until the sorcerer's cavern is chaotically awash. But McHugh and his colleagues didn't release these powers. They were in motion anyway.

Revolutions were coursing like tsunami through Western countries. Antinuclear campaigns, gay rights and feminism; Vietnam war protest and civil rights; violent student anarchy and marshmallow hippie love. They sucked away accepted surfaces, crashed through the existing social fabric, and left new landscapes behind. There was crazy drug-taking, and strict embracing of eastern religions, and partying only surpassed in intensity by political awakening. People were impossibly idealistic and honestly convinced that they, personally, could change the world—and some did.

Different cities drew in like minds. San Francisco nurtured hippies, Paris attracted radical left students. Of all places, Vancouver on the Pacific coast of Canada spawned the movement against whaling. Accounts of the time portray a backwater city that drew a vibrant counter-culture, fed by young Canadians who came west, US draft dodgers who fled north, all meeting local ancient indigenous people and established Quaker and Asian communities.

Success has many fathers. In the campaign to save whales, beyond question one of them was Paul Spong. A bright, intense New Zealander, at age 29 he was assistant professor of psychiatry studying brain function in

captive Orcas—Killer whales—at Vancouver aquarium. Spong's Eureka moment was given to him by his subject animal.

An adult female Orca named Skana was induced by food to distinguish between ever more closely spaced lines, to test her power of visual resolution. After many trials Skana could detect spacing down to millimetres, about 90 per cent of the time. Then the whale suddenly switched to getting everything wrong. Once Spong overcame his frustration, he realised that far from being 'dumb', the animal was brainy enough to show that she was bored. Skana gave the wrong answers repeatedly, on purpose.

'This is the first time in the history of behavioural science that a lab animal so obviously refused to do something it knew how to do,' he concluded. Spong's path changed. In mid-1968, he turned against the incarceration of such an intelligent animal, lost his job and began to devote his life to observing wild Orcas from a hand-built island home. The Canadian wildlife author Farley Mowat found Spong, and encouraged him to campaign against whaling.

Another clear claimant to paternity was Bob Hunter, a hippie columnist on Vancouver's daily newspaper. He moved beyond local protests against city reconstruction to become involved in 'Don't Make a Wave'. The Quaker-based group decided to transfer the religion's philosophy of peaceful witness against wrongdoing into a protest over US nuclear tests on Amchitka Island in the Aleutian chain. It was feared that an explosion could trigger a real tsunami there. Hunter led a group who steamed to the Aleutians in a chartered fishing boat, the *Phyllis Cormack*, in 1971. The group failed to stop the test, but raised a momentum that prevented any more.

Returning from the Aleutians, Hunter recalled seeing whales appear before the boat. 'At least two members of the crew had taken LSD while listening on headphones to Roger Payne's *Songs of the Humpback Whale.*' Someone suggested calling them in to the boat. 'We began to fill our heads with the most loving thoughts and images.' Hunter was straight enough to remember that one whale did change course. Through Spong he became hooked on the creatures he called 'armless buddhas'.

Paul Watson came to the cause from an animal-loving childhood in a Canadian fishing town, by way of a hard adolescence in which he left home

at fifteen. Watson's worry about Amchitka was its effect on wildlife. 'I wasn't a people person,' he said.

His polar opposite was a nuggety man who grew up in the rich part of Vancouver. A most unexpected activist was David McTaggart. After the Aleutians success in 1972, 'Don't Make a Wave' transformed its name and goal. By then McTaggart was a 39-year-old failed construction businessman living on the yacht *Vega* in Auckland, New Zealand. There, the father of his nineteen-year-old girlfriend told him about a protest against the French at Moruroa Atoll in the Pacific planned by a Canadian group called Greenpeace.

'I don't like limits on my personal freedom, don't like anybody telling me what I can and cannot do,' said McTaggart. 'So somewhere right around this point my personal rights and the planet's, my outlaw self and this quite righteous crusade, came slamming together and held fast.' *Vega* sailed out into the Pacific under the Greenpeace banner with McTaggart at the helm.

As the consciousness of this disparate bunch was rising, so the global slumber over the environment was ending. Articulate scientists spread popular warnings. Rachel Carson's clarion *Silent Spring* on the effect of pesticides was the first direct hit on industry—the chemicals business. Zoologist Paul Ehrlich foreshadowed tragic consequences for a planet with too many people in *The Population Bomb*. Cellular biologist Barry Commoner assembled data on the effects of atmospheric nuclear tests. The 'Paul Revere of Ecology', *Time* magazine called him.

Scientists began to work together, the Club of Rome publishing in 1972 *The Limits to Growth*, which drew the earth as finite. In the United Nations, the first conference on the human environment was held at Stockholm. Naturally, it being the time that it was, the Merry Pranksters had a hand in things.

Functioning, often barely, on the edge of sanity, Ken Kesey's Merry Pranksters laced the sixties with LSD, anarchy and artistic experiment. They were an ultimate Californian band of hippies. One of their number, Stewart Brand, thought up the Great Trips Festival of 1966—a Super Acid Test for hundreds. Blown away by the early satellite photographs of partial Earth from space, Brand drove coast to coast across the United States selling buttons with the slogan: 'Why Haven't We Seen a Photograph of the Whole Earth Yet?'

Brand became rich with the *Whole Earth Catalogue*, a sort of Google on paper for tools of the counter-culture. He funded a festival at Skarpnack, Stockholm, to coincide with the UN conference. Through it, the Save the Whale campaign was launched to the world. 'In its way, the Skarpnack Village symbolized the dominant American approach to the environmental crisis in all its apolitical, naively romantic, transcendental glory,' said the UN conference's chronicler, Wade Rowland.

The gloomy Europeans wrestled with the 'isms': colonialism and imperialism, capitalism versus socialism—root causes behind environmental woes. Young Americans at Skarpnack instead went for symbols of resource depletion. Let off the hook, the US delegation embraced whale saving. It offered impassioned support for the notion of a ten-year moratorium on whaling. This wouldn't be the last time that a government adopted the whale as a convenient cause—a fig leaf for naked failures in environment protection.

At Stockholm the IWC's embarrassing ineptness was trailed across a different world stage for the first time. A florid debate unfurled in which the US hardened a conference resolution that had proposed that the IWC decide what to do about its own crisis. Instead the Americans wanted an urgent call for a ten-year moratorium. They got the change up, 51 to three with twelve abstentions. Japan, Portugal and South Africa voted against it. The Soviet Union was not there.

Within weeks the pitiful state of the IWC as a conservation organisation was exposed. At its annual meeting the commission rejected the world's moratorium call by four votes to six with four abstentions. Norway switched its Stockholm vote from 'yes' to 'no', and Iceland came off the abstainers' bench to vote against it as well.

'While it was clear to all [Stockholm] delegates that several species of whales were in serious danger of extinction, it was just as obvious that the IWC, the only body capable of controlling the harvest, would no more consider an immediate moratorium on killing of all species than General Motors would consider a moratorium on automobile production,' Rowland said. Word of an incapable IWC was spreading.

After Stockholm, the group of founding scientists in Friends of the Earth drafted a chilling explanation of what had happened to whales, which they saw as an allegory for other global environmental failures. It was the tragedy of the commons, a bleak view of human nature that looks back to medieval over-grazing of common ground.

Whales belonged to no one in particular, and for that reason nobody in particular would defend them, so the argument went. 'This means that the profit someone can make by killing a whale is bigger than the loss he suffers by there being one less whale in the world. For the whole profit is his alone, while the loss is shared by everyone. Thus, from his point of view, it seems best to kill a whale, and another, and another . . . until there are no more.'

In such a selfish world, commonly agreed control such as the IWC's, was the only option. Unless of course you didn't believe people were so callous, and instead could be altruistic. That they might just save whales because they were worth it.

Paul Spong convinced Bob Hunter to trust the special nature of Orca intelligence by putting his head inside Skana's fish-breathed, toothy mouth. Early in 1973 Spong proposed that Greenpeace should take on a new cause after antinuclear campaigning, and send a boat out to intercept the whaling fleets.

Never shy about cataloguing their successes, Greenpeace histories thoroughly detail what went into building this first confrontation. An allegory of the times, it was a mixture of canny business, hard-bitten activism, eastern mysticism, fairytale luck, and what the whalers were so good at: deceit.

Hunter was convinced that whales had become chic, even handy with the girls. 'Whale freaks had a lot of sex appeal in the counterculture.' McTaggart was involved in the antinuclear campaign, and thought Hunter's band of merry men 'flaky'. But he knew a winner when he saw it. 'I'm not really an animal person, but I was starting to see the value of a warm and fuzzy issue that appeals to people emotionally . . . The whales are a real people magnet, and in democratic societies if you've got the people behind you, you've got the power.'

Some Greenpeacers were hardening their activism. Paul Watson was with besieged native Americans occupying Wounded Knee, South Dakota, in 1973 when he felt a federal marshal's bullet whistle past his ear in the dark, and realised his mortality. 'Once you overcome your fear of death, you can do anything you want,' he said. Watson came back to Vancouver to help prepare *Phyllis Cormack*. It took two years to fund the ship, load it with a wild bunch and send them to sea. Before they left though, they needed to know where in the wide blue North Pacific to look.

Paul Spong was certainly not alone in searching for answers in the *I Ching*. George Harrison is said to have drawn 'Gently Weeps' as a message for a new song when he threw three coins and referred the results to the ancient Chinese texts. Spong first went to Japan with a slide show to convince people, against all odds, of the value of live whales. Then given the task of finding the whaling ships' usual routes, he took the slide show across Canada to Iceland and Norway. Like a cloak and dagger spy he closed on the obvious target, the Bureau of Whaling Statistics in Sandefjord, Norway.

Under the guise of a scientist interested in studying Sperm whales in the North Pacific, he asked whether the factory fleets' past records showed where the Sperm might be found. Initially he was refused this sensitive data. But after a little fibbing, he was given access. Spong copied out pages of coordinates for the Japanese and Soviet fleets. He found the *Dalniy Vostok* fleet had taken a course out to sea from California in the previous June. Greenpeace had a place. If they got it right, their timing would coincide with the annual IWC meeting.

It took *Phyllis Cormack* weeks of oceanic meandering to reach the fleet, listening to a radio direction-finding beacon in the hope of catching Russian voices. Every rainbow was auspicious. At one point when time was critical, a musician and 'inter-species communicator' among the crew took the wheel for a night watch and decided to follow the line of moonlight on the water, steadily taking them far off course. Spong, in London waiting to drive home Greenpeace's message, faced a restive press. On the last day of the IWC meeting, 27 June 1975, Greenpeace found the fleet above Mendocino Ridge, a subsea rise just 40 miles west of California.

Within half an hour Watson was standing on the small, dead Sperm whale, marked with a radio beacon for later collection. A Soviet whale chaser spotted the hubbub near its kill and steamed over. Watson glowered there in mid-ocean, as a crewman on the chaser readied a large fire hose.

He was disinclined to leave, even as others on the *Phyllis Cormack* shouted at him to get back in the Zodiac. 'I wasn't too happy with what I was seeing,' he said flatly. But he did clamber back into the dinghy. A whale hunt was underway, and Greenpeace went about 'bearing witness' with activist and camera.

Under IWC rules, a Japanese observer on the pelagic fleet should have been watching for undersized animals. Hunter, the expedition leader, said: 'If the very first whale we spotted proved to be undersized, it meant only one thing: the Russians routinely ignored the rules and slaughtered whole pods of whales en masse, right down to the children. "Whale management" could therefore only mean, in truth, whale massacre.'

Greenpeace soon put the first Zodiacs between harpoon and whale, briefly delaying a chaser's shot. They claimed to have saved eight Sperm that swam away, and saw close-up the deaths of two. The first to be harpooned was a small female, drawn in thrashing to the catcher. According to their account the second was an enraged adult bull that charged at the bow of the whaler, and was harpooned in the head. Watson recalls that moment's anguish more than his lone stand on the first whale.

Riding in an inflatable with Hunter, Watson was almost crushed as the Sperm thrashed convulsively close by. 'The whale wavered and towered motionless above us. I looked up past the daggered six-inch teeth into a massive eye, an eye the size of my fist, an eye that reflected back an intelligence, an eye that spoke wordlessly of compassion, an eye that communicated that this whale could discriminate and understood what we had tried to do . . . On that day, I knew emotionally and spiritually that my allegiance lay with the whale first and foremost over the interests of the humans that would kill them.'

Hunter radioed the encounter with the Soviets to Vancouver, it was passed on to Spong in London, and the first attempt to intervene against whaling duly broke as world news. Greenpeace spent two days trailing the *Dalniy Vostok* fleet, decided it had enough film, and headed for San Francisco to show it. The gold standard for trusted television in the US was the CBS Evening News with Walter Cronkite, and it ran Greenpeace's footage. In London, Spong became a media darling. Reporters for the first time sharply questioned the Soviet and Japanese delegations.

At that meeting, the IWC approved catches of 32 478 whales around the world including 19 040 Sperm. A sub-committee investigating the 'alleged killing of an undersized Sperm whale by the Soviet whaling fleet' would later find that 'a comparison of the reports of the Japanese observer and the Greenpeace Foundation, who made the charge, yielded no evidence upon which to base a claim of violation'. Whale savers still had far to travel.

9

HEARTS AND MINDS

Sometimes you say things in songs even if there's a small chance
of them being true.

Bob Dylan, _Chronicles_, 2004

Another Zodiac hanging onto a chaser on a different whaling ground.
Another pair of protesters crouched in a small bouncing hull, breathing
outboard motor fumes for hours. They were supposed to have a back-up
fishing boat, but it hadn't appeared. A plan for a 22-metre mother ship
never came closer than a newspaper report. The Australian coast had
disappeared long ago. Their compass, better for boy scouts on land, was
spinning in all directions. They dipped between big, heaving, glassy
Southern Ocean rollers, fetched up in late winter from far away.

The chaser _Cheynes II_ had headed due south for hours without whaling.
Not so much as a stroll to the bow by the master/gunner. The protesters
were following 80 nautical miles out to sea in a 4-metre-long rubber
bubble. Bob Hunter had come to town boasting of having the world's first
ecological navy. This time it seemed Greenpeace might need the whalers
to save them.

Albany in August 1977 was angry over the greenies. This last bastion of
whaling was not looking as if it would be taken lightly, and the campaign
against it looked more freakshow than serious challenge. Kase van der Gaag
insisted it was not a pre-planned ruse to lure the dinghy away from the real
whaling.

Aboard it was the protest's exotic financial backer, Jean-Paul Fortom-
Gouin. A small, tanned and rich French national who lived in the Caribbean

and Florida, Fortom-Gouin breathed whale-saving like oxygen. Impressed by Greenpeace's North Pacific work, he had phoned Hunter in Vancouver out of the blue, and paid for him to come to Australia. A couple of months earlier, Fortom-Gouin was at the annual IWC meeting, coincidentally in Canberra, on Panama's delegation. He backed anti-whaling protests with an inflatable whale that travelled around the country in the lead-up to the meeting, and linked up with the Australian branch of Project Jonah, which campaigned through public education and well-connected lobbying. They lost in Canberra. The IWC lifted Cheynes Beach's quota from 624 to 713 Sperm.

Jonny Lewis, a Sydney photographer who adored dolphins, went along to the meeting and was captivated by Fortom-Gouin's passion. Lewis had a piece of pop art: a cartoon of the Phantom water-skiing behind his dolphins. 'I gave it to this fellow. As I said, "I think you're a bit of a Phantom of the IWC ".' By meeting's end Fortom-Gouin had handed him US$2000 to crank up a campaign against the Albany station. 'We called ourselves the Whale and Dolphin Coalition. But we called ourselves anything to make it look like there were thousands of activists percolating under the surface.'

Hunter and Fortom-Gouin duly met at the campaign headquarters, Lewis's rambling loft in Sydney. They bought boats and gear, and ran a picture opportunity for the media with the Zodiacs zooming along in front of the Sydney Opera House. The jetsetter did not impress Hunter by deciding to fly to Albany. The Canadian and a few others were left to drive a clapped-out truck and a station wagon over the mind-numbing Nullarbor with the gear, road-killing kangaroos in the name of a higher purpose.

The protest drew an awkward collection of dissenters. Like karma from California, one of Kesey's Merry Pranksters floated in. Pat Farrington, an inventor of the peace-building New Games, wanted Albany flower children playing whale games. She eventually resorted to a hunger strike, sitting outside the whaling company's Perth head office. The increasingly odd former Labor deputy prime minister, Jim Cairns, appeared at a rally looking beatific, with his exotic companion, Juni Morosi. Walking a fine local line, the Albany Conservation Society voted for a phase-out of whaling but declined to publicly back the protest.

There were a handful of young Australians, like Lewis. 'We were just a bunch of joint smoking hippies who had a bit of a social conscience, a sense of adventure, and felt very strongly for the whales.' But they were not much of a force against the whalers. On the chasers, the crews were openly hostile, baring their bums at the protesters when the cameras weren't around. Paddy Hart had to dissuade his excitable ship's cook from dropping a harpoon grenade into a Zodiac that came too close. Van der Gaag cooled down a crewman who wanted to throw a lighted cigarette into the rubber boat with its fuel tanks. Ashore the anti-whalers navigated past a bikie gang called God's Garbage whose members formed the core of the flensing crew. Townspeople refused to sell the protesters a bed or repair their vehicles.

At least the Gauloises-puffing paymaster was willing to get into the thick of the protest, as the frolic tailing *Cheynes II* in the rubber duckie with Lewis showed. 'I had no idea where we were,' said Lewis. 'And I didn't seem to worry about it too much. Not too much. We'd hyped ourselves up to the point where there was no backing down. I think from Kase's point of view, if they could get us into trouble, they would, and rescuing us would be a public relations coup.'

Having teased the rubber duckie along until lunchtime, *Cheynes II* halted and put out fishing lines. 'We stopped and they came close and had a bit of a yak,' van der Gaag said. 'Then I asked permission to stay out overnight from the company. They said that was OK. But we had a crew of reporters on board. So I thought, oh well, I'd better go back. I gave the course to the blokes in the rubber duckie. But they didn't believe me. We headed back and they stayed next to us until they could see land. Then they were gone. That same night the weather was something shocking. They could not have survived.'

Lewis stepped ashore with Fortom-Gouin, walked up to the whalers' pub, the White Star, and ordered a drink. 'It was so surreal. For me it was like walking on the moon. I went into the loo and I remember looking at my face. It was bright red and had a film of white salt on it. This weird person had come back from the sea. The whalers checked us out. There was a bit of an acknowledgement that "this is serious".'

The other Cheynes Beach chasers had watched the Zodiac roar over the horizon in pursuit of *Cheynes II*, then turned west in search of Sperms spotted from the air. 'I think we ended up with fifteen whales,' said a first mate, Mick Stubbs. 'Kase just led them on a goose chase.' They weren't going to be stopped by any old Zodiac. Two harpoons fired awfully close to the activists proved that.

In the most frightening confrontation, Paddy Hart, master/gunner on *Cheynes IV*, was being annoyed by Fortom-Gouin and another young Australian, Tom Barber. 'They were between us and the whales, and I managed this particular day to sort of outfox them. Because as the sonar operator is calling out directions, the normal thing is to follow and sit behind on the tail of the whale.' Instead Hart, up at the cannon, signalled to the helmsman to run up a little to the right of the whale—slightly between the animal and the fast-moving Zodiac.

'When it was time I just ran along and spun around and shot this whale. That whale died in an instant. These blokes came along with the duckie and they drove over the line. They made the claim that it died in agony. If that whale hadn't been killed instantly it would have dived, the rope would have shot up out of the water and tossed them 100 foot in the air.'

Fortom-Gouin buzzed with anger at the closeness of the shot. He flourished a statement to the local newspaper about the charge that police would bring against Hart for firing a harpoon near them.

'The skipper and the whaler kept the harpoon gun on the boat aimed at us while we were zigzagging in front of the boat's bow for several minutes,' the Frenchman said. 'I then heard a detonation, and the harpoon from the gun on the bows of the boat shot across our bow and the harpoon cable slapped the water a couple of yards ahead of us . . . At the time the harpooon was fired, I was about 50 yards from the whale chaser, and about 15 yards from the whale's right rear.'

Nothing happened about it. Not in Albany. The company was publicly cleared of blame.

Within a few days, Barber and Jonny Lewis were in an inflatable awfully close to a Sperm when another harpoon was fired. 'I remember saying to Tom, "Slow down, the whale's coming up underneath the boat." Then there was the noise. It's a large explosion. And you see bits of whale blown out. It's quite ghastly. I remember feeling totally and utterly wasted. There's nothing you can do.'

The whale was pumped with air, marked with a radio beacon and the chaser steamed off for the next hunt. Barber and Lewis idled by. 'We took it in turns just running our hands over the sides of the whale's body,' Lewis said. He had never before seen up close the creature they were trying to save.

The protest folded up with mixed feelings. Lewis, who soon moved on to indigenous and human rights issues, was proud of its pioneering activism. Hunter was depressed that the whaling hadn't been stopped. Some saw what was ahead. In the White Star hotel, van der Gaag had met Hunter and Fortom-Gouin. The Dutch master/gunner listened, sadly, to these new pioneers.

'They believed in what they were doing. I talked a lot to that Bob Hunter. I talked also to that Frenchman, and he was totally obsessed with saving whales. So we talked. He said the Sperm whale has got the biggest brain in existence. Their language is very complicated. Anyway I wasn't ever happy to kill them. That really gave me the push. I left in October.'

The protests had fingered the whalers through camera and pen. Hunter knew the power of the act of whaling transferred through McLuhan's 'hot' medium of television. 'The only thing besides sex, politics and sports that grabbed its attention, excited it, made its juices run, was violence.'

Extraordinarily, the Cheynes Beach Company took the media out on its own boats, day after day during the protests. Perhaps it boldly felt it had nothing to hide—after all, tourists crowded to watch the horror show at the flensing deck. Maybe its costly public relations advice was that it would be better to control the media on company boats, rather than have them steam around on their own. Van der Gaag got sick of reporters and cameras. He knew what they were seeing was damaging. 'For a start, it's cruel. Then as long as they have the press coverage, they have Greenpeace hanging around.'

Before the protest few Australians knew whales were still being shot off the distant windward edge of the country. Even fewer knew first-hand about whales. By the seventies they were mainly giants from the past.

Through the Canberra IWC meeting and Albany protests, harpoons and the case against them filtered into homes and schools around Australia.

Like others her age, a sixth-grade girl at boarding school named Phoebe wore a Save the Whale button. She asked her father about whales. 'Didn't he think they should stop being shot? . . . When Dad was next questioned about it by someone, he said, "Oh yes, Phoebe's been tackling me about the whales"—and the press picked it up and ran. It was blown out of all proportion.' Dad was the Prime Minister, Malcolm Fraser. An adviser to Fraser has no doubt that his strong-willed youngest child sparked his conversion. It took a little longer to arrange the politics of change.

Fraser's ruling conservative coalition was being niggled by dissidents who formed a pale green party called the Australian Democrats. On the other side, with an election due three months after the Albany protest, the Labor opposition couldn't organise a coherent policy. Four years earlier in government, Labor had backed a ten-year moratorium at the IWC. In Albany in 1977, the local Labor candidate was against 'indiscriminate killing of whales'. But he reassured locals that the party wouldn't move against Cheynes Beach until fishing could be expanded.

Fraser had personal evidence that whaling was a dinner table topic, and the backing of his party's federal council for a moratorium. He went to voters promising an inquiry—the usual defuser of a hot topic—and the issue played little role in his re-election. Returned, he fulfilled the promise. Like many good Australian official inquiries, the outcome was no surprise. The value lay in what it brought to light along the way. It was the first government inquiry anywhere in the world to logically tease out what whaling involved, and whether it could be justified.

The royal commissioner was Sidney Frost, a courteous and inquisitive former chief justice of Papua New Guinea who didn't much take to the sea. Paddy Hart recalled welcoming him aboard the *Cheynes IV*. 'You know, the man hardly ever got on deck? He was sick from the moment we left harbour. Now how could he get up and give accurate detail of what happened?'

Frost's overriding term of reference was to recommend the best way to 'preserve and conserve' whales, and next to decide whether Australian whaling should 'continue or cease'. He mined data far and wide, and his report became a compendium on modern whaling. The gold he dug up was on the ethical treatment of whales.

A bushy moustached young philosophy professor at Monash University in Melbourne sent in his own submission to Frost, including a copy of his recent book, *Animal Liberation*. Peter Singer wasted none of his 1000 words explaining what whales were, what whaling was, and why it was ethically indefensible.

Whales, he said, were social mammals with exceptionally large brains, capable of enjoying life, and of feeling physical pain much as we do. Whaling could cause feelings akin to grief among them; their killing was often neither quick nor painless; and it was not required for any important human need.

Ethically, Singer said, animals should not be killed or made to suffer significant pain *except* when an overriding need could not be met any other way. So it followed that whaling should stop, particularly because of whales' often slow and painful deaths.

> It is instructive to ask what we would think of a slaughterhouse which killed cows by a method which took, on average, between two and five minutes—and sometimes much longer. There is no doubt that to kill animals by such a method in any Australian state would be regarded as cruel and obviously wrong. It would also probably be illegal. The fact that in the case of whaling the killing takes place offshore and away from the eye of the public may explain how the whaling industry has been able to continue using such methods for so long, but it cannot justify their use.

All the Cheynes Beach Company could do in reply was to mount an argument that just because whales had special behaviour and brain structures, they shouldn't be seen as 'idols'. Nor should the whale species' different characteristics be combined to create a 'near human' animal.

What tore at Frost's conscience was the 'most horrible' method used to kill whales, and the significant number of the deaths that, by Cheynes Beach whalers' own evidence, were not instantaneous, but took at least three minutes, and up to seven.

'Our conclusion then, as to whether the method used to bring about the death of a whale is inhumane or not, does not admit of doubt,' Frost said.

'The death of a whale is caused as a result of the organs being shattered by iron fragments from the head of the harpoon. We leave on one side the fear and terror of the chase, and the exacerbation of pain as the whale is being winched into the boat.' Those that didn't die straight away, he said, died most inhumanely. 'The fact that these cases are a significant proportion of the total leads to the inevitable conclusion that the technique for killing whales at present used is not humane.' Such a slow and painful death inflicted on whales was blatantly insupportable. 'Upon all the evidence, it cannot now be said that whaling can be justified as the only means of satisfying important human needs.'

The judge duly found that Australian whaling should end, and the government oppose it around the world. He drew his conclusions firstly because whale stocks were so badly depleted. No surprise there. But his second reason showed how much a rational man's heart had reached out to whales. Whaling should stop, because of 'the special nature of the whale itself, including the real possibility that we are dealing with a creature which has a remarkably developed brain and a high degree of intelligence.'

Seiji Ohsumi, who dominated Japanese whale science at the IWC for decades, once looked at the effect of sonar, which he called ASDIC, on behaviour. 'When ASDIC is used, baleen whales swim faster and do not dive, but Sperm whales dive for longer and do not swim on the surface.' Did the big Sperm bull that Gordon Cruickshank's sonar man tracked south of Albany 'know' what the tinny metal noise meant? Is that why it stayed down and hid? Did it dread the ping?

'The highest intelligence on the planet probably exists in a Sperm whale, who has a 10 000-gram brain, six times larger than ours,' said John Lilly, a Californian medical practitioner who was a sixties pioneer in the study of cetacean brainpower. 'I'm convinced that intelligence is a function of absolute brain size.' This is something that later scientists discount. Lilly also experimented heavily with LSD and other synthetic drugs, invented isolation tanks, and was the inspiration for the Ken Russell movie, *Altered States*.

Brightly coloured personal credentials are like battle ribbons in the politics of whaling.

Take Fortom-Gouin. The jetsetter with the hazily explained cheque book was briefly Panama's commissioner on the IWC, and several times its adviser. He carried a photograph of a Sperm whale brain into some meetings, a model into others, parading them sombrely around the room.

Or Sidney Holt. In a previous life he was a fish stocks scientist, one of the Three Wise Men that the IWC sought counsel from in the early sixties. He became an elder oracle from a greener Mount Olympus. White hair and beard flying, he shifted openly to environmentalism. He also retained serious credibility in the IWC—enough, for example, for one of his treatises to be included in a Scientific Committee report without the need for a single referenced footnote. The last words of that paper anointed the Sperm as: 'what some people suspect is a species of exceptional intelligence'.

Fortom-Gouin and Holt put a case to the IWC that no female Sperms should be killed at all. 'The Sperm whale brain is characterised by an extraordinary quantitative and qualitative development,' they said. Nothing in its long mental evolution had prepared it for the new threat of whaling. Perhaps like some human populations under extraordinary attack, it might even lose the will to reproduce. 'Is it not possible that such psychological effects could be found in some cetaceans, as well as in other higher primates?' Melville's grim antagonist was being re-cast as a vulnerable thinker.

Project Jonah's Californian founders considered whales to have 'a mind anatomically like ours, but profoundly different, a Mind in the Waters'. If only the IWC could break its thumb-sucking obsession with the maths of stocks and yields, and grasp the simple ethics of killing such awesome animals.

Fortom-Gouin took the case on. He arranged for neurophysiologists to outline the special nature of the whale brain to the IWC Scientific Committee in 1978. Then he followed it up himself. 'If whales are intelligent, then whales are people, people from the oceans. If whales are people, then whaling is not the harvesting of a resource, it is murder.'

The IWC was stone-faced. An item called 'Consideration of the ethics of killing cetaceans' made it onto the meeting's official report. It sniffed:

'Some members felt they were no more qualified than any other body to comment on the general ethics of killing animals'.

Pushed, the organisation did sanction a workshop in Washington on Ethics and Intelligence where the Orca advocate, Paul Spong, was an official rapporteur, or record-keeper. The notes he kept stand like the opening volleys of a war still being fought across a cultural battleground today.

University of California Professor Harry Jerison said the larger whales had 30 billion neurons in their cerebral cortex—three times more than people. 'What they are doing with it, with this capacity, we don't know,' he said. 'But to propose that they are doing nothing with it is a stupid conjecture.' The Humpback specialist Roger Payne detailed one use: complex songs exchanged between groups. Killing such animals could only be done by people who believed they were of a lower status, Payne said. Like slaves.

Back shot Japanese scientists, warning of the dangers of excessive animal protection. Ryu Kiyomiya said: 'Our concepts of ethics and justice differ, and it is impossible to establish a standard throughout the world.'

Sidney Holt would have none of this. 'The purpose of this body is precisely to search for a global ethic; that is why we are here.' Not according to the IWC majority, it wasn't. The workshop asked the commission to 'develop a dialogue with philosophers on the ethics of whaling'. The proposal sank at the July 1980 IWC meeting without a vote, while catches of 23 341 whales were sanctioned.

Barely two years earlier both Spong and Fortom-Gouin had watched in shock in Sydney at a special IWC scientific meeting on Sperm whale quotas. Japan succeeded in talking up the North Pacific quota for Sperm from 763 to 6444. This meeting at the CSIRO in Cronulla was a last hurrah for the whalers. They were finding it much harder to get their arguments past the obstacle that had been such a help in the past: the IWC's three quarters majority. By 1980 there were several failed votes before they could engineer a Sperm whale catch limit of 890 in the North Pacific.

The global ethic Holt had held up to defend whale intelligence was spreading. There was life in the big romantic notion of a moratorium on killing these creatures. Terribly damaged though great whales' numbers were, it was their hunters who increasingly were under attack. The decrepit

Soviet fleet and ocean-straddling Japanese companies were being hemmed in by new international laws. Cold fury hardened protests as the scourge of pirate whaling was exposed. The IWC, trying new ways to safely manage whale stocks, found its numbers being stacked—against the whalers.

'Like it or not, the whale is now a symbol of mankind's failure to manage the world's resources responsibly,' the New Zealand Government warned. 'The attention of concerned people throughout the world now focusses on the decisions of this commission with an intensity none of us would have thought possible.'

For years governments wrestling with ideas of maximum self-interest, versus the common heritage of mankind, had looked out at all that boundless ocean and the wealth in it. The United Nations Convention on the Law of the Sea (UNCLOS) adopted in 1982 had articles formally demanding cooperation for the conservation, management and study of cetaceans.

With UNCLOS came the spread of 200 nautical mile Exclusive Economic Zones (EEZ). Offshore waters once free were suddenly off limits. Distant water fishing companies from countries like Japan had to pay to fish inside them for the first time. The IWC's founding document might cover all the world's oceans, but places such as, say, Mendocino Ridge off California, where the Sperm whales gathered in mid-summer, were suddenly inside EEZs too.

The widening library of international law around Antarctica meant the region's place as a zone of peace and scientific research gained stronger conservation overtones. Perceptions of the place had changed with the 1959 Antarctic Treaty. It spawned a seal protection convention and then in 1982 the fisheries-directed Convention on the Conservation of Antarctic Marine Living Resources (CCAMLR). This had a remit of conserving the southern marine ecosystem as a whole.

Globally, there was also a new Convention on International Trade in Endangered Species. Most great whales were natural inclusions on early CITES protection lists, and dozens of conservation-minded countries adopted CITES membership after it was opened in 1974.

This new, boxed-in world was driven home to the last Australian whalers within weeks of the Albany protest. A 1200-tonne shipment of Sperm whale oil had crossed the Pacific for Europe when it was unexpectedly blockaded in the United States. The tanker *Stolt Llangdaff* planned to offload the palm oil it was also carrying in Portland, Oregon, but US Customs ordered it out beyond the new 200 nautical mile limit because Sperm oil was illegal. The tanker was refused passage through the US controlled Panama Canal, and the oil was last heard of in Vancouver. It was forward sold, so the Cheynes Beach company had its money, but its buyers had good reason to doubt future supplies.

The last US coastal station was wound up in 1972 in Monterey Bay, California: whales ground up for Cal Can brand dog food. A Marine Mammal Protection Act sharpened the anti-whaling attitude, and the long arm of American law began to reach other countries through people like Congressman Tom Pelly. A Republican from Washington state, Pelly listened to fishermen who resented foreigners catching 'their' salmon further out to sea. He sponsored an amendment to the Fisherman's Protection Act that set out a series of steps leading to a Presidential ban on imports from a country that harmed international fishery conservation, or endangered marine species.

New domestic US law let Washington impose sanctions by cutting another country's fisheries allocation inside the American EEZ. The Packwood-Magnuson Amendment meant at least half of a foreign country's allocation could disappear if the Secretary of Commerce certified the foreigner was whaling to the detriment of the IWC.

This international legal net began to encircle Japanese fishing companies who were also whaling. The three main whalers all had much bigger operations in global fishing: Nissui's trawlers and longliners worked off the North American west coast, Kyokuyo ran factory fishing fleets in the North Pacific, and Taiyo pioneered trawl grounds off the tropical waters of West Africa. Formerly free fish were suddenly costing these corporations cash. Their oceanic freedom was trammelled by international fisheries agreements. And the US was developing law that might also lever whale protection out of them.

Watching on the outer limits of protest was Paul Watson. Pensive and bearish, he was not the kind of person to trust slow-growing legal systems to save whales. After Watson stood on that undersized Sperm, he turned to anti-sealing campaigns. Greenpeace had been back in the North Pacific twice and harassed Icelandic whalers without him. To most of them, Watson was too much warrior and not enough rainbow. When finally he broke from Greenpeace, he went after pirate whalers in order to sink them. 'Everything else was failing,' he said. They were natural enemies: Watson a maverick wildlife crusader who formed the Sea Shepherd Conservation Society, and the outlaw whalers.

Since the days of Onassis in the 1950s, pirate whalers had scuttled like crabs around the fringes of the whaling pool. There were catcher boats refitted with stern ramps, converted factory trawlers, and coastal fishing boats that could bolt a small harpoon gun to the bow. They hid in quiet corners of the Atlantic and Pacific, some trading to local markets, most freezing and shipping their whale meat to Japan. None was likely to obey any IWC rule about size or species. Humane killing was not in their equipment.

Exposing them and their crevices of international business took gumshoe investigation. A British wildlife advocate named Nick Carter gave Watson his first target by lodging a report with the IWC in 1975 on MV *Sierra*, a pirate so bad that its own crew turned on it. The *Sierra* was a former 650-tonne Dutch whale chaser modified at the stern to drag aboard and process whales. Carter found it operated from 1968, first as MV *Run* under Norwegian directors, exporting its best meat to Nissui in Tokyo and second-grade products to Britain as pet food. Operation of the ship shifted to South African-based Andrew Behr in 1972, a contract was signed with Taiyo Canada to supply whale meat, and its plundering continued from the port of Freetown, Sierra Leone.

Carter tracked *Sierra* through government and financial records, and looked under the rocks of the maritime world. He took a chance on placing a small advertisement in an engineers' journal, seeking a leak. Wonderfully, a response came from a marine engineer working on *Sierra*. 'The engineer bravely videotaped the piracy, including an endangered humpback whale being dragged up the slipway, butchered, and boxed for the Japanese market.' This whistleblower's indelible evidence survives in

Carter's small history of pirate whaling. A Humpback already protected by the IWC for twelve years was pictured on *Sierra*'s stern in 1975, skewered on cables, an unmistakeable pectoral wing flat on the deck.

The IWC made noises of official disapproval of the *Sierra* in a resolution against pirate whaling in 1977. The same interests thumbed their nose at the regulators. They acquired other ships: the *Tonna*, poetically capsized and sunk by the weight of a dead Fin in July 1978; the last South African legal chasers, renamed *Susan* and *Theresa* like Behr's daughters; and a refitted Japanese trawler, *Astrid*. The South African government legislated against the pirates, and their business links were brought to light in US Congressional hearings before the Packwood-Magnuson Amendment clanked into gear. It threatened Japanese fishing interests with expulsion from US fisheries. Tokyo responded by passing its own law against receiving meat from non-IWC countries.

Still the *Sierra* whaled on until Watson came riding over the horizon in *Sea Shepherd*, thinking of the extinction of the Great Plains bison, and how he had once fantasised about having a Sherman tank to take on the buffalo hunters.

'*Sierra*, *Sierra*,' Watson called over a marine radio on 15 July 1979. 'Goddamn you, you whale-killing son of a bitch, your career is going to end today.'

Having tracked the ship to the harbour at Leixoes in northern Portugal, Watson powered *Sea Shepherd* up to ram it. With a few minutes of fury he changed the face of anti-whaling direct action. The 779-tonne former North Sea trawler, its stem filled with concrete, first hit the *Sierra*'s bow and then starboard side, staving it in. *Sierra* reached dock heavily damaged but afloat. The only person injured was a former *Sea Shepherd* crewman who was beaten when he later went to apologise to *Sierra*'s crew. Watson was briefly arrested. Rather than have *Sea Shepherd* confiscated, he scuttled it. *Sierra* was repaired, but when it seemed it might go whaling again, three unidentified saboteurs with military skills sank it with a limpet mine.

'We traded a ship for a ship, but it was a great trade because we also traded our ship for the lives of hundreds of whales that would be spared from the *Sierra*,' Watson said. Within a few months other pirate vessels in this fleet were out of business, two seized by South Africa, and *Astrid* fleeing to the less hazardous tuna business, encouraged by a Sea Shepherd Conservation Society reward posted around Canary Island docks offering a bounty for its sinking. Within months, more unexplained limpet mines sank two Spanish whalers.

The destructive scourge of pirate whaling appeared elsewhere. Carter tracked non-IWC whaling in Chile, Peru, South Korea, Spain, the Philippines and Taiwan that he linked mainly to Taiyo, then the most influential member company of the Japan Whaling Association. 'These operations have been so dependent on Japanese capital, vessels, equipment and expertise, as well as the import markets for whale meat, they have been little less than Japanese whaling colonies.'

All this made the politics of whaling look increasingly messy and uncontrolled—like the litre of red liquid the Australian animal activist Richard Jones poured over Japanese and Icelandic delegation papers, splashing suited delegates, at the 1978 IWC in London.

It was not the way mainstream environmentalists wanted to go. Uninterested in the risk that forceful protest could damage broad public support, they decided to change the IWC's numbers instead. As David McTaggart, the antinuclear adventurer who thrust his way to the top of Greenpeace, put it: 'It's an age-old strategy: if you can't beat them, join them . . . and then beat them.'

A compulsive image-maker, McTaggart liked to paint the membership changes as a green coup—the dozy club of IWC nations shaken up by environmental non-government organisations (NGOs). In truth numbers had been growing steadily since 1973, when there were just fourteen members. Countries with no whaling history but interests in globalism, like Sweden and Switzerland, took a seat at the table. Others converted, like Australia. Turning on its own history with alacrity, it became a crusader for the cause.

There were signs of recruiters at work on both sides. Needled by attacks on pirate whalers, some countries who supplied whale meat to Japan outside the IWC decided it was time to turn legitimate. Other small countries were clearly encouraged by the anti-whaling side. No more were the environmentalists wafty hippies who played flutes to whales. People like McTaggart, Holt and Fortom-Gouin pulled strings for the Big Idea, the global moratorium. A trial run came with a scheme to protect the entire Indian Ocean as a whale sanctuary.

As a young man, Holt had co-authored a classic on fisheries science, *On the Dynamics of Exploited Fish Populations*, that pointed to the importance of 'refugia' or sanctuaries in the marine world. Thirty years later, he reached into green networks to dream up a pan-oceanic shelter the size of whales. Holt knew Lyall Watson, a nature writer in Seychelles who had links to equally exotic people, from the Shah of Iran's rich brother to Paul Spong. He connected Holt with the left-wing Seychellois president, Albert Rene, and to the initial mystification of Japan, the small island jewel joined the IWC.

Soon Holt sent a jubilant postcard to Spong announcing the Seychelles planned to put the Indian Ocean Sanctuary on the agenda, together with a moratorium on all Sperm whaling. 'This is a *great* day,' Holt wrote. He watched from an observer's seat at the IWC in 1979 as the Seychelles, with Lyall Watson running the delegation, proposed and won the sanctuary vote, 16–3–3 (sixteen for, three against and three abstentions). It extended from the Gulf of Oman to the sub-Antarctic. The Soviet and Japanese pelagic fleets were excluded. Among the whales protected, the Albany Sperms were safer than they had been for more than a century.

If proof were needed that environmentalists could make change at the highest level, this was it. The sorcerer's apprentice that the American, John McHugh, worried about back in 1971 had magicked whale protection using the power of a national government. Surely no one thought such audacious behaviour would be cost-free? The Seychelles found it wasn't.

'My government is facing difficulties in co-ordinating divergent views concerning the extension of such a grant to your country,' the Japanese ambassador wrote about fisheries aid in the Seychelles. 'In particular the fishery industry in Japan strongly oppose the grant in view of your government's attitude at the IWC.

'Therefore, in view of this, all I can say at this time is that if in future your government should change its attitude at the IWC towards Japan, there would be the possibility of my government extending the grant to Seychelles.'

At about this point, the tawdry IWC vote race began. The grim politics of global numbers ended the little organisation's days as a closed whalers' club. Instead the action moved down the road to the trash-and-treasure market of international deals. Clearly the club had failed whales appallingly. But from here on, the animals might be bought or sold by countries with no real knowledge of them at all.

For the IWC's members it was a quick education in nuts-and-bolts diplomacy. Australia's IWC commissioner, Derrick Ovington, found that his alphabetical neighbour from Argentina was amiable but had little scientific background. On tricky issues, Argentina was content to rely on Ovington, a botany professor who ran the National Parks and Wildlife Service. On the other side, Brazil's commissioner proved harder to crack. He liked being duchessed at dinner. But in the end Ovington thought it best to persuade volatile Brazil to abstain from votes.

The burden of taking on strident Japan was shared by anti-whaling nations. Though Prime Minister Malcolm Fraser was committed, Ovington didn't want a complaint about him rocketing back to Canberra behind his back.

'I got on well with Lyall Watson. Sometimes I could get the Seychelles to say something we would then support. Sometimes we would take the running, rather than the Americans, who didn't want to offend Japan.' He stopped short of recruiting new members to the IWC. 'To my knowledge there was never any movement for the Australian Government to enlist people.'

Seychelles withstood Japanese pressure over the Indian Ocean sanctuary. But for every win on the protection side, there was a loss on the other. Panama dumped Fortom-Gouin from its delegation and then vanished completely from the IWC after a sugar deal with Japan was threatened. When anti-whaling nations did go for a moratorium in 1980 they were badly rebuffed. Needing a three-quarters majority, the vote was lost 13–9–2. Japan argued furiously that it would directly contradict the IWC's founding convention. Newer members, whaling nations Peru and Chile, South Korea and Spain, were whipped into line.

McTaggart was brooding on defeat with the British naturalist, Sir Peter Scott, a founder of the World Wildlife Fund, when they decided it was time to lift the recruitment pace. Fortom-Gouin had flashed a brown bag of cash at Spong two years earlier before heading into central America and the

Caribbean. McTaggart and Scott were more subdued. They settled into the bar at the Metropole hotel in Brighton, England, where the meeting was held, wrote names of possible new members in a notebook, and began to think about who could reach them, and how.

A year later in the same bar, environmentalists were putting the best face on failure again. All the pre-IWC travel to distant lands, all the private meetings and night-time dinner talk at the rambling Metropole, failed to yield enough votes. Four new members sided with them: India, Jamaica, St Lucia and St Vincent. Another, China, went against. The hard reality of a three-quarters majority struck them. The moratorium vote was lost 16–8–3.

In spite of that, 1981 *was* another great year for Sperm whales. Pointing to CITES and European Economic Community bans on trade in Sperm products, anti-whaling nations called for a 'zero quota' on the species. Japan could not stomach this. It claimed there was a Sperm whale population of 738 500 in the Southern Hemisphere alone. A fleet-satiating 644 300 of them were said to be over minimum size. All Japan won was the right to catch a small Sperm quota in the western North Pacific; likewise there was a concession for Iceland's coastal whalers. Otherwise, this little understood 'mind in the waters' was protected everywhere.

The Japanese industry blamed Lyall Watson for this iniquity. 'Watson especially loved Sperm whales. Ever since he appeared at the IWC, he tried every possible means to ban the harvest of Sperm whales,' snapped commentator Yoshito Umezaki. Watson was said to have told Japan's Commissioner, Kunio Yonezawa, that he would consider compromising on Minkes, if Japan abandoned Sperm. 'This is an example of how the leader of anti-whaling power can manipulate the IWC and whales like private properties.'

The most protective decision ever made about whales went back to the Metropole again in late July of 1982. The other favourite IWC city, London, was a nightmare that week. An IRA bomb had killed nine people outside Hyde Park Barracks. Images of dead horses were strewn across television screens. Brighton at least had an excuse for a diverting marine character. The briny English Channel was just over the road from the Metropole, dumping its scummy wash on a scree shore and swirling around tattered amusement piers.

It was a sign of the meeting's polarity that, by this time, Sidney Holt had shifted to the Seychelles delegation, and from his old United Nations Food and Agriculture Organisation (FAO) seat a scientific ticking-off was given to those who wanted a global moratorium.

'This is a completely unselective measure,' said British fisheries scientist John Gulland, who was the designated FAO observer. 'Given the differing status of the various stocks, and the fact that virtually all those species or stocks that are seriously depleted are already receiving complete protection, there seems to be no justification for a global moratorium. Justification for a complete cessation of whaling can be put forward on aesthetic or moral grounds, but these seem outside the terms of reference of the Commission.'

Countries lined up to prove him wrong. There were five separate proposals for an end to commercial whaling from Seychelles, Britain, USA, France and Australia. They were distilled down to one Seychellois plan, for a three-year phase-out to the southern summer of 1985–86, when 'zero catch limits' would come into force. By 1990, the plan said, the IWC had to 'consider' other catch limits.

'I think the feeling was, that if you could stop whaling for a number of years, the Japanese ships would rust and rot away,' said Derrick Ovington. 'The culture of eating whale meat would decline, and the bureaucracy that supported it would go too. The moratorium was seen as the forerunner of an end to commercial whaling.'

Hectic encouragement by environmentalists had paid off, particularly in the Caribbean, Europe, and around the Indian Ocean rim. There were ten countries at the meeting for the first time. Two, Jamaica and Canada, had left the IWC. Energetic on the conservation side the previous year, Jamaica's departure was sudden and unexplained, and the country was missed. Canada's vote was confused, and confusing.

IWC votes are by voice, called on a rotating alphabetical roll. The call was under way when the Japanese delegation theatrically rose and walked single file towards the door. McTaggart watched from a Greenpeace International observer's seat. The unsinkable Fortom-Gouin was back, neatly attired, in the St Lucia delegation. Holt and Watson were at the Seychelles seats. The dark suits of the 34-member Japanese delegation kept on exiting. Was Japan physically leaving the IWC? . . . No. One person stayed behind to cast the Japanese vote.

The moratorium got there, barely. It was a 25–7–5 vote. Excluding the abstainers, a three-quarters majority was 24. McTaggart, who understood the media need for a neatly packaged outcome, declared: 'The whales are saved!' Fortom-Gouin pulled a bottle of champagne out of a paper bag and broke it open, splashing it around with a huge grin. Girls kissed Derrick Ovington. The Japanese Whaling Association huffed that the decision was irrational, and its only option was to 'leave the conference'.

On the other side of the Earth at the same time, Albany's derelict factory was being turned into a tourist attraction, Whaleworld. Gordon Cruickshank and Paddy Hart long had an amiable dispute over who shot the last whale in 1978. Its skeleton is mounted in a former storage shed at Whaleworld, jaws agape in a disconcerting monster smile.

Life for the whalers diminished. Kase van der Gaag went away to drive tugs, but came back to Albany, his 'best place in the world'. He lived alone with household animals. I watched him lean out of his car to politely ask a miniature pony to move, so that he could use the driveway. The pony wasn't inclined. So the man who shot 1000 whales sat there, car engine idling, waiting in slight embarrassment for the little animal to amble clear in its own good time.

Gordon Cruickshank found walking difficult but, trouser braces taut, still made it out to the back yard to garden until 2006, when he died. When I first met him he was pottering among plants where he had erected his own statuary: mounted harpoons. Welded atop metal posts, two were sunk into concrete. From next door came the noise of children playing. Indeed at first glance, the harpoons looked like rusted old-time play equipment.

Paddy Hart had a hard time of it. There was no cushioning financial package when Cheynes Beach factory shut. 'I think we were bushwhacked,' he said. With five children, he needed work. The man who'd commanded a ship and fired its harpoon went to work on a cattle feedlot, then as a boiler attendant in a woollen mill. Eventually he retired happy with his family and big garden where he battled to save the goldfish in his pond from raiding birds.

Mick Stubbs, the first mate, came back to Whaleworld where he worked at maintenance. He made a consummate guide, gently pointing out the obvious. Much of the old factory was carefully restored, but the stray detritus of whaling still surprised. Beside the deck where whales were flensed, Stubbs nodded his head down at a natural gutter in the rock. It was chock full of bright orange objects that looked like battered seashells. 'Grenade fragments,' he said. Shards of metal that had shattered the insides of whales, and were kicked aside by the flensers. Still there, welded by waves into the rock.

PART IV · MINKE

(*Balaenoptera bonaerensis*)

10

A DOZEN DEAD OCEANS

The history of whaling is made up of a number of chapters . . .
Each begins with a new discovery and hopeful enterprise,
passing through a phase of fierce competition and ruthless
exploitation with improving techniques and ended at length
in diminishing resources, exhaustion and failure. Man has been
both blind and ignorant in the pursuit of the whale.

Frances Ommanney, *Lost Leviathan*, 1971

On southern Australia's Jan Juc beach, a rising tide was bringing the white
surf closer to George Baxter Pritchard. A high cliff of crumbling, sandy rock
rose above him. Its base was undermined by wave-scoured caverns, and
piles of fallen boulders were heaped on the sand. The shattered rocks were
dusted with scraps of ancient animals fused over geological time into
brittle stone. In the lower face of the cliff were long ribbons of shell—sea
floor millions of years old.

Drawn by a hint of bone protruding from the rock, Pritchard, a 63-year-
old geologist, and two colleagues walked around from a nearby beach with
a ladder in January 1932. They climbed about 4 metres up to attack the
rock with pick, hammer and chisel. Spurred on by the tide they worked free
a lump of rock big enough to enfold in a man's arms. This they struggled to
lower carefully to the sand, helped by curious onlookers. 'It now became
necessary to move on with our prize or get a thorough wetting,' said
Pritchard. Trousers rolled, they escaped the waves.

The lecturer at the Melbourne Workingmen's Institute took the rock to
nearby Torquay, and chipped away at it until he'd exposed the remains of a
45-centimetre-long skull that still held eleven teeth from a whale of 'small
and delicate make'. Examining the teeth closely, Pritchard thought he had

hit a fossil jackpot, with 'an exceptionally interesting and important as well as ancient form'. He named it *Mammalodon colliveri* after Stanley Colliver, a young man who helped him.

The fossil lay in a Melbourne collection for 50 years before Pritchard's belief was vindicated by a New Zealand palaeobiologist, Ewan Fordyce. Rather than concentrate on the teeth that mesmerised others, Fordyce read the bones of the skull and noticed how some lay separated in the fossil. The blunt V-shape of the palate, he believed, was like a filter-feeding baleen whale—a mysticete. The jaw bones' position in the fossil hinted that in life, they were connected by tissue in the same way as are mysticetes today. Yet strangely, some parts looked like the archaeocetes, extinct early toothed whales.

Fordyce reconstructed a streamlined whale no more than 2.5 metres long. It may have had an early form of baleen in its jaws as well as the teeth. There were also, in miniature, the bones of today's baleen whales. At one point Fordyce thought this the most primitive mysticete ever found. '*Mammalodon colliveri* is important because it bridges the structural gap between . . . archaeocetes and other mysticetes,' he decided.

The richness of Jan Juc for marine fossils was confirmed in the late 1990s when an inquisitive teenager, Staumn Hunder, was drawn to reflections in a small beach boulder there. Instead of glass he found teeth and bone in another fossil skull. 'It was an incredibly lucky find. The boulder had been uncovered by storms, and the sun was shining at just the right angle on the rock,' said Erich Fitzgerald, who described *Janjucetus hunderi*, a longer-toothed swimming companion of *M. Colliveri*. 'Both are novel experiments in the early evolution of whales.'

These whales lived in the late Oligocene epoch, around 30 million years ago. Globally it was a time of rapid evolution in a warm climate. A young and food-rich Southern Ocean flowed, as continents like Australia drifted further from their old places in the supercontinent, Gondwana. Cetaceans took advantage of this kind of grand scale oceanic change, and this is a lesson they have to offer us. Many hundreds of fossils have been recovered from old sediments around the world—enough to build a history of growth and success among cetaceans. They took to marine lives better than any other group of mammals. Profound change to their bodies let the air breathers excel underwater. Their family lines branched again and again, so that around 84 species in fourteen families reach into every sea today.

Near blind dolphins poking around tropical river mouths and open ocean travelling Sperm bulls share the same land ancestor, as do the largest Blue and the smallest Minke. It was long thought to be a dog-sized mammal called a mesonychid, living in a tropical climate on the fringes of shallow waterways. Then in 2000, University of Michigan paleontologist Philip Gingerich's team found fossils of primitive early whales in Pakistan with ankle bones—whales with feet. The shape of these bones confirmed a link instead with ungulates, a group that includes cows and deer, and the whales' closest living relative: the hippopotamus.

The earliest known whale, *Himalayecetus subathuensis*, probably lived an amphibious aquatic life in the now-vanished Tethys Sea of the Northern Hemisphere. A meagre handful of tooth and bone fragments prised out of oyster shell deposits in northern India's Simla Hills in 1998 are the oldest cetacean fossils. Reconstruction of a jaw, study of its place in the rock, and of oxygen isotopes in the bones, unlocked the age. It extended the fossil record of whales by about 3.5 million years to the middle Eocene epoch, 53.5 million years ago—around ten times the age of the earliest hominid ancestors of man.

H. subathuensis was one of a group of amphibious early whales, around 2 metres long, called pakicetids, hunting the Tethys before it was closed up by continental drift. 'The origin of whales is commonly explained by availability of fish as food in highly productive shallow marine waters of the eastern Tethys,' said the scientists who reported the oldest find, Sunil Bajpal and Philip Gingerich.

In this cradle of whale evolution emerged things that make a cetacean what it is today. On the Egyptian shore of the Tethys 40 million years ago, dauntingly big basilosaurs' forelimbs had converted to flippers, though they still had remnant hind limbs. At Wadi-Al-Hitan, a desert sand valley studded with a whale fossil legacy as rich as any Pharoah's tomb, whole skeletons were chipped and brushed out of the sand. *Basilosaurus isis*, up to 21 metres long, may have preyed on compact, dolphin-like *Dorudon atrox*, that swam through the mangrove fringed estuaries and coastal lagoons of the valley.

These smaller archaeocetes had already developed a whale's distinctive equipment for fast, enduring propulsion. A strong vertebral frame held massive muscles that heaved water away vertically. They had a 'mechanism of considerable strength for propelling themselves by upward and downward strokes of the flukes, after the manner of living whales', said the great hunter of ancient whales' bones, Remington Kellogg. Today the fastest human swimmers mimic this efficiency at every turn of an Olympic race.

Archaeocetes spread easily into the new seas. Basilosaur fossils were found in the Gulf Coastal Plain of the United States and in New Zealand. They were lastingly successful, living for around 19.8 million years to the end of the Eocene epoch 33.7 million years ago. But in the end, all they had was teeth. They could not light up the dark sea with sound-like emerging odontocetes. Nor could they gulp masses of prey, as would mysticetes. Archaeocetes faded out as the ancestors of modern cetaceans arrived.

Ewan Fordyce believes this happened in a part of the world that would be their great stronghold through time: the Southern Hemisphere. In the Oligocene epoch its expansive waters were so plentiful that, in the absence of marine reptile competitors, both toothed and baleen whales flourished. In wide, temperate seas like those where *Mammalodon colliveri* and *Janjucetus hunderi* lived, prey was in an abundance that would persist as whales modernised over the next 30 million years.

Early in the warm climate of the 10-million-year Oligocene, and through to the early Miocene epoch 23 million years ago, whales split into their two great lineages: first the odontocetes, and soon after through beginnings as modest as the Jan Juc whales, the giant baleen whales.

Fossil skulls tell this story. Without much vision underwater and lacking facial expression, whales used noises for hunting and communication. Bones of the skulls telescoped out, making space for intricacies like the communication system in today's great Sperm whale. Nostrils migrated along the top of the head to the rear, forming the blowhole that gives long-distance travellers like the Blue a quick way of taking a breath on the run. The tooth substitute, baleen, grew astonishingly long in species like Rights in order to skim planktonic riches. They developed insulating blubber layers, and massive size. These helped reduce heat loss in cold waters, but the scale could also have been an anti-predator aid, or minimised drag during swimming and diving.

Palaeontologists last century found enough big animal fossils to form a view of their evolutionary message: great size is usually not sustained. They need much more food and space than the small, so they tend to be rarer anyway. 'It seems to be generally conceded that gigantism is one of the indications of approaching extinction,' said Kellogg before he went on to help found the IWC.

Today's whales have held their place in the marine world for a long time. Modern baleen whales, for example, first appeared in the late Miocene, more than five million years ago. Around that time, one of the ancestors of man, *Ardipithecus ramidus*, may have been thinking about walking upright. Tracing the genes of the Antarctic Minke, Stanford University's Steve Palumbi found that the population reached back more than one million years. About then, *Homo erectus* had moved out of Africa and was walking across Asia.

Cetaceans lived in adaptable ecological harmony in every sea. 'Ice ages, sea level change and even local food sources did not interrupt their lives,' said Palumbi. 'Living in a fluid environment they could move to new areas of productivity and find food even as the climate around them changed.'

Then in the blink of an evolutionary eye this ended, with a force perhaps only exceeded by the meteor that took life from the dinosaurs. After 53 million years of growth and change, great whales were rushed to the brink of extinction in just a few hundred years. Said Palumbi: 'Whales have shown a remarkable resilience to cataclysmic events—until the last one—which is us.'

It would take a bleak view of the intricate patterns of life on earth to think that these were just more giants whose time had come; that commercial whalers were only doing what comes naturally.

Counting back is hard. No log was kept by whalers who could not write or did not want their catch known. Other records were lost or falsified. Little account was taken of whales struck by a harpoon and then lost, to die some time later unknown. For those who want to look though, forensic work is glimpsing the true scale of what was taken from the oceans.

Historical records claimed that around 20 000 Humpbacks and 30 000 to 50 000 Fins lived in the North Atlantic before hunting began. DNA sequencing by Joe Roman and Steve Palumbi told a very different story. They figured that in order to have created the genetic diversity now present in these stocks of Humpbacks and Fins, their populations had to be around ten times larger than the historic count.

Better records were kept of the single largest slaughter, of Southern Hemisphere whales at the peak of industrial whaling last century, even if 94 027 deaths were disguised by the Soviets. When tallied, modern whaling in the far south accounted for 2 039 621 whales. The species hardest hit was the Fin: 725 116 were killed. Another 401 670 Sperm died, and 360 644 Blues.

Very, very recently in evolutionary time, our oceans were alive with whales. Their role in the marine ecosystem was intact. The glorious statements they made to watchers above the surface—the breach and the blow—might have been as regular a sight as a passing flock of birds, or the afternoon sea breeze. Out at sea, they might have gathered in uncountable numbers.

When the moratorium was agreed in 1982, they were largely gone. No species was made extinct, but off many coasts of the world, they totally disappeared. No longer did the Right whale swim its slow, restless passage along the Atlantic coast of western Europe. Perhaps a few tens of them hid in the eastern North Pacific, along with a precarious population of Gray whales. The globe-straddling Sperm did better than most, but was reduced to a fraction of its former scale: from 1.1 million whales to around 360 000 spread right across the world's oceans. Humpbacks lived in small, unknown numbers. The Blue was an arithmetical figment in much of its former Antarctic range, and the Fin little different. There was just one animal left in commercial abundance for the harpoon.

December 23. In spite of its being Sunday we harpooned a small whale, called in the Arctic language a Mencke whale, after a German who accompanied Mr Foyn on some of his voyages. Under a commotion and uproar worthy of a Right whale, the animal is killed and brought along-side; its value is very small, except for the practice it gives our men, and the excellent steaks which it adds to our larder.

Today when speed and efficiency count for so much in what we think of as aesthetic, the great expression of whale design lives in the *Balaenoptera* genus: Rights, Sperm, even the close relative, the Humpback, look ungainly beside them. The five *Balaenoptera* rank like a model series from a luxury car maker: the same long, sea-galloping shape and identifying features, a few variations in colour—and of course, size. Down through the genus, whalers chased them.

After the Blue and the Fin, they turned to the less abundant and smaller Sei and Bryde's whales, worth six to a Blue Whale Unit. When they reached Minkes, the BWU was reduced to its most absurd. One Blue equalled 30 Minkes. If Svend Foyn's nineteenth-century crewman mistook one for the other, as legend had it, no wonder his name was a byword for foolishness among whalers. Mencke's whale was thought of as just that: a joke, until Japanese whaling companies began killing it seriously in the Antarctic in 1967–68.

I was asleep on a rock in Antarctica when I heard my first Minke. As our ship had neared the continent, a few surged quickly across the bow—in panic or in play I was unsure. There was a little blow and then their hooked fins and dark backs flashed before they plunged back into the water and sped away. We reached Australia's deeply isolated Mawson station, to resupply it as *Aurora Australis* moored in the natural granite arms of Horseshoe Harbour. Tired in perpetual daylight, one afternoon I copied the local seals and had a doze in the sun on the smooth rock of the west arm.

The PHOOO-aaaahhh! of a whale breath woke me. I looked up and glimpsed a Minke cruising close by. This was a humbling moment for a human. The whale was at peace among the ice that stretched in a seascape edged by ice cliff to a far horizon. It swam unhurried around the floes, and gradually worked its way out to sea again.

Enough images of harpooned Minkes exist now for us to be almost familiar with the look of the little piked whale. It *is* small as baleen whales go. Females might reach 10 metres and 13 tonnes at most. Its acutely pointed snout is like a Fin's in miniature. Global in range, with several sub-species, in the Antarctic the Minke's dark back gives way to a silver-white underside. Rows of rorqual pleats furrow the belly sleekly, and a thin tail stock runs out to flukes shaped like a sickle moon. As I look at one image, what surprises me about these flukes up close is their texture. It's not smooth like the wetsuit skin of a beached pilot whale I once touched. Instead a rich network of blood vessels runs under the surface. It reminds me of nothing so much as the back of my hand.

Minkes are fast, with good endurance. Records of their being chased by Orcas off the Pacific coast of North America had them reaching 30 kilometres per hour in bursts, and averaging around 20 kilometres per hour in sustained pursuits. As long as the Minke kept on running and wasn't trapped in a bay, it would outlast any Orca snapping and squealing behind.

Early whalers also had to either steal up on Minkes or corner them. Boat engines meant Norwegians could take some from local waters in the early twentieth century, and they were part of a small pre-World War Two catch by Japanese coastal whalers. Oil was the main objective of industrial whaling, and Minkes were a waste of time, boiling down to a measly couple of barrels. Hundreds disappeared into Soviet factory ships that would consume anything, but Minkes weren't much in the thinking of an IWC focussed on other crashing stocks. An extensive whale species status report by its scientific committee in 1968 didn't even mention them.

Like a bystander swept up in a passing parade, the Minke, the whale no one had bothered with, became the point of a defining international environmental struggle.

Unable to find bigger *Balaenoptera* in the Antarctic any more, Japanese whalers aimed at the mammal with 'excellent steaks'. They had quietly counted Minkes at least since 1966, consistently finding large numbers in the same waters south of Australia and New Zealand where General MacArthur first sent them after World War Two.

Pressure was coming from the Japanese fishing industry to make the most of this whale. It had dedicated one of the whaling fleets, the five-ship *Jinjo Maru* group, to catching only them. The result of its first voyage, the meat of 3000 Minkes, brought an encouraging price when it reached fish markets early in 1972. At the annual IWC Scientific Committee meeting a few months later, Japan's scientific chief, Seiji Ohsumi, waded in, bent on obtaining approval to take many more. Bad luck for Japan it was the year that the discredited Blue Whale Unit was finally replaced by individual species quotas in a greening world.

Only the Japanese were doing detailed Minke population work, and Ohsumi's opening bid was to double the abundance estimate. Calculating the number at 150 000–200 000 in 1971, he revised it to 299 999 in 1972, figuring this meant a maximum sustainable yield (MSY) of 12 230, which was the quota Japan wanted. MSY is the largest catch that can be taken without damaging a stock's ability to renew itself. Had the IWC agreed with Ohsumi, the Minke could have been exterminated at a pace much like the larger species before it.

Other scientists proposed a much more conservative quota of around 5000. South Africa's Peter Best said any estimate so radically revised upward on just a single season's sightings had to be 'provisional'. Japan acquiesced and the quota was set at 5000. That was the theory. Then came the reality as Japan pushed for more. It went over quota in 1972–73 by 745 whales. Next meeting when the quota came up again, the Soviet Union and Japan held out for a catch of 8000. Only these two nations were in favour, and a vote held it to 5000. At this, Japan and the Soviet Union used the IWC's universal get-out clause: the objection.

Any member who disagrees with a major IWC decision, a Schedule Amendment, has 90 days to lodge an objection. Then it is automatically free of the decision. The two remaining Antarctic whalers decided to catch 4000 each, and took a total of 7713. In 1974, the IWC majority gave ground. Though the Scientific Committee was unable to agree on a stock size and urged conservatism, a quota of 7000 was set. Strangely, that was exactly what the whalers would say they caught—3500 each.

About as many Minkes were being taken as all other baleen whales combined. The Fin would still be hunted in small numbers in the North Atlantic, but it was almost a memory in the Antarctic. In all the vastness of the Southern Ocean, there were only enough Fins for the IWC to set a last quota in 1975–76 in a neglected corner of the south-east Pacific. It yielded a catch of just 206—the last of nearly three-quarters of a million.

Thousands of Sei and Bryde's whales were still being processed, but as the 1970s closed, the IWC was getting a grip on the geographically separate stocks of individual whales. With their catastrophic state too clear to be ignored, more stocks were being protected each year. Two species still held out a future to the industrial whaling machine: Sperm and Minke. According to IWC reports, an average 9997 Minkes were taken annually around the world in the seven years leading up to the moratorium, and the killing didn't end then. IWC delegates had barely left Brighton in 1982 before objections to the moratorium were lodged. Japan, Norway, the USSR and Peru each exempted themselves. In retaliation, attempts to stop whaling moved beyond the IWC and into the hazier world of global politics.

Each of the four objectors showed in a different way why the IWC was failing. As part of a wide push into the high seas, the rich Japanese fishing companies had a well trained domestic market tied to whaling. Small-scale Norwegian fishermen hunted local Minkes in the North Atlantic for domestic consumption and export, and these fishing families presented a solid bloc for Oslo's politicians. The Soviet fleet might have been decrepit, but a West-hating command economy ran it. Peru and other small countries outside the IWC whaled for the Japanese.

Peru fell over first. Its operation backed by Taiyo Fisheries had been taking whales in a shabby shore-based business since 1967. Many were undersized in an industry operated with Japanese management and little Peruvian government supervision. Under pressure of US fisheries sanctions Peru had joined the IWC in 1979. It killed its last Bryde's whales, 181 of them, in 1984, and two years later dropped its objection.

The country that US President Ronald Reagan described as 'the evil empire' was having trouble sustaining its whaling. The youngest Soviet ships were in the rusted *Dalniy Vostok* fleet fingered by Greenpeace in the Pacific. The number of targets its whalers could find were a mockery of the years in which Solyanik puffed himself up for exceeding the plan.

Moscow knew its whalers were being closely watched. Those mad environmentalists had steamed over the horizon year after year in the

North Pacific. And it was impossible to resist IWC demands for foreign observers aboard whaling ships. There was a hint of collusion in the flat dismissal by a Japanese observer of the claim that the Sperm whale Paul Watson had stood upon was undersized. There were more hints in the records of some Soviet catches. They were exactly on quota in an industry, and by a nation, chronically unable to stop going over quota.

As whales disappeared and fleets retired, Soviet Sperm whaling ended in 1979. Under the objection it stuck to Minke whaling, and could not resist pushing past the quota in the phase-out years. The White House loaded the legal artillery. The Soviets refused to hold to their share of the Antarctic Minke quota in the summer of 1984–85, declaring 3027—more than 1000 over limit. In response the US halved Soviet fisheries allocations and put the squeeze on Japan not to import excess Minke meat.

Reagan stopped short of using his full power to embargo Soviet fishery products under the Pelly Amendment because it could have affected a $12 million US joint venture. Clearly though, brazen Soviet whaling was history. Forces much more powerful than the toothless and ill-informed IWC of the 1950s were at work on Minkes. The Soviets quit commercial whaling at the next IWC meeting in Malmo, Sweden, in 1986. The delegation said it would end by 1987 and belligerently refused to lower its kill before then. Still, today, its objection to the moratorium remains on the IWC's books.

The world was then left with two kinds of incorrigible commercial whalers: the company men of Japan and the obstinate Norse fishers. They wanted the Minke, and its millions of dollars of useable flesh.

11

BRAVE NEW SCIENCE

All our science is a cookery book, with an orthodox theory of cooking that nobody's allowed to question, and a list of recipes that mustn't be added to except by special permission from the head cook.

Aldous Huxley, *Brave New World*, 1932

Masayuki Komatsu was an enigma to the West, and probably many of his countrymen too. He was nothing like the usual poker-faced Japanese suit that made Westerners nervous. They knew where they were with Komatsu. And it was usually somewhere bad.

He was among Japan's best and brightest. He grew up bold in the provinces to climb Tokyo's bureaucratic ladder in a country where government apparatus is for the elite. He became an international champion for Japan, denouncing the deceitful, soft-headed West. Such passion seemed incongruous for the small, dapper man with the soft, wary face. But he was so effective and his country so determined that Komatsu was sometimes a ringmaster around which the entire IWC circus performed.

He was the child of a part-time fisherman at Rikuzentakata in Iwate prefecture. Japan's main island, Honshu, is fringed with black volcanic rock and sand. The small fishing town on its cool northern Pacific coast is famous for its crescent of pine-fringed, white sand beach.

As Komatsu tells it, in Rikuzentakata many fishermen had foreign wives. That was why he found it easy to communicate with the foreigner—the *gaijin*. He graduated from Tohoku University, a well respected regional college in Sendai, about halfway between his home and Tokyo, and joined the Fisheries Agency in 1977. A few years later, marked for greater things, he was sent by the government to the US Ivy League college Yale, to take an MBA. For a 30-year-old with such a background it was a formative time.

Japan's postwar economic miracle had made it a global leader in heavy industry, cars and consumer products. Its top companies were starting to move overseas. Honda opened its first US plant in 1984, the year Komatsu graduated from Yale. At the same time in Washington, Japan was engaged in a furious dispute over whaling and fishing.

An ultra-conservative, Yasuhiro Nakasone, was prime minister, and the Fisheries Agency was strategically important. His countrymen were eating around 12 million tonnes of fish annually. Local fishing was the mainstay of this protein mountain. Sardine, Mackerel, Bonito and Squid underpinned it, but the sea brought much else: Saury and Pollock, seaweed and clams.

Navies of small fishing boats crowded inside harbour walls along the coast of a country that counted nearly 7000 fishing villages. More than 400 000 fishermen and their families formed a solid political constituency. Nakasone's Liberal Democratic Party had been in power almost without interruption since 1948. And one way it stayed there was to hammer home the message that only by electing LDP candidates would rural districts get infrastructural improvements. All those typhoon-proof harbour walls . . .

The fishing companies were also powerful. Despite the growing barriers of Exclusive Economic Zones, around 2 million tonnes of fish came from far seas fisheries around other countries. Diplomats made bilateral access deals for keenly hunted species such as Southern Bluefin tuna. Like whales, catches of this Tokyo fish-market prize were falling by the early 1980s. A prodigious 81 000 tonnes of Southern Bluefin were caught in 1961. By 1984 it was less than half that figure.

Yet that year the 37 000 tonnes of Southern Bluefin roughly matched the entire whale meat supply to the Japanese table, both in price and quantity. Whale comprised about 0.28 per cent of the entire Japanese seafood consumption—a tiny fraction. For most, its taste had drifted into the past. Tuna—Bluefin, Bigeye, Albacore and Skipjack—were preferred in the high-end raw seafood market. The three companies that went whaling were much busier spreading fishing nets and longlines around the globe than they were at firing harpoons. Still, whaling remained so important to the companies and government that they would make it a matter of national pride to somehow keep the hunt going.

When most whales had disappeared and stock quotas began to be enforced, the companies kept business ticking over by cutting ships and jobs. The three big whalers, Nissui, Taiyo and Kyokuyo merged their whaling operations into a single company: Nippon Kyodo. It ran one fleet to both the Antarctic and North Pacific, and kept on whaling during the moratorium using the objection.

Inevitably, this drew an attack. As Komatsu was broadening his mind among clever, wealthy Americans at Yale, US environmentalists forced the pace against the Nippon Kyodo fleet. Despite warnings from Washington, the fleet took 3908 whales in 1984 to put Japan on collision course with American domestic law. Under the Pelly or Packwood Amendments, Japan could lose fishing rights or face trade sanctions if the Reagan Administration decided it was diminishing the effectiveness of the IWC.

The way the iron negotiator Komatsu remembers it, the stakes included a million tonne Alaskan Pollock fishery. The threat of its trawlers losing access to these shoals made Japan bow to US demands and withdraw the objection. This was undue interference in Japan's national sovereignty. 'The United States phased out the fish allocation anyway,' Komatsu said. 'Thus Japan lost both—whaling and fishing.'

Actually there was a little more to this story. The Nakasone and Reagan administrations struck an agreement that Japan could still take some whales for a few years if it dropped its objection to the moratorium by 1988. Just before their agreement was finalised in 1984, the environmentalists went to the District Court in Washington to have Pelly and Packwood enforced. They won there, and at an appeals court, before the US Supreme Court finally decided 5–4 in favour of the Japan Whaling Association.

It was an empty victory for the whalers. Before the case went to the Supreme Court, the Japanese Government had guaranteed to drop the moratorium objection if the appeals court's order was reversed. The

Supreme Court decision came down in June 1986. Nippon Kyodo's fleet took its last commercial haul of Minkes, Bryde's and Sperm in the North Pacific the following summer. Then it went scientific whaling.

Japan wasn't the first. Australia, Britain and the United States were some of the more enthusiastic early users of scientific permits. As if there weren't enough opt-out clauses disabling the IWC's founding convention, many original member countries tried Article Eight on scientific whaling. It seems to have floated into the treaty from another, mythical, time when scholarly science and devious politics were strangers.

The wording is unmistakeable. Absolute power is given to any country to issue a 'special permit' for lethal scientific research on as many whales as it wants. It requires the whales to be processed, and the 'proceeds' to go where the government sees fit. All an IWC member country has to do is say promptly what was killed and what research was done. Even this basic demand was ignored. Of sixteen special permits issued in the first eight years of the IWC, covering 150 whales, very few scientific reports reached the commission.

A series of permits were issued in Australia through the government research organisation, CSIRO. Some were defensible, others dubious. The pioneering Humpback biologist, Graham Chittleborough, applied to take a small number of lactating cows and their suckling calves in the 1950s. Mothering Humpbacks were normally off limits, even though the species was still widely hunted. 'Norwegian gunners didn't like doing this, as a matter of fact,' Chittleborough said. 'I explained that I wanted to see if females had post-partum ovulation—how soon they could mate again. This would have a big bearing on their rate of recovery. I found out that it does occur, but it seldom results in pregnancy.'

Later Australia became more adventurous with permits, notifying the IWC of a plan to take 25 undersized Bryde's whales, thirteen undersized Blues and 48 undersized Sperm in 1962. It persisted in granting permits for undersized Sperm, another 56, in 1963. In this Australia boarded a crowded bandwagon. Around these years South Africa gave permission for 350 undersized Sperm to be taken, the US issued a permit for a 'harem' of Sperm; Canada and New Zealand wanted them as well.

Japan dreamed up a reason to join the Sperm whale scientific flurry, wanting three whole schools including 'undersized whales, calves and suckling whales and females accompanied by calves and suckling whales'. What was so interesting to science about undersized Sperm whales? There was some honesty to it. With IWC rules only allowing catches of large females and adult males, these permits allowed science on ageing through teeth, and checks on pregnancy rates among 'nursery' schools, according to Australian scientist, John Bannister. But a permit was also a ticket for commercial whalers who hauled in animals below regulation length. 'It certainly boosted land stations' numbers,' Bannister said.

IWC commissioners couldn't stop the rule-bending but they did point to it publicly, and try to rein it in through the oversight of the Scientific Committee. Enthusiasm for special permits waned until 1976 when the Japanese fleet decided to take 240 tropical Bryde's whales in the Pacific as part of a three-year program. Its scientists pushed out a detailed paper on this kill, but the IWC Scientific Committee was unconvinced of its value, and successfully argued that any more permits should go before them first for comment.

Considering this long record of doubtful science, it's hardly surprising that after the surviving whalers were blocked by the moratorium, they looked at their costly whaling ships and factories and turned longingly to Article Eight. 'The government will do its utmost to find ways to maintain the nation's whaling in the form of research or other forms,' said the Japanese Fisheries Minister, Moriyoshi Sato. He was walking a fine line, as he found when the US twisted Japan's arm to withdraw the moratorium objection. Article Eight might give sovereign right to whale 'for science', but there could still be consequences.

Iceland and South Korea made scientific pitches to get past the increasingly focussed anti-whaling nations who pointed out plans by Icelanders to trade whale meat, and an absence of the most basic science in the Korean offering. Then steaming out of Japan in 1987 came the largest bid yet to whale in the name of science. A twelve-year research program in the Antarctic would take 825 Minkes and 50 Sperm annually. For a reduced

Japanese fleet, it was a barely viable half of the previous commercial kill.

Of course the program was opposed. Eloquent arguments about the value of the science wafted back and forth across the IWC meeting room in Bournemouth, England. A resolution was passed condemning it. But the IWC couldn't stop it. Once again the United States was left to take it on, and half-heartedly the Reagan Administration did. The scientific catch was cut to 273 Minkes, but still the Japanese lost access to their only remaining US fishery: 5000 tons of Pacific whiting, and 3000 tonnes of sea snails. By weight and value of seafood, the Japanese had the worst of it. Reagan baulked at trade sanctions under the Pelly Amendment—not with the Asian economic powerhouse. So the Kyodo Senpaku fleet began its years of chasing whales for science.

The way a ricepaper wall in a traditional Japanese house gives a notion of privacy, so the different Japanese components of scientific whaling were separated. The big fishing companies folded their joint operation, Nippon Kyodo, into a new business, Kyodo Senpaku Kaisha Ltd, or translated: the Ship Partners Company Ltd. It owned the fleet and was represented by the Japan Whaling Association (JWA).

On the other side of the screen stood the Institute of Cetacean Research (ICR), which chartered Kyodo Senpaku's fleet and ran the whaling. Set up in 1987, it collected revenue from sales of whale meat and answered to the Fisheries Agency in the Ministry of Agriculture, Forestry and Fisheries. It also employed scientists, but most of this work was done on contract to outside institutions.

The office workers of JWA/Kyodo Senpaku occupied one floor of a plain white building fronting a reclaimed reach of Tokyo Bay. Staffed by ranks of young male clerks and office ladies, the place could have been an insurance company if not for the ship models and harpoon sitting on the carpet in the entrance lobby. Ricepaper screens were replaced by a lift. One floor below were the offices of the ICR.

Encouraged by this artificial division, a language arose as well—one that would have found favour with Humpty Dumpty.

'When *I* use a word,' Humpty Dumpty said in a rather scornful tone, 'it means just what I choose it to mean—neither more nor less.'

'The question is,' said Alice, 'whether you *can* make words mean different things.'

'The question is,' said Humpty Dumpty, 'which is to be master—that's all.'

The factory ship was not the factory ship. It was the research fleet mother ship. There were three chasers, only they weren't chasers. They were sighting/sampling vessels. The gunners shot harpoons that occasionally missed the quick Minkes. It wasn't a miss though. It was a sampling error. When a Minke was boxed and frozen, it wasn't whale meat. It was the by-product of research. Japan wasn't commercial whaling, it was conducting scientific research. It was master of the word.

At first skirmishing over this adventure in logic was confined to science journals. Japanese researchers said they needed to collect whale's earplugs which are ringed, like trees, with age. They said they wanted to do this to estimate the natural mortality of Minkes—an obvious key factor in any calculation of sustainable yield. 'Our ignorance about the biology of whales is delaying any informed discussion about the practice of commercial whaling,' said the director of the ICR, Fukuzo Nagasaki.

The Australian, Bill de la Mare, replied in *Nature* that the way they were going about answering this question offered no prospect of resolving the problems of managing whaling. Instead they had set out on a program that would need truckloads of earplugs to find an answer. 'Some Japanese researchers seem reluctant to accept analyses showing that these estimates will be cripplingly imprecise . . . unless the research were to continue for decades, with total samples of tens of thousands of whales.'

Governments' treatment of Japan in the IWC was a gentle tut-tutting. Ritually, anti-whaling nations 'invited Japan to reconsider'. So it did and decided the program was about right, feeling 'resentment and regret that so many countries now joined the bandwagon' against it.

But brave new science did also imply obligations. A serious nation would want to dutifully share its research. Each year Japan brought some of the results of its program back for IWC scientists to discuss. It also detailed forthcoming surveys. Intelligence like this was useful for the most vocal opponents of Japan from Greenpeace. It was taken onto

MV *Gondwana* to help track the fleet down in the first action against scientific whaling.

Under David McTaggart's infuriating and inspiring corporate leadership, Greenpeace's gentle hippies had been pushed aside and replaced by a generation of cold-eyed activists. The leader did wear jeans—pointedly he wore jeans. And like a denim favourite, Greenpeace became a managed global brand with multi-million-dollar finances, capable of turning up anywhere on the planet.

It was out campaigning for Antarctica when the chance came to seriously harass whalers for the first time in years. The ice-strengthened *Gondwana* already had a busy schedule in the summer of 1988–89. Its activists occupied the construction site of a penguin-killing French polar airstrip, checked on a deteriorating Soviet base, and were bound for their own World Park base on Ross Island. Then out of the icebergs north-west of the Ross Sea sailed the Japanese fleet in its second season of scientific whaling.

Expedition co-ordinator Paul Bogart remembered this as one-quarter planning and three-quarters luck. 'We set a course for our ship that would traverse where we thought they might be at that point in the season. It was a needle in a haystack—100 000 square miles of ocean—narrowed by the season, and commonsense. Luck intervened and we found them something like a day into our course.'

The factory ship then was the 22 000 tonne *Nisshin Maru No.3*, a wheezing old monster that had been consuming whales since the late 1940s. *Gondwana* had no trouble keeping up and was soon willingly engaged, even nosing in behind the stern ramp to block the transfer of dead whales.

'The stern ramp could accommodate much larger whales than the relatively small Minke, and brought home the realisation that there wasn't much left for this beast to devour,' Bogart recalled. 'Instead of being mothballed as a relic of another era in some Japanese shipyard, she was here in the Southern Ocean devouring a few Minke whales under the guise of science.'

Greenpeace campaigner Naoko Funahashi listened to radio exchanges in Japanese between ships of the fleet. Chasers complained about being picked on by Greenpeace, and were urged by *Nisshin Maru No. 3* to be patient and show restraint. When Bogart called the *NM-3* by radio in English to formally argue the case, the reply was unsurprising. 'There was a long silence, followed by a "Well, I'm just a scientist".'

A Japanese account claimed *Gondwana* bumped the stern of the catcher *Kyo Maru No. 1* in 'another dangerous act' by Greenpeace. Bogart said: 'They bumped *us*, but of course they would view it the other way. In any case, no harm was done to either vessel and the stern ramp blockade ended up being the most effective way of stopping the whaling.'

It was a short encounter, around a week. In the early years of satellite communications and the internet, Greenpeace was at the cutting edge. It could process and send still photographs out over the Inmarsat line and exchange internal email. It wasn't possible to send today's horrific colour video footage, but images went to IWC scientific committee members as the hunt took place. The immediacy was new and attractive. The impact was enough for Greenpeace to think about returning. Three summers later the ex-salvage tug MV *Greenpeace*, nicknamed the Black Pig, made the first dedicated attempt at interrupting the kill.

The 1991–92 season began with Greenpeace caught out. Expecting the old *Nisshin Maru No. 3*, the activists found it had been replaced by a new *Nisshin Maru* one third the size. This converted stern trawler was sold into Kyodo Senpaku by its leading shareholder, Nissui, after sitting idle when US fisheries access was lost. It was faster than both the old factory ship and MV *Greenpeace*. Instead of dogging the whalers all the way south as they planned, the activists had to try to surprise them down there.

Using the IWC data and the advice of the long-time whales campaigner, John Frizell, MV *Greenpeace* sailed to the 100th degree of longitude, southwest of Australia, and waited. It idled on the edge of the retreating pack ice zone, and in the middle of a 3500-kilometre diameter elongated loop that the fleet planned to sail off the Antarctic coast. Two days later, contact was made.

Detailed accounts were kept on each side, from the time a scouting chaser came upon MV *Greenpeace* until the campaigners left the fleet 52 days later. Greenpeace's Keiran Mulvaney and Japanese freelance journalist Toshio Kojima watched each other's ships come and go.

Mulvaney brought a wry English approach to the voyage. Crossing the equator on a perfect evening, he nodded coolly at his Greenpeace predecessors: 'I half expected to see a rainbow suddenly appear and a flock of doves fly past.' Kojima shed a little light on the whalers, but was contemptuous of Greenpeace. He saw the activists as wastrels, lolling on deck or speeding by in inflatables like teenagers on holiday.

Formal messages passed between the two sides as if they were encamped on a medieval jousting field. Mulvaney proposed fancifully that *Nisshin Maru* and MV *Greenpeace* rendezvous at an agreed time and place to discuss their differences. The ICR director, Nagasaki, sent a letter to Greenpeace's head office in Amsterdam protesting against the dangers and demanding their withdrawal. The rivalries opened with skirmishes in which the chasers took turns to tail MV *Greenpeace* for weeks. Not equipped with a helicopter for reconnaissance, and sailing in entirely the wrong direction much of the time, the increasingly flustered campaigners did not find *Nisshin Maru* until 4 January 1992.

When the two ships did come across each other, they gave no quarter. In a gentler era in the 1970s, the whale seer Paul Spong docked an inflatable at the stern slipway of a Soviet factory ship in the North Pacific, walked up the ramp and asked the amazed flensers to please desist. This time, despite below freezing temperatures, inflatables buzzed beneath the catchers' bows and their occupants pushed grimly past fire hoses to reach *Nisshin Maru*. It was dangerous work. In the most intense moment they tied the small boats to lifeline rings at the bottom of the factory ship's slipway. Their ropes were grappled by the whalers, and one inflatable momentarily hoisted out of the sea, almost capsizing before the line was cut.

Greenpeace's campaign mood seemed to swing between anarchist collective and naval discipline. Aboard *Nisshin Maru*, the sight of Greenpeacers depressed the whalers visibly until they overcame the first attempt to blockade a transfer, and broke into cheery, relieved laughter.

Logistics needed to make the protest worthwhile had improved. Mulvaney lost an enormous amount of sleep on the end of a satellite phone to Australia, New Zealand and Europe. He wired out black-and-white pictures, even posted a videotape with a passing Australian ship. But Greenpeace had no helicopter and most of the images lacked fire.

Photographs of harpooning had to be taken at sea level. *Nisshin Maru's* flensing deck, lined with canvas wind screens, was still a mystery to Greenpeace when they called it a day and sailed north.

If the whalers breathed a sigh of relief then, it was too early. There *was* a helicopter further down the whaling fleet's voyage track, in Prydz Bay, eastern Antarctica, and the people aboard it were no friends of the whalers.

From the air in summer, this wide embayment named after a Norwegian whaling manager looks to be pure wilderness. The Lambert glacier sweeps an Amazon of ice out of eastern Antarctica to float over the head of Prydz Bay. Great tabular icebergs scatter to the horizon. Tracts of pack ice shatter into a floating geometric carpet. Emperor penguins convene on ice floes like ornate priests. Smaller Adélie penguins waddle about imitating Charlie Chaplin. It is home to scrofulous moulting elephant seals, and to pure white snow petrels, to Minkes and to Australians.

Australians have known Prydz Bay year-round since 1957, when Davis Station was built in a line of hazardous plywood huts on its eastern shore. A fortress of primary coloured, triple-glazed steel sheds now stands against the cold. It's near the heart of the Australian Antarctic Territory—42 per cent of the continent, 5.6 square million kilometres of iced land with a 7000 kilometre coastline.

Like mainland Australia, it is a place where most life clings to the coast, and inland is a wide trackless desert. Scientists stalk among the birds and seals, monitor the Lambert's shifts, mutter over rocks, and occasionally find something very new. In the unvegetated brown gibber hills behind Davis in 1985, the director of science at the Australian Antarctic Division, Professor Pat Quilty, urged me to look at a piece of straight-grained stone.

'That's bone!' he said, bursting with the thrill of discovery. He had just found the fossils of what would be identified as a new genus and species of dolphin. A depression in the hills called Marine Plain turned out to be a cetacean graveyard 4.5 million years old. Fragments of a small Right whale and large vertebrae from an ancient baleen whale lay exposed there.

In February 1992, after seeing off MV *Greenpeace*, the Japanese whaling fleet headed south-west. It swept back and forth across Prydz Bay for several days before steaming inshore near Davis, a chaser after a Minke, and *Nisshin*

Maru a little further out to sea. When the Australians caught sight of it, they exploded as if violated.

James Shevlin was an Antarctic Division voyage leader running the hectic Davis resupply by the ship *Icebird* when the catcher hove into view. He took a helicopter up to look, and what he saw made his blood boil. 'I can only liken it to video footage of a group of white policemen beating up one black man,' he said. 'Just the total lack of contest in it; the anger you feel that something defenceless is being mercilessly hunted.'

He watched, and photographed a chase. 'The chaser was in hot pursuit of a Minke that was surfacing fairly regularly. As it zigzagged, so did the ship. As it tired, it had to surface for air more often.' The cannon fired just ahead of Shevlin's camera shutter. His picture shows the grey chaser at speed peeling out a white wake like a frigate. A puff of smoke surrounds the gunner, and the harpoon slices through the water slightly above a wash where the Minke dived. It missed. 'We hoped the helicopter being there might have put the harpooner off,' Shevlin said.

He flew back to Davis to refuel, checked with officials in Canberra, and was told to fly out again and investigate *Nisshin Maru*, which by then was rafted up to a cargo ship. Shevlin used his camera to take some of the first pictures of this factory deck seen in the West. A Minke made a pathetic sight being peeled to the backbone. Flensers worked with knife, gaff and winch amid a small lake of blood. To one side lay fins separated like pieces of a plastic model. Big blue buckets, one overflowing with innards, stood on the deck. The Japanese had expected to be photographed sooner or later. A small cabin had a sign above the door painted in English: RESEARCH ROOM.

Australia had just proclaimed a 200 nautical mile Exclusive Economic Zone in waters off the Australian Antarctic Territory. The country's Whale Protection Act covered these waters. Here was a fleet brazenly operating within sight of shore. Surely something could be done?

In Canberra it was a diplomatic fizzer. The Hawke Government's angry Environment Minister, Ros Kelly, said the 'abhorrence of all Australians to whaling' should be made known. The acting Japanese ambassador was called in to the Department of Foreign Affairs, which suggested Japan should have shown 'more restraint'. That was the limit. It was decided that the Whale Protection Act only applied to Australians. The fleet sailed north-west out of Prydz Bay, then in another loop taking the ships back through Australian Antarctic waters again, unopposed. The Prydz Bay encounter widened the gulf between Australia and Japan. Both Greenpeace and Australia lifted a corner of the veil over scientific whaling. Next season another foreigner showed the rest of the world what it actually meant for a Minke on the end of a harpoon.

No one had sailed with the Japanese scientific fleet before and publicly told the story later, and Mark Votier is still not entirely sure why they agreed to let him aboard. The British photo-journalist made his first inquiry at the Fisheries Agency, just as the MV *Greenpeace* was making life harder for the whalers. The man on the other side of the table at the initial meeting was Komatsu, recently returned from a posting to the Japanese Embassy in Rome where he had worked on the UN Food and Agriculture Organisation.

'He gave me about an hour of his time,' Votier said. 'He was very frank and courteous. He struck me as reasonable, in a Japanese sort of way.' It was the beginning of many trips to Tokyo, and much careful listening by Votier about what would be expected of him. Nine months later they agreed to a contract that forbad him from filming 'unsightly' scenes, and required prior ICR approval for the use of any film he shot.

'I suppose ultimately they decided that I, or rather Granada, could go with them because they didn't really have anything to lose,' Votier said. 'The reputation of the Japanese at the time was so so bad it probably couldn't have got much worse.'

For seven years after leaving the Royal Navy the tall, curly haired Briton had lived in Japan, and been warmly treated by its people. 'They have, I think, a far more inclusive society than the UK. Terribly hard-working. Terribly committed and conscientious to their jobs and families, and very welcoming.' Unusually his friends were actively green. At their request Votier had pitched to Granada, the British television production company, the idea of making a documentary about the indigenous Penan people's battle against logging in Sarawak. It was a success and they decided on whaling next.

Granada at the last minute switched projects to focus on the closer, cheaper, Norwegian whalers. But Votier had already quit work as an English teacher in Utsunomiya, a home of Honda north of Tokyo, given notice on his flat and sold his car. He decided to go south as a freelance cameraman anyway and the whalers agreed. 'In fact I think they were happier I was doing it on my own, because probably they expected a greater control over what was produced.'

Nisshin Maru left from Tokyo Bay on 7 November 1992 with Votier aboard, and was joined by the rest of the ships soon after. He was given the run of the fleet. He took his camera everywhere, from the crow's nest of the chaser *Toshi Maru 25*, past the flensing deck of the factory ship to its Stygian freezer hold.

'If you're asking me whether I was treated with suspicion, the answer is no. Because in a typical hierarchical society, once the decision has been made by the people at the top for me to film and document what was going on, other people didn't question what I was doing. I had completely free access.'

Aboard ship he found a microcosm of Japanese life, starting with exercise on deck at 8.00 am, and finishing with an evening drink. Work was determined by the stage of the voyage. On the three-week passage south, the crew chipped and painted the ship or maintained factory machines. In rough weather, the whalers became cabin-dwelling television zombies. When whaling began, flensing and processing might continue to midnight. A whale must be carved up quickly if it is to be used safely for human meat, and a Minke could be in a box in a blast freezer less than half an hour after it came aboard.

While it was being reduced by flensers and winches, scientists took measurements and samples, from precise length and weight, to extracting a fetus or an earplug. 'The scientists believe in what they are doing,' Votier said. 'It's not a sham in the sense that they nod and wink and say "we don't really care about it." They are doing it because they are genuinely interested.'

In the far south, Votier spent four weeks aboard *Toshi Maru 25*. Each day one of the chasers steamed off on a sightings cruise along a pre-determined track to count whales. The other two were killing them in a quota that had bumped up to 330.

The choice of a target Minke was random. 'They have to take these animals on a scientific basis. So the scientist who's on the catcher boat, usually a kid in his twenties, has a book of random numbered tables. Let's say they spot a school of five whales. The scientist looks up the page marked five and the next random number. If the number is three, they have to take the third largest whale.

'It can be extremely difficult, because once a whale disappears you don't know where it's going to bob up again. But generally they got it right. The take reflected, I think accurately, the size composition of the whales. They didn't just shoot at the larger whales.'

It was a bad year for Greenpeace. Mulvaney led what he called The Voyage from Hell. Despite having a helicopter, MV *Greenpeace* made only brief contact with the fleet after two and a half months of searching. Votier said that as soon as the activists turned up, the fleet scattered to different points of the compass, to meet again several days later.

As *Nisshin Maru* steamed back to Japan at the end of the season with another load of scientific Minke meat, Votier joined in the tropical drinks parties. The whalers had worked for nearly six months in the Antarctic, and their karaoke machine was blasting fully. He watched the tipsy crooners on whom he was about to blow the whistle.

He had loved the Antarctic: the mesmerising iced seas and the skies without sunset that he first saw with the Royal Navy after the Falklands War. He liked shipboard life. 'There is an esprit de corps. It's the same with any ship's company. You're out on the sea and you're all together on the boat with one objective. You bond.'

What he couldn't stand was the inhumanity. Minke hunting was, to him, atrociously cruel. Less than half the whales he saw harpooned were dying outright. At least the same number were only wounded. Then the ghastly horror of slow whale killing was being repeated. He believed the fault lay in the scientific demand to recover a head undamaged in order to extract the whale's earplug. The harpooner had to aim deliberately away from the head, and hit a vital organ. Too often that didn't happen.

When they first turned to Minkes, the whalers found heavy harpoons with big grenades meant for Fins and Blues were too powerful. The shaft regularly blasted right through the slim animal. If the grenade exploded internally, much of the meat was damaged with shrapnel—not a welcome addition in the markets. So the whalers left the harpoons 'cold', or grenade-less. Superhuman accuracy was needed to repeatedly hit the target, the heart or brain, for instant death.

In 1981, against whalers' complaints, the IWC set a two-year deadline to get rid of cold harpoons. Japan pushed that out a year as it came to grips with a new penthrite grenade. Black powder—ordinary gunpowder—was used in harpoon grenades for a century. Its explosion burned and haemorrhaged and it had about half the detonating velocity of the standard explosive, TNT. The newer Pentaerythritol Tetranitrate had a much bigger bang, about 1.66 times greater than TNT. Whalers claimed it killed straight out by shocking the nervous system. It also made them nervous for their own safety, and they undercharged the grenades.

When the Japanese adopted penthrite, they told the IWC that the Minkes' average time to death in 1983–84 was two minutes and 26 seconds, almost half the cold harpoon's time. But they also said a 'secondary' method of killing was still needed. Some countries favoured another harpoon as a secondary method, others a high powered rifle. The Soviets tried an anti-tank gun, and Japan developed the electric lance. It wasn't working, and Votier had evidence of that on film.

'If a whale wasn't killed outright, it would start to labour and thrash as the barbs of the harpoon opened out inside it, gaffing and clawing at its innards. It would be winched to the front of the catcher boat, and if it was still moving, then lances with detachable electrodes would be produced.

'The animal would be speared, and the electrodes would sink into its flesh. Then they turned on the juice. On this particular catcher it was 100 volts and five amps, which is not sufficient to knock out a whale quickly. It was just a very, very horrible sight to see. The longest time I saw a whale take to be killed was 23 minutes.'

The electric lance was already on the IWC's watchlist. At the annual meeting a few months before Votier's voyage, Japan had been attacked over humane killing. Australia's commissioner Peter Bridgewater said whale killing was, actually, still very often inhumane, and there were serious concerns about the lance. Japan said that humane killing was not in the IWC's remit, but was reluctantly prepared to discuss it. This was Komatsu's first meeting of the commission, and he found nothing like the reception he had received at the FAO. 'I was shocked to find much of what Japan said was being ignored,' he said.

Votier remembered the fleet's arrival back in Japan to the usual fanfare from politicians and Fisheries Agency officials. 'All the crewmen, lined up like little soldiers on the deck.' He had made good friends after five and a half months on the voyage. But he was about to cut those friendships short.

He had already shown footage of the botched electrocutions to *Nisshin Maru* crew on the way home. When the ship arrived in Tokyo, he offered to hand over his 30 hours of film to an ICR official, who squinted through Votier's camera viewfinder for a few hours, sampled some tapes and went away.

The remaining film went to London and quickly became the heart of a British documentary exposing the electric lance's failures. It was screened on the ITV network in prime time, aired in Japan, then in Australia, Germany and the USA. Afterwards Votier returned to the nation that he still admired, and made a point of visiting the people who approved his trip. 'There was no intention on my part to deceive the ICR,' he said.

Some took the chance to vent their anger. 'The worst moment came at the ICR when Dr Nagasaki shouted at me: "I am a scientist. I am not concerned with humane killing."' Komatsu was more relaxed. 'It was clear that he felt the electrocutions were wrong, and he didn't give me a particularly hard time. I think also he found my embarrassing so many of his ICR colleagues amusing.'

Across the range of Japanese attitudes, Votier believed there were more Nagasakis than Komatsus. 'Unfortunately the Japanese didn't just treat whales badly. In the Japanese hierarchy, animals did not count. People counted. Animals were often treated very, very badly. Any dog lover who lived in Japan would despair, seeing them in tiny cages 24 hours a day outside their masters' homes. In a Japanese farm just about every animal had something through its nose to chain it up.

'Cruelty to animals did not register. It wasn't an issue—in the same way, it has to be said, that prisoners of war were treated so badly. They were the lowest of the low.'

Japanese officials at the IWC would disagree. They expressed their respect for the life of animals to the meetings. The whalers conducted ritual services of respect, such as pouring a bottle of sake over the first whale that came aboard *Nisshin Maru* each season. The country might lack space, but pets were treated with doting care. A few weeks after Votier's story broke, the Japanese went into the annual meeting to say that humane killing was still a non-issue, and Japan was continuing its research.

There have been many rounds in the heavyweight contest at the IWC between Japan and anti-whaling nations, and the punch-up over the electric lance was an early, representative one. Along the way we would see each side's underlying approach. The conservationists would win on points. Then Japan would shrug off the loss, and whale on.

They called themselves 'like-mindeds'—the group of anti-whaling nations who had a coordinated position in the IWC. Australia, New Zealand, Britain, France and the United States were at its core; others like Brazil and Italy close at hand. Spreading diplomatic risk, they took it in turns to lead on different issues.

Against the electric lance, the campaign's backbone lay in the work of a New Zealand scientist. David Blackmore of Massey University tested the effect of electric currents on tissues of stranded, dead whales. He found that rather than ensuring a quick death, the lance probably added the pain of electric shock to the original harpoon wound.

The UK weighed in with the law, written and unwritten. It was universally accepted that an electric killing method that didn't immediately stun was inhumane. A European Council directive on animal welfare clearly laid out correct methods, none of which could be carried out at sea. Australia took on debating points. There was no need to kill whales for research, but in any case science demanded the highest standards. Killing methods could not be partially humane. It was like being pregnant—either you were, or not.

Pressure intensified until 1996 when Komatsu was Alternate Commissioner for Japan, effectively manager of its business in the IWC, and its chief spokesman. The case Japan put started by saying that the issue of whaling was no concern of the IWC, and finished with an ultimatum. There was a jab at cultural difference. What about the killing methods used on deer and kangaroo? And a nod to the war legacy. Use of a rifle was not allowed on Japanese ships. Finally there was a warning: an attempt to ban the electric lance would frustrate 'future cooperation and collaboration' by Japan.

Supporters of Japan made their voices heard. The bass-voiced Commissioner for Antigua and Barbuda, David Joseph, raised the doomsday prospect that loose talk about the issue of hunting methods could end global fisheries. When would fishing be regarded as inhumane? And what a threat that could be to developing countries! Along the way we also learned that Japan's whalers were killing fewer than a third of Minkes instantaneously in 1995/96, and only half were dying within 30 seconds.

A year after saying that it would not give up the electric lance, and under the pressure of an IWC vote, Japan relented and said the rifle would be introduced. Minke catches were also raised as the fleet began to take them from the North Pacific, giving it work in the Northern Hemisphere summer. Mark Votier was served with a summons at his British home. The ICR prosecuted him in a Japanese civil court for breach of contract.

Resort to the civil courts is rare in Japan, and prosecution of foreign journalists almost unheard of. Votier believes the ICR was profoundly embarrassed by his film. It sought 10 million yen in damages and 20 million yen costs, a total of around US$450 000 at the time. This was 'a little scary', Votier said. He found a London lawyer who could advise on Japanese law, and was told that as long as he stayed out of Japan he could not be arrested nor have a judgement enforced.

At the House of Commons in Westminster, 116 MPs signed a motion supporting Votier and opposing scientific whaling. Their case was put by an acid-tongued vegetarian Labour MP named Tony Banks who railed against 'Japanese butchers' and wished sanctions could hit their cars and electronic goods. 'That might concentrate their warped little minds,' Banks said.

In the trial, a judge in Tokyo finally made a three million yen (US$45 000) order against Votier, a sum that he felt showed disdain by the court for the case. Still a sometime photo-journalist and unable to set foot in the country he admires, he regrets the broken friendships, and believes that is Japan's fate too.

'The Japanese have never had a chance to become friends with anybody. Every time Japan has had some sort of an encounter with foreigners, it's been bad.' From first contact with the West to twentieth-century wars—all ended in sorrow. 'They have never had any emotional rapport, or bonding, with the rest of the world. When it comes to logging, or tuna fishing, or whaling, the rest of the world might simply be Mars or Jupiter. They do not give a toss.'

12

BEING JAPANESE

Butterfly: They say in your country
if a butterfly is caught by a man
he'll pierce its heart with a needle
and then leave it to perish!
Pinkerton: Some truth there is in that . . .

Madama Butterfly, Giacomo Puccini, 1904

Cultural bedrock did matter to Japan. Again and again whaling's defenders reached into the past to justify the present. When the West tightened its grip on the IWC in the early 1990s, Japanese diplomats became strident about others' imperialism.

'No one has the right to criticise the food culture of other people,' said Komatsu. 'When we Japanese eat our food such as fermented soy beans and sashimi we accept some people may think such food is weird. It is *their* business to think so. But we would be angry if they forced us to stop eating it.'

As he became the public face of Japanese whaling, Komatsu increasingly argued that attempts to stop his nation were based on cultural arrogance. Some people eat wild animals, he said, some eat livestock, and others eat whale. In Japan it was not difficult to strike a chord with this approach. 'Sentiments run deep in Japan', said Robert March, an academic who consults to Australian businesses wanting to link with Asia. 'Whaling is obviously a very emotional issue for the Japanese, and their two most commonly used arguments are that Japanese culture is under threat, and that the Japanese are being treated unfairly.'

This is a country where Buddhism at one time prohibited the eating of unclean four-legged animals, and at another called for a symbolic whale grave to be built in one of its temples. Where, to get past the taboo against mammal eating, the whale was named *Isana*, or brave fish. In a denial of reality, whales were regarded as just different fish—amorphous resources of the sea, like squid or sea urchins.

'It is almost an article of faith among Japanese that their culture is unique,' said the Dutch academic Karel Van Wolferen, as he decoded the country. 'Not in the way that all cultures are unique, but somehow uniquely unique, ultimately different from all others.'

Local cuisine is a heartfelt identifier in this culture. Arguments over the best noodles focus on Sapporo and Nagasaki. Green tea reaches its apex in the nirvana of Japanese tradition, Kyoto. The poisonous blowfish, Fugu, is detoxified best in the port of Shimonoseki. There is even a daikon radish town: Tano. Urbanised and globalised like the rest of us, Japanese sigh nostalgically for the home town and its symbolic tastes even as they enjoy 'Aussie Beef' and canned drinks. So whaling's advocates pointed to the half dozen towns with this tradition and defended their right to cultural survival. Never mind the reality that ordinary Japanese had nothing to do with whales at all.

Taiji on the south-east coast of Honshu is one of these towns of fond memory. It hugs the Pacific coast below pine wooded hills that slope sharply into coves and bays arranged just *so*, like an old oriental watercolour. On a wet summer Saturday I was driven under two happy fibreglass Humpback whales arched across the highway at the town entrance. We stopped at a whale museum crammed with skeletons and outsized anatomical specimens decaying in formalin. Young couples staying out of the rain gasped at the giant organs in jars.

Down the hillside from the museum, a bored-looking Orca amused itself by diving to the base of its sea pen, and rising to toss mouthfuls of black sand in the air. A shrine to the whalers stood at a lookout point on a head-land. We drove up and peered out over the coast into the warm drizzle, trying to imagine it as a place where generations of spotters spied whales.

Apart from the tourist attractions, these days Taiji is home to drive hunts for Striped Dolphin and Pilot whales, and a remnant coastal whaling industry. In a hotel lounge a few of the 'old boys' agreed to speak. They had a grievance—not enough whaling to do—but they did not appear to be the poorer for it. Their clothes were comfy afternoon club attire. Their cars were flasher than any of the Albany whalers'.

Among them was Yosihiro Kogai, whose trim blue 32-tonne coastal whaler was moored at Taiji port with a 50-millimetre cannon mounted on the bow. Kogai was an Antarctic gunner in the 1960s who killed Sperm, Sei, Humpback, Fin, and even Blues. Nearly deaf from too many cannon explosions but otherwise strong, he was just back from waters north of Japan, where he'd quickly picked up a quota of four Baird's beaked whales. A whale of the North Pacific and outside IWC control, Baird's may exceed 12 metres in length and 11 tonnes—much larger than a Minke. And when you can only take four, Kogai pointed out, you do go after the biggest.

He also had a local quota of twenty Pilot whales, and since 1988 had been asking the IWC without success to let him take Minkes locally as an 'indigenous whaler'. He and two other gunners chatted about the task that Kyodo Senpaku's fleet faced taking Bryde's and Sperm in the newly expanded North Pacific hunt. Bryde's were as lazy as goldfish, they concluded. Sperm were slow, and not as smart as Baird's. Kogai laughed throatily.

I had been nervous about meeting these gunners. Back in the whaling company's Tokyo office, a dozen industry men had gathered to scrutinise me, eyeing me as if I were Exhibit A of The Lying Western Media. Adding to my alarm, behind them on the wall in the meeting room loomed a wildly dark painting. A bunch of bearded whalers, clasping gleaming knives, were about to spring from their boats onto floundering, harpooned Pilot whales.

The Taiji gunners looked remarkably unlike the painting. They looked like ordinary fishermen, with the same weathered faces, wiry frames and toughened hands that you would find on any Australian wharf. They cracked the same jokes about their quarry. Through an interpreter I asked Kogai how it felt to hunt the great whales.

'He is saying it's a sort of awesome experience,' came the reply. 'But he thinks of his experience when he went hunting in the forest with a rifle. He looked into the eyes of the bird, and then he couldn't shoot that bird. He supposes that if he looked into the eyes of a big whale, he wouldn't be able to shoot that either.'

A couple of years later in Taiji, Sea Shepherd activists documented a Striped Dolphin kill. Boat-borne hunters drove dozens of them into one of the pretty local coves, and the waters turned red as the animals were butchered with knives and hooks over the following days. After attempting to free some dolphins, two activists spent 23 days in prison. When too much media attention was drawn to the hunt, local authorities declared it illegal to film, and put up canvas screens to hide it from cameras.

I thought again of the dark painting at the Kyodo Senpaku office, and of Kogai's quota of Pilot whales. To Australians, a Pilot whale is something you save. Deep ocean dwellers with well-developed sonar capabilities, they are like miniature Sperm. Navigators of the black. I had helped once when these animals were stranded in Tasmania, an event that drew strangers to an unspoken common purpose like passers-by first on the scene at a bus smash.

I shut my ears to the guttural groans of dying whales up the beach and waded in to help the rescue. At one point we lifted a calf into deeper water, and I was left to steady it in the low swell. The tightly muscled, sharp-toothed, 150-kilogram animal whistled unendingly at high pitch in clear distress. It resisted my guiding hands and turned back to its nearby mother. Determined to swim past me, it was strong, wild and upset. Yet it offered no threat. It just kept pushing. Luckily its cries and the work of other rescuers were enough for the cow to shrug off the sand. The pair made for deeper water, blowing softly. I watched, bemused by the rare and precious chance to be able to touch, let alone aid, creatures from such a different world.

While Kogai and others might kill Pilot whales, most Japanese had different attitudes to whales, if they thought of them at all. Outside Taiji I saw whale symbols that were current Japanese pop images. The spare wheel covers for Toyota Rav 4s on Tokyo streets had a diving whale's tail flukes, and the homily in English: 'Preserve Nature'. In southern Japan's Kochi city, where Miroku made the cannon and harpoons, smiling whales with flawless teeth advertised petrol and homewares. The local fishing fleet at nearby Ogata did a useful sideline watching for Bryde's whales, to the delight of school children on excursion from Osaka and Kobe.

A MORI poll in 1999 found that a statistical blip—just one per cent—of Japanese ate whale more than once a month. A Gallup poll in 2006 found a combined 83 per cent had not eaten it in a long time, or never. Only in pushy, pro-whaling polls was there support for 'sustainable whaling'. Yet Japan became a hardline scolder of anti-whaling nations, driven by the Fisheries Agency and industry. Even as it bent IWC rules to its own needs, official Japanese grudges mounted against the perfidious West.

According to Tokyo, these countries played fast and loose when a chance came to overturn the moratorium and legitimately hunt a plentiful species. They stonewalled development of a new blueprint to safely manage commercial whaling if it resumed. The wretched 'eco-terrorists' kept on harassing the Japanese fleet in the Antarctic. And to cap it all, this most productive global ocean was being fenced off.

The first chance to overthrow the moratorium on commercial whaling came only four years after it was enforced. The original IWC resolution said its effect on whale stocks, and on new catch limits should both be considered by 1990 at the latest. As the IWC met that year in Noordwijk, south Holland (another grey European beach town), Japan took this resolution to mean that the moratorium *would* be lifted if there was clear evidence a whale stock was healthy. Anti-whaling nations were never going to do that. Their only question was how soon this industry would wither and die.

Japan claimed strong scientific ground to resume. Assessments had put Antarctic Minke numbers up to 761 000, robust enough to set a new catch limit. The North Atlantic fishers, Norway and Iceland, swung in behind. A skirmish erupted when the Swedish chairman, Sture Irberger, declared it was possible to vote on new catch limits. Irberger's ruling was slapped down by anti-whaling nations. First you had to vote to change, they said. Only *then* could you set new limits. Japan spitefully concluded: 'The Commission does not keep the promises it had agreed upon, nor act on the scientific advice it receives.' Iceland stated the obvious: the moratorium was becoming indefinite.

Whalers had another reason to complain about delaying tactics when some of the finer scientific minds ever to be applied to whale management had their work shelved. It took eight years to develop the Revised Management Procedure (RMP), a plain name for a carefully wrought piece of mathematical elegance. At its heart was a formula that forced a whaler to be certain about the safe yield of a stock. In a world of devastated whales, the RMP was caution burned into a computer program.

It was officially accepted by the IWC in 1994, but agreement was missing on the over-arching Revised Management Scheme (RMS). This was meant to give the IWC the teeth lacking in the bad old days. But how many teeth? A system of independent observers seemed a good start. Who would pay for them though, and what sort of information would they collect? Would they be standing on a chaser's deck with a stopwatch counting the whales' time to death?

Disputes about the RMS became snarled in dozens of inconclusive meetings. To countries like Australia, the RMP already stood like a harpoon ready to be loaded into the cannon of commercial whaling. Canberra wanted no whaling, and for some time refused to talk about the RMS at all. This kind of treatment was insufferable to the British chairman of the IWC's Scientific Committee, Philip Hammond, and he quit. 'What is the point of having a Scientific Committee if its unanimous recommendations on a matter of primary importance are treated with such contempt?' he said.

Worse for Japan, the anti-whaling numbers were on a roll in the IWC. Forever colourful, Komatsu blamed the 'Goblins', groups like Greenpeace whom he accused of secretly manipulating the commission. 'Unfortunately many governments of the Western world have sold their souls to appease these organizations,' he claimed. To the West, campaigns that joined environmentalists and governments were less a pact with a devil than an expression of democracy. Nowhere was this better seen than in the crushing defeat of Japan over the Southern Ocean Sanctuary.

David McTaggart called it 'seeing the movie'. Conjuring a big idea, dead simple and with wide appeal. That was the easy bit. Movies take years to produce, and by far most work happens behind the scenes. A film also needs the right connections if it is to get made—links of the kind that infuriated Komatsu.

Brice Lalonde was a leader in the May 1968 uprisings that heralded the awakening of French student political power. He went on to run Friends of the Earth in France, where he met McTaggart, and the two sailed into anti-nuclear protests in the Pacific. Just after Lalonde ran unsuccessfully for election as president of France, they spent 40 days on the yacht *Vega* off Mururoa Atoll waiting for the government to fire an underground explosion.

'Each time you sail in that sea, you can go swimming with whales,' Lalonde fondly recalled.

By 1991, his time had come. He was appointed Environment Minister in the government of former fellow student activist, Michel Rocard. 'He, and I, were horrified by the *Rainbow Warrior* bombing in New Zealand,' Lalonde said of the sinking of the protest ship by French military saboteurs, which killed the photographer, Fernando Pereira, and led to a US$8.1 million settlement to McTaggart's Greenpeace in 1987.

'(Rocard) wanted France to be very active in the field of environment, and especially in the South Pacific, to try to be forgiven as much as possible. So he asked me to be minister in his government.' Lalonde helped to negotiate with Australia an Antarctic mining ban, which was also a passion of McTaggart's. Just as this was being realised, the new movie popped up.

Its genesis is obscure. Some say it emerged from the French Government. But it first saw the light of day in 1991 at the Italian farm-house home of Sidney Holt, the scientist and environmentalist who was so important for the Indian Ocean Sanctuary. Also in the room with McTaggart were the Australian scientist Bill de la Mare, Cassandra Phillips from the WWF, and John Frizell from Greenpeace.

'Bill and Sidney start spouting off about how, if we get a Southern Ocean Sanctuary, we've got a crack at saving most of the world's remaining whales,' McTaggart said, recalling it as a moment of absolute clarity. 'The sanctuary idea is big, but it's simple and winnable in a short time frame.'

The concept was grand. It meant drawing a line around the surviving whales' main habitat—one quarter of the global oceans. South of 40 degrees south, the latitude of Bass Strait, Wanganui in New Zealand, and of the Right whales' Peninsula Valdez, no harpoon might be fired. Not only was this reassuring for the endangered great whales. Surely no self-respecting country would kill Minkes for science *inside* a sanctuary?

Leaving Holt's farmhouse, McTaggart made quickly for Lalonde. 'He suggested that, as I was lucky enough to be in office, France could introduce the idea of the sanctuary to the IWC,' Lalonde said. 'We wrote the proposal together. Just think, the French Government and Greenpeace working together!'

Komatsu was appalled. Attending his first meeting of the IWC, in Glasgow, he saw the emergence of the sanctuary as an underhand conspiracy. He seized on the existence of the original text in English rather than French, and on Holt's role as an advocate of its science. This was evidence France had become little more than a proxy for environmentalists. 'It is a matter of concern to anyone with sensitivity for justice that the IWC has been operating in such an unfair and irregular manner,' Komatsu said.

Rocard's socialist government collapsed before the Glasgow meeting and Lalonde resigned his portfolio. But he still went to Scotland to speak for the sanctuary, and put it on the agenda. Big IWC changes often take a few meetings to achieve as diplomats taste the idea, take it back home to chew over, then decide whether to spit it out or swallow. Anti-whaling nations, whipped on by green groups, kept the sanctuary afloat. At the next meeting in Kyoto in 1993, the chasm between Japan's pressure groups and the West was there for all to see.

Set out with precise and austere gardens and temples, Kyoto is a shrine for Japanese traditionalists. The IWC meeting was in the Kyoto International Convention Centre, a vast, concrete, modernist interpretation of the city's traditional temples. Its forecourt was blockaded daily by a convoy of ultra-nationalists in darkened buses. Far right groups flourished in Japan. In a convoy of shiny buses they toured the country, amplified slogans spouting from loudspeakers on their roofs. These raised verbal harassment to rock concert noise levels. Outside the meeting, the ultra-nationalists exchanged triumphal choruses with pro-whaling groups, who also had buses, billboards, and a platoon of women in kimonos as cultural props for the cameras.

This was a welcome change to Japanese officials, after years of running the gauntlet of ragged hippie environmentalist battalions outside meetings in the West. The single green protestor, Yoshio Kamejima, stood a safe distance down the road and was careful to arrange himself beside a policeman for the best pictures. Already looking dangerously thin, the 25-year-old Tokyoite staged a hunger strike.

How well he symbolised environmental protest in Japan. Its Government had no internal pressure against whaling. Non-government organisations cared about prisoners in foreign jails or feeding impoverished African children. Some were quite specific in their cause. There was, worthily, the Association for Sending Picture Books to Lao Children. But in Japan, NGOs were few and powerless. Most lacked tax deductibilty or legal status, and in a conformist society they were seen as slightly odd. They did not target government policies. The Japanese umbrella NGO organisation, JANIC, politely explained that unlike Christians, Buddhists were not instinctive evangelists. The Japanese also relied more happily on their government to make decisions for them.

Environment issues did get serious, but they were local. Passions heated up over excesses of industrial pollution, or the siting of airports and highways. The only noticeable activity for fauna came from the 45 000-member Wild Bird Society, Japan's biggest environmental NGO. Broad policies on something like climate change came down from the government. Starved of local funds, powerful groups like Greenpeace and WWF had to rely on their global finances to campaign in rich Japan. Any challenge to whalers was for determined dissidents.

At Kyoto the whale huggers, as Komatsu called them, were out in the cold. The meeting's social high point came with a 'cultural evening' hosted by the fishing industry. On stone piers over carp ponds, delegates watched Kodo drummers thunder out rhythms that vibrated in the stomach. Japanese television cameras swooped close when it seemed a Westerner might be about to swallow Minke with noodles, stewed, or as sashimi marinating in its own blood.

Faroese, Icelanders and Norwegians had a jolly time of it. Others said, 'If not now, when?' The IWC's scientific editor, a friendly Irishman called Greg Donovan, had little trouble. 'Sure I'll eat whale,' he said. 'If I didn't, when I went on field work to Greenland I'd starve. That's about all they eat up there.' My young colleague, Canadian journalist Maryse Cardin, tasted it in a broth with noodles. 'You take a bite and it's just like steak, and then all of a sudden a fishy taste swims in,' she said. 'It's really tender.' I couldn't grasp the concept, headed for the salad bar, and lost a front page opportunity.

Sans the Rocard Government and Lalonde, the Southern Ocean Sanctuary was lucky to get out of Kyoto alive. A line was drawn early when Kazuo Shima, the stony-faced Japanese commissioner, called it a political proposal lacking in science that could force Japan to quit the IWC. France tried too soon to bring it on, and embarrassingly gained only its own vote. Australia's gimlet-eyed commissioner, Peter Bridgewater, put up a lesser target, a resolution endorsing the 'concept' of a sanctuary and proposing an inter-sessional meeting to move it ahead. That was backed 19–8–4. Shima complained: 'The IWC has become an international organisation for the protection of whales.'

He was only slightly ahead of himself.

For the inter-sessional meeting, Bridgewater shut delegates away on bucolic Norfolk Island in the South Pacific, where the cattle have right of way on the road. All of the frontline anti-whaling nations were organised as co-sponsors by the time they came off the island. In the run-up to the next full IWC meeting in Mexico in 1994, backing extended to the point that a Scandinavian whaler like Denmark gave its support. Even Norway flirted openly with the idea if there might be a deal to approve the RMS in exchange.

Surely, facing such weight, a defeated Japan would accept the global verdict and end its scientific whaling inside these protected waters? A gentle prod was offered by Bridgewater. 'I think many people feel the concept of a sanctuary would suggest scientific whaling really shouldn't be taking place there, though I'm not sure it would stop immediately,' he said. Off the record he warned Japan against the international ill-will it would find if it ignored the decision.

The buzz was good for environmentalists among the palms and pools at the Westin Resort in Puerto Vallarta, Mexico. Sidney Holt, his long white hair flying atop a rumpled cream linen suit, bowled along the pathways chasing delegates. McTaggart, perpetually smoking cigarettes, watched from the sidelines with his blue eyes alight. Japan waited to see who it could count on.

Surprisingly two jet-lagged Solomon Islanders turned up. The Melanesians worried the anti-whalers. Along with other small island nations from the Caribbean, they formed a serious bloc of votes for Japan. The three-quarters majority needed to record a Schedule Amendment and create the sanctuary meant that every vote against was worth three in favour. But it quickly became clear that Japan would struggle for numbers when it sought postponement of a decision, and that was rejected 22–6–4. Key countries were abstaining from the fight.

The greatest trouble that the anti-whaling nations had was in deciding what the boundaries should be. Loaded with politics though the sanctuary was, the IWC's founding convention demanded that it 'shall be based on scientific findings'. Oceanic convergences—well-defined borders in surface sea temperatures—seemed to make sense. The maps started with the sub-tropical convergence below 40 degrees south, were wound back to the Antarctic convergence, then pushed out again, except around South American countries worried about territorial seas.

This was hardly the best science. Independent American scientists commissioned to review the sanctuary ten years later found it could not be ecologically justified, and was even unhelpful for whales. Mark Zacharias and colleagues called it a 'shotgun' approach to conservation. 'In reality this large scale sanctuary does little more than provide a false sense of security by assuming that protections for whale populations are in place.'

At the time though, it was a high-water mark for anti-whaling forces in the ebb and flow of IWC contests, covering an impressive circumpolar 48 million square kilometres of ocean. In the vote even Japan's whaling ally Norway withdrew from the meeting, leaving it the lone 'no' ballot in a 23–1–8 result. Kazuo Shima looked like an angry piece of granite as Japan voted alone. Environmentalists celebrated long and hard. Sidney Holt was pictured among cheering greenies, smiling contentedly. McTaggart was thrown into one of the resort's many pools.

Sir Peter Scott, who died five years before the Southern Ocean Sanctuary was achieved, once reflected on how to safeguard whales. He likened the task to a tug of war. 'If you have a cause that you want to advance, you start pulling . . . hard. Other people are pulling the other way, and if you pull harder than they do, the middle position comes over towards you. The only thing you mustn't do is pull so damn hard that you bust the string. Because if you do that, it rebounds the other way and you're discredited.'

It was a difficult and ambitious struggle to create the Southern Ocean Sanctuary. When it came Japan was left spectacularly isolated. Any string of cooperation left in the IWC was busted.

I flew out of Puerto Vallarta on a rattling old American jet that had members of Japan's delegation aboard. Seated next to me was Shigeko Misaki, an interpreter whose earnest voice the IWC's English speakers craned to hear. She was the daughter of a postwar agriculture minister, and steeped in that era's need for whale. A close colleague of Komatsu's, she co-wrote and translated with him a series of books on Japanese whaling.

On the jet she busied herself with papers, but we chatted. She told me about an apartment she owned in Sydney, where she had gone to university and still had friends, and of her plans eventually to spend more time in Australia's glittering city.

As our aircraft came in to land at Los Angeles, it seemed to be flying faster than usual. I looked out of the window to see us touch down without the wing flaps extended, and then just as quickly lift off. We headed out over Malibu, where we circled and learned a hydraulic system had failed. The good news was that there was a back-up system. The crew cranked it into action, and an hour later we approached the runway again. The jet landed fast and shuddered to a halt mid-runway surrounded by fire trucks.

I was wide-eyed at all of this, but Misaki kept on reading her papers and I remarked at her coolness. She told me she had been on British Airways Flight 009, when the Boeing 747 lost power in all four engines after flying through a cloud of volcanic ash over Java in 1982. The aircraft glided, brick-like, for fourteen minutes before the engines miraculously cleared, were re-started, and against all odds landed safely in Djakarta.

'This,' she said, barely glancing at the flashing lights outside at LA airport. 'This is nothing.'

Such were the people who carried the flag for Japanese whaling. It duly lodged an objection to the inclusion of Minke whales in the Southern Ocean Sanctuary. Scientific harpoons kept on killing Minkes inside the new protected zone. The whole implacable campaign for a return to commercial whaling stepped up. As an obstacle to Japanese progress, the sanctuary was nothing.

13

KEIKO GOES HOME

What aligns wolf and primitive hunter more strongly than
anything else is that to live, each must hunt and kill animals.

Barry Lopez, *Of Wolves and Men*, 1978

With 4 tonnes of Killer whale powering through the water at his
small wooden skiff, only one course of action seemed sensible to Arild
Birger Nesthaug. Flee. His twelve-year-old daughter Hanne and two family
friends also in the boat were of the same mind. 'They were very scared,'
remembered Nesthaug's partner, Lindis Oloni Kornis.

In Norwegian, Orcas are known as *spekkhogger*, blubber pecker, or
våghund, the bay dog. This big black-and-white beast swam out of nowhere
to break the peace of a Sunday morning fishing trip at Korsnes Fjord in
south-western Norway in the late summer of 2002. Nesthaug started the outboard, turned the boat and ran for shore with the *spekkhogger* close behind.

After the group scrambled ashore and turned to watch the animal, they
noticed electronic devices attached to its floppy dorsal fin. It was also swimming around tamely, as if it might have been familiar with people. Enough
confidence returned for the Norwegians to climb into their boat again and
motor back to Nesthaug's nearby fishing cabin.

'He followed them,' Kornis remembered. 'He stayed at the dock all night
with my children. It seemed that he wanted company and someone to talk
to, and he was not dangerous. Hanne went for a swim with him. She was
very excited. And he was happily eating fish that we gave to him. It was an
amazing experience. At first they didn't know it was Keiko.'

Captured in Iceland 23 years earlier and flown from one artificial tank
to another through the Americas for most of his life, Keiko became an
animate symbol of the gulf between whale lover and whaler. His release

after enormous effort and expense brought him back to waters where some of the world's most determined whalers still hunted. They were not still killing Orcas by then. Nevertheless, he was a sentient cetacean who knocked on their children's door and said hello.

'In ways I wouldn't have understood when I started, the Keiko phenomenon put a face on the whale issue which was extremely powerful,' said David Phillips, of Earth Island Institute, the environment organisation that managed the freeing of Keiko. 'It wasn't about *this* whale. It was about all whales.'

This was a great hope to saddle Keiko with. Orcas have uneasy relations with people, not least in the North Atlantic. Down the street from Phillips's San Francisco office, the Beat-era poet Michael McClure performed his first piece of projective verse in 1955, an early manifestation of changing attitudes to whales. The short, angry, poem responded to news that American servicemen stationed in Iceland were enlisted to bomb and machine-gun Orcas: 'Like sheep or children'. The whales were blamed for eating all the local fish.

Keiko was born only a year or two after Norwegian fishermen killed their last Orcas to feed pet dogs, and foxes grown for their fur in 1975, and he was young at the time of the first North Atlantic protest by Greenpeace in 1978. In that action, David McTaggart watched a Fin whale take an hour to die off Iceland and concluded: 'I'm not one of those people who's seriously soft on animals. I don't think they are individually as important as human beings. But this is disgusting.'

When the moratorium on commercial whaling was agreed, Keiko was a captive, swimming in a pool on the Canadian side of Niagara Falls. Netted in Iceland in 1979, he was sold to Marineland, Ontario. The animal park near Horseshoe Falls still keeps Orcas, and bills itself as 'the largest whale habitat in the world', its enthusiasm exceeding even the oceans.

Keiko did not fit though. He was sold on, and flown to Reino Aventura in Mexico City. As the moratorium came into force in 1986 the group hunter from the North Atlantic was alone, performing for thawed fish in a warm pool in a corner of a Central American adventure kingdom.

Back in his home waters whalers had refused to give up business. Puttering around the fjords, foraying out of rock harbours into this cold grey ocean, using the midnight sun and seasonal fish runs, the Norse had scoured the North Atlantic for centuries. This was the cradle of global industrial whaling. Even when they ran out of whales in distant waters, they would not stop at home.

Norwegian fishermen who chased cod and mackerel in the colder months mounted harpoon cannon on the bows of their boats in summer and stalked the shy local Minkes in their coastal waters, and Iceland's want for export krona kept it chasing bigger whales. In the Danish dominions, Greenland and the Faeroes, there were traditional hunts that could be argued to have some basis in need, but Norway and Iceland? These were rich, First-World countries, civilised leaders in human rights and social justice. Their children were thrilled to swim with an Orca. Why could they not part with something as apparently outdated as whaling?

I looked for an answer to the Norwegian, Egil Ole Øen. A veterinarian with an inventive mind and a serious face, Øen is probably the world's leading developer of whale killing methods. He grew up in 'the valleys'—in nostalgic, rural Norway. When he is not working on improving times to death, when he has time off, he takes to his own forest and logs it for recreation. Or he hunts.

Around 47 per cent of Norwegian men hold hunting licences. So do a substantial number of women. The country has a long tradition of outdoor life, of hunting and fishing. Moose, red deer, reindeer, grouse and other birds are felled each year by the tens of thousands. 'Being a good hunter is the same as getting the whale,' Øen said. 'It is the satisfaction that you are clever. Every hunting society I have met they have actually been clever.'

The culture of rural providers also carries political weight. Twice rural opposition has swayed Norwegians against joining the European Union. As Øen's mentor in whale science, Lars Walløe, put it: 'Most people have their parents or grandparents in the countryside, and they are farmers or fishermen. In the summer holidays they go back home, as they say—even if they haven't ever lived there. And this is part of the country's identity.'

Across the Norwegian Sea in Iceland, a thread of whaling runs through an ancient history. It was to this volcanic land surrounded by marine life that Northern Europeans looked for their early education about whales. Part of it was recorded in the thirteenth-century Norwegian treatise, *The King's*

Mirror, a mixture of superstition and nature study listing all whale species found in Iceland. It includes the Orca, or grampus, which 'gather in flocks and attack large whales, and when a large one is caught alone, they worry and bite it till it succumbs'. It also talks of the 'fish driver', the whale that herds fish before it, 'as if appointed and sent by the Lord for the purpose'. Was this the Minke, the whale that in Icelandic folklore was also to protect humans against 'bad' whales?

More recently Icelanders have persistently shouldered their way into the story of whaling. Some of the great early catches were in its waters, and the oddest people passed through it. There was the nineteenth-century Dane, Jorgen Jorgensen. He was the adventurer who believed the Right whale would keep on sailing up the Derwent in Tasmania, into infinity. Later he overthrew the governor of Iceland and installed himself as ruler in a reign that lasted a few months in 1809.

And there was the twenty-first-century Icelandic performing artist, Bjork. She collaborated with her American partner, Matthew Barney, for the artistic event, Drawing Restraint 9. Part of a series by Barney exploring concepts of physical restraint, this elaborate film and sculpted performance was mainly set aboard the *Nisshin Maru*.

Bemused Japanese whalers posed in their uniforms while Bjork and Barney paraded through the ship. 'In the gruelling climax, they grasp a pair of flensing knives and slowly cut away the flesh from each other's limbs. Tails and blowholes appear on their bodies and they transform into whales.' They swim away, the only whales ever to leave *Nisshin Maru* in better shape than when they arrived.

When the moratorium came into force, Norway and Iceland kept on whaling with a dour solidity.

There was no doubt that IWC rules backed Norway. In 1982 it had filed an objection to the moratorium decision, so it was exempt. Its quota for Minkes might not have the IWC's approval, but it did have a scientific basis. And Norway appeared to have the strength of will to back its claim.

In the prime minister's office was the European left's Margaret Thatcher equivalent, Gro Harlem Brundtland.

But when Washington threatened the use of the Pelly Amendment restricting trade access for fisheries products, Norway folded. It suspended the 1986 commercial whaling season and reduced the 1987 quota. Catches drifted down in number, hastened by a second Pelly certification, until in 1991 Norway caught none.

Iceland had been a small, delinquent violator of IWC rules before the moratorium, and was ready to clamber through the science loophole afterwards. At stake was a four-catcher commercial whaling fleet and shore factory owned by a businessman, Kristjan Loftsson. According to a report to the IWC, Iceland killed hundreds of undersized Fin and Sei whales between 1977 and 1983 and exported the meat to Japan. A small local appetite for whale was met by Minkes.

Reykjavik's ancient parliament, the Althing, voted 29–28 not to object to the moratorium—under pressure from Washington, the whalers claim. Soon after, the whaling company and the government began to draw up plans for a scientific hunt. A draft contract between Loftsson's Hvalur HF and the Ministry of Fisheries scheduled a take of 40 Blues and 40 Humpbacks, both species in parlously low numbers in the North Atlantic. Eventually the whalers settled on a kill of Fin and Sei whales in 1986.

So clear was this rule-bending that it is little surprise the first serious violence against whaling in the North Atlantic came to Reykjavik. The increasingly militant Paul Watson believed the floodgates were opening to 'pirate' whaling and claimed the Icelanders had ignored his warnings. He sent two Sea Shepherd 'field agents' to Reykjavik. Rodney Coronado and David Howitt worked covertly for weeks, watching the whaling operations and gathering tools. One November night as a snowstorm howled outside, they spent four hours vandalising the Hvalur factory. Then they opened the sea cocks on two of the catchers, sank them at their moorings, and caught a flight to Europe.

Watson proclaimed: 'My men delivered an $8 million punch to the Icelandic pirates, and they were reeling.' He went to Iceland two years later to accept responsibility. A wary Ministry of Justice refused him his day in court. 'At questioning, Paul Watson has admitted that he has given some remarks that connect him with sabotage, but in spite of this he now claims that he neither took part in the planning nor the execution of the sabotage,' said the Ministry. It deported him.

Hvalur whaled on with its remaining ships. It took 368 Fin and Sei whales under scientific permit from 1986 to 1989. Against IWC resolutions that the permit meat must be utilised by the whaling country itself, Iceland exported up to 77 per cent to Japan, which was still driving the market.

Watson had further plans for the North Atlantic whalers. Adopting the Killer whale as a mascot, he painted it onto the bow of his ship and formed a cadre of activists called the Oceanic Research and Conservation Action (ORCA) Force. His attention turned to the other side of the Norwegian Sea, where the woman known as the Green Queen was in charge.

Gro Harlem Brundtland had some of the best environmental credentials in the world when she regained the prime ministership of Norway in November 1990. Her name was on the landmark UN report, 'Our Common Future'. It first popularised notions like sustainable development—meeting 'the needs of the present, without compromising the ability of future generations to meet their own needs'.

Outside Norway it was unthinkable that someone so strongly identified with global environmental change could wind back the clock on great bio-diversity gains against whaling. But in Oslo, the medical doctor with the fierce smile came under strong domestic pressure from the fishing constituency to continue whaling. Her long-time friend and colleague, Lars Walløe, said Brundtland was forcefully reminded of her own argument.

'There was a possibility that because of the opposition in the world, she would pay the whalers and close it down. That of course is what the US wanted us to do. But the other course was to follow the principles. Why shouldn't we go whaling if it can be done sustainably? It was difficult for her not to agree with her own principles back home, when she had given this advice to the rest of the world.'

Walløe was asked to chair a long-term study of Minkes in the North East Atlantic as Brundtland wrestled with the politics. 'She wanted to have the scientific evidence. If the evidence said so, then close it down. But if not, it should come back.'

In 1992 Brundtland announced that Norway's small fishermen would resume commercial whaling the following year. Walløe's best estimate of the Minke numbers in the North East Atlantic was around 86 700 (later to be revised down to 75 000). The Norwegian fishermen were given a quota of 296.

Committed anti-whaling nations failed to understand Brundtland's decision. Australia's Environment Minister, Ros Kelly, was horrified. 'Hunting and killing whales has no place in the commercial or scientific activities of civilised countries,' she said. In Britain the acerbic Labour MP Tony Banks was ashamed to describe her as a socialist—particularly one who boasted of green credentials. 'That is rank hypocrisy, and I cannot wait to tell Mrs Brundtland so again, next time our paths cross.' Cementing bipartisan opposition in Westminster was the Norwegians' own evidence that many of these whales were dying extended deaths.

Brundtland brushed away the rhetoric. 'When did the international community decide to stop hunting and using animals for human consumption? . . . It is impossible to continue with international cooperation on the resources of the ocean, or any other resources . . . if preservation alone dominates the issue.' Once Brundtland had received a delegation of American politicians and diplomats who expressed their disapproval of her pro-whaling policies. 'I think the Americans thought it would be very easy to pressure this girl,' Walløe said. 'She reacted very negatively to that kind of pressure from old men.'

Instead she aggressively sold the decision. Norway set up a US$1.5 million international public relations budget. With the same conviction of right as the Albany whalers, fishermen of the Lofoten Islands were organised to meet foreign media, some of whom watched the whalers shoot Minkes. On a visit to Washington, Brundtland pointed to an American double standard for allowing an indigenous hunt of endangered Bowheads by Alaskan Eskimo while opposing Norway's sustainable catch. The Clinton Administration baulked at using the Pelly Amendment.

Then Sea Shepherd came out of the night to the village of Steine in the Lofotens on Boxing Day, 1992, and Minke whaler Jan Odin Olavsen's 22-metre fishing boat *Nybraena* went to the bottom of the harbour. Once out of the country, Watson publicly proclaimed his involvement with two others, and Norwegian justice began to chase him. Olavsen took up the fight publicly as chair of the Norwegian pro-whaling group, High North Alliance; he raised his boat and kept on whaling.

The following winter Sea Shepherd returned to southern Norway with the same result. Activists, who Watson said were former US Navy Seals, crept into an outer reach of the capital's Oslofjord, where they tried to scuttle the whaler, *Senet,* at its moorings. It too was salvaged in time to go whaling through the summer of 1994. Out in the North Sea the owner/skipper, Arvid Enghausen was met by boarding Greenpeace activists who cut loose a whale he had harpooned, but he whaled on.

On the same day, further north, Watson played out the hair-raising Battle of the Lofotens. He steamed his converted British seismic survey ship, *Whales Forever,* up the Norwegian coast with a yellow mini-submarine on the deck, wanting to see whalers flee 'like rats' back to harbour in fear of the sub. Instead he was met with the strongest force that the Norwegian Coast Guard had ever used on another ship.

Watson disputed that he was in Norwegian territorial waters when he was ordered to halt, under arrest by the 2200-tonne cutter *Andenes.* He refused to stop, and instead faced down an increasingly frightening attack. The cutter circled *Whales Forever* trailing a thick hawser, trying to snarl its propellers. The two ships soon collided, the Norwegians shearing off the bow of the Sea Shepherd ship, which gouged a scar deep along the forward hull of the cutter. Each disputed fault, though clearly the *Andenes* initiated the tight manoeuvres.

The rope briefly crippled Watson's ship but the crew freed it, and *Andenes* began firing live warning shots from its 57-millimetre cannon. In response the activists lined the deck of their ship, daring the Coast Guard to hit them, and Watson kept on steaming. He saw off the *Andenes'* helicopter by firing a signal flare, and maintained his course when the Norwegians sent a fast dinghy out to drop depth charges in front of *Whales Forever.*

'I decided to call their bluff,' Watson said. 'Norway had too much to lose if they killed us.' He set a course for the British Shetland Islands and eventually *Andenes* gave up the pursuit. The Coast Guard claimed it had full legal authority to sink *Whales Forever,* but held back. 'Even though

Mr Watson's actions were insane, a reaction that could have led to injury or loss of life was not justified,' said Commander Torstein Myhre.

Two years later Norway did catch up with Watson. Passing through Amsterdam's Schiphol Airport he was detained on an Interpol warrant over the sinking of the *Nybraena* in 1992. The Dutch held him for 80 days, the sentence he would have served in Norway, but would not hand him over to Oslo.

This was the stark difference between the North Atlantic and Antarctic protests. Whalers' boats might be small and more easily blocked, but policed territorial waters gave them powerful protection. In 1999 when open conflict broke out again, the Norwegian Coast Guard made sure there would be no repetition of its embarrassment with Watson. It sent three ships to protect a whaler from two Greenpeace vessels. The guard arrested and held the ship *Sirius*. A Greenpeace activist was seriously injured when he was hit by a Norwegian inflatable. And then he was prosecuted.

The lines were clearly drawn. The Norse would defend their whaling. It was into these waters that the blubber pecker splashed down.

Warner Brothers paid a fee of US$80 000 to Reino Aventura for the use of Keiko, the animal star in *Free Willy*. It must rank as one of film-making's better deals. The movie's worldwide revenue was around US$153 million.

'It started off as a low budget kids' movie,' said David Phillips. 'All of a sudden it becomes a real hit.' Such was the success that two sequels followed in which Orcas, either mechanical or not Keiko, struggled against ocean-fouling oil tankers, and sashimi-chasing pirate whalers. If evidence was needed that public affection for whales was peaking, then here it was.

When Keiko was found by the film-makers, the whale was sick after seven years of swimming around a tank that was shallower than he was long. He had a chronic papilloma virus, was underweight, listless and weak. He couldn't even accomplish the basic trick of a performing Orca: to splash the children. After the film became a hit, it took a short time for the star's sad state to become publicly known.

'So Dick Donner calls me up,' said Phillips. 'He says: "Dave, you've got to help us. We're dying down here".'

Richard Donner, a maker of cash-rich action films and *Free Willy*'s executive producer, was talking about a public relations death, not the state of Keiko's health. His cry for help from Hollywood began what Phillips recalls as an incredible wild ride, nothing less than a bid to turn a movie fiction into a reality. 'We wanted to give the whale a shot at rehabilitation, and going home.'

Donner had known Phillips and Earth Island Institute from a previous collaboration on a dolphin-safe tuna campaign. Encouraged to help, Phillips flew to Mexico City and was depressed by what he saw. 'I thought: "What have I got myself into?" Keiko would lie on top of the water and loll around. It was kind of like seeing a dog neglected for a long time. He didn't look like a wild whale at all.'

Freeing Keiko cost around US$20 million, and years of work. Donations came in from thousands of children, and from an electronics tycoon moved just as strongly as any ten-year-old by the plight of the whale. Other animal welfare groups, and Warner Brothers, gave money and resources. Coordinated by Phillips, the Free Willy Keiko Foundation built a halfway house, a US$7.3 million rehabilitation tank in Oregon. The Orca was flown there in 1996 after 27 000 Mexicans filed past his Reino Aventura pen, farewelling him as they might a local saint.

In Oregon the papilloma rash went away and Keiko put on nearly a tonne of weight. He was retaught to catch and eat live fish rather than his thawed Mexico City staple. He had less contact with people, as trainers explored the notion that he might soon find other whales for company. Phillips began to look for a place in the North Atlantic to take the next step.

'Of all the negotiating, the thirteen trips to Mexico City, raising money for Oregon, really the hardest thing I had to do was convince Iceland to let him back in. By that point, Keiko was larger than life. He had become an emissary for whales, a symbol for why we should protect the ocean environment.'

In Iceland they couldn't see that at all. The country had quit the IWC in a sulk in 1992 after the organisation had voted repeatedly against lifting the moratorium. Icelanders were promoting an alternative organisation of

Nordic whalers and sealers, the North Atlantic Marine Mammal Council. 'The key was convincing the prime minister,' Phillips said. 'All the inter-mediate levels of government told us, rudely, to get out of the country. Eventually we were able to get to David Oddson.'

As well as leading the government Oddson was a writer, an intellectual leader of the 290 000-strong population. Phillips's pitch was that there was really no alternative. Keiko came from Iceland, so he needed to go back there if there was to be any chance of him finding his kin. An obstacle was the possible spread of the papilloma virus, but Oddson agreed and sold the idea to his people. 'He told them they couldn't stop it happening. Keiko would swim back to Iceland anyway if he wanted to.'

Around this time Phillips must have felt giddy. He rang the US Air Force to order a C–17 Globemaster. Able to lift 77 tonnes of cargo off an airstrip only 1 kilometre long, the plane flew Keiko and his entourage directly from Newport, Oregon, to the island of Heimaey in Iceland in September 1998. Heimaey, 'home island', has special significance to Icelanders who live with volcanic fire. Only a generation earlier the people of its town, Vestmmanaeyjar, had turned pumps and hoses onto an eruption that would engulf many of their homes. As the American writer John McPhee recounted in *The Control of Nature*: 'There came a moment in 1973 when Thorbjorn said to Magnus, "We cannot defend the town and the harbour at the same time." Magnus said instantly, "We must defend the harbour. There is no use of any town if we don't have a harbour."'

The hoses prevailed, cooling the lava. In an outer arm of the harbour they saved, Keiko was lifted gently into a sea pen.

Across the North Atlantic, Norway had weathered all protests. Even so, it was left to deal with one weakness: humane killing.

Egil Ole Øen began work on whale killing in the early 1980s, and was astonished to find that only one in six died instantly at the end of a har-poon. 'The rest took several minutes, or a longer time. This was actually a very inhumane method.'

With a reputation for his work immobilising wild animals on land for rescue, Øen shifted his skills to euthanasing the largest wild animals at sea. A lance with compressed gas, an electric harpoon, drugs, high velocity bullets and explosives—all were tried. There was the old trick of cutting the sharp end off a harpoon, making the weapon less likely to skip across the ocean's surface. 'Immediately, instant killing went up to 25 or 30 per cent, but that was not satisfactory.' What did work was the penthrite grenade, with its great explosive shock.

By the turn of the millennium, Norway was claiming to kill 80 per cent of whales instantly. There were veterinary inspectors aboard each boat, meaning the figure was reliable. But the overall average time to death was still two minutes and seventeen seconds. The kind of hit that stretched out times was caught on tape off Vardo Island in the Lofotens, north Norway, in 2005.

Activists on shore from British organisations, the Environmental Investigation Agency and the World Society for the Protection of Animals, videoed the little red fishing boat *Wilson Senior* with a long lens as its crew hunted and shot a Minke about 1 kilometre offshore.

Always a quick, cryptic target, in this case the Minke was being hunted through pitching seas and 20-knot winds. *Wilson Senior*'s skipper picked a meandering course along the coast for hours before finding a chance. The Minke blew a chimerical puff about 30 metres ahead of the boat, the harpoon cleaved the water, and the watchers set a clock ticking over the video. More than three minutes passed before the whale resurfaced. Apparently maddened, it kept rising on different sides of the boat, which had to back away to keep the line clear of the propeller. After eleven minutes, the whalers fired the first of seven rifle shots at the animal. The last sign of life, a tail beating the surface, came fourteen minutes and 30 seconds after it was struck.

The video's narrator concluded: 'It must have been subjected to a great deal of pain. Clearly there is no humane way to kill a whale at sea.' Øen told the IWC that this hunt took place in unfavourable weather, and the hunters did not follow recommended procedures. But the government couldn't overrule the whalers' choice to go hunting.

'We try to get them to understand how to kill an animal,' Øen told me. 'But they are human beings. You have some boats where there are 100 per cent instantaneous kills. Some are not so good.' To encourage marksman-ship, he set up a prize for the best gunner. 'They pretended they didn't care very much, but when the prize should be awarded, they were all there. I know them all, and they are very, very proud of their whaling.'

Even so, less would be revealed about the killing of Norwegian Minkes, not more. Until 2006 a veterinary inspector was aboard every whaling boat, logging its effectiveness. Then electronic vessel monitoring was installed instead. Under this system, time to death was only sampled randomly by the inspectors, though the hunt increased.

Many Minkes were taken inshore along the northern coast, but the Nor-wegians' small, tough boats also cruised up into the Arctic, to the Barents Sea and off Svalbard; they dipped and rose north-west through the swells to the foggy mid-ocean Norwegian EEZ around Jan Mayen Island; and into the crowded North Sea closer to Britain.

The kill was based on their own assessments of sustainable yield. There was a kill of 388 in 1996, and ten years later 523 whales were taken in a quota of 1052 as the market topped out and wholesalers could sell no more. Was it just a bad summer, or was the Norwegian taste for Minke declining? Its advocates said it was eaten as steak, meatballs, pizza toppings. What they really wanted was to export it.

Norway and Japan tried repeatedly to have Minke stocks' global protection reduced for trade. Its listing on Appendix One of the Convention on International Trade in Endangered Species meant there could be no transfer. Like the whaling convention, CITES has an objec-tion loophole, and both nations registered that. For years they restrained themselves from using the objection, and taking a fight from the IWC into another organisation.

Whale trade pressure rose when Iceland elbowed its way back into the organisation it had left a decade earlier. It rejoined because outside the IWC it had no prospect of trade with Japan, nor of obtaining Norway's penthrite grenades. Hvalur needed both in order to go commercial whaling.

The attempt to rejoin was initially rejected because Iceland wanted to sign up with an objection to the moratorium already in hand. Finally it was allowed to vote itself in during a confused debate brought on at a special

IWC meeting called on a different subject, where some members were absent. This international legal trickery drew gasps from anti-whaling countries, but they were defeated. Iceland also joined CITES with reservations against the listing of all its target species—even the Blue and the Humpback. To the Icelandic Government, whales equalled fish. 'As whales are a part of the marine ecosystem, utilization of whales can only be a natural part of a sustainable fisheries policy,' said the Foreign Minister, Halldor Asgrimmson.

Out at Heimaey as Asgrimmson spoke, Keiko had been returned to a substantially free life. Nearly four years after arriving in Iceland he was free of the confines of his sea pen, and of a larger netted bay as well. The Orca that used to float listlessly around the surface of a pool too shallow to dive in was regularly heading down to 75 metres in the open ocean. He foraged for himself, and swam at times with other whales.

In the midsummer of 2002 Keiko took off from Iceland, swimming out into the North Atlantic where his minders tracked him with a mixture of pride and horror. 'As he got closer to Norway, I thought please, don't go there,' said Phillips. 'You've got to pick *another* whaling nation?

'But he had the same effect there when he arrived. For some reason he had an amazing attraction to kids. If you had 100 adults around a pool, and one eight-year-old, he would come up to the eight-year-old. I saw these pictures of kids swimming with him in Norway and I thought: Where are these kids' parents? Why are they letting their children do this?'

Keiko was in good shape when he arrived—'fat and sassy', as Phillips put it. But it had to be admitted that re-wilding him had not worked. A CNN anchor, Daryn Kagan, bantered: 'Well how many times have we heard the story before? You get a big movie, become a big star, go into rehab, have issues and can't quite get on track.'

His carers had tried to keep Keiko's arrival in Norway quiet, a plan that came to nought when he bounced up the fjord to greet the Nesthaug skiff. Instead there was global attention. Tourists headed to the town from around Europe. A psychic animal interpreter channelled his thoughts, and an eight-year-old girl played the movie's tune to him on a harmonica.

After a couple of months Keiko was led by boat to Taknes, a quieter, ice-free fjord nearby, in the hope that he might still meet and be attracted to more wild Orcas. A year later he was still there, and drawing children. At the same time, Norwegian Minke whalers resumed selling whale to Iceland and were celebrating a likely deal with Tokyo. It was only delayed, according to Lars Walløe, by the growing stockpile of uneaten whale in Japan.

Iceland began a scientific whaling program aimed at taking 250 whales a year. That proved too ambitious. Small numbers of Minkes were taken until in a hasty late season hunt that caught environmentalists by surprise, Hvalur began to kill Fins again. Its winches dragged seven ashore in October 2006, describing the largely unsold meat as 'eco-friendly'.

Despite all the attention given to Keiko, the number of captive cetaceans rose. Orcas still performed through the Americas and in North Asia, some finding smaller local campaigns to free them. Dolphin petting and 'swim-with' pools were newly popular in resorts and hotels. A cloak over the trade in wild dolphins was lifted when 28 were flown out of the Solomon Islands for Mexico in July 2003, embarrassing the Mexican Government enough to ban more imports.

Approaching a second winter at Taknes and still under care, Keiko sickened suddenly, beached himself, and died on 12 December 2003. He was at most 27—not very old for an Orca—and was taken by a mammal's long-time foe: pneumonia. His body was brought ashore at night in a snow-storm by an earthmover and tractors, and buried beside Taknes beach. Early in the New Year local people organised a midwinter memorial service where dozens of Norwegian children, colourfully dressed against the cold, each laid a single stone on the grave.

His carers could claim success. 'A great opportunity was imperfectly dealt with,' said Paul Spong, the father of Orca studies. 'Keiko never made it back to his family group. But he died in the ocean. That's the bottom line.'

Indisputably, Keiko reached children globally, and probably many of their parents. It was no mean achievement for an animal that did little more than be himself. 'The trainers used to say that he really aimed to please,' David Phillips said. A Canadian anthropologist, Ann Brydon, studied Keiko's effect on Icelandic culture. She thought that, briefly, he undermined the political solidarity behind Icelandic whaling. 'I am suggesting that what they glimpsed in Keiko was themselves, in all their frailties, reflected back in the mirror of nature.'

Perhaps for a moment the Norse whalers paused as they recognised the wolf of the sea. Then they turned back to their own hunt.

PART V · HUMPBACK

(Megaptera novaeangliae)

14

EXPLOSION AND ITS MEANING

'You've started going to church again . . .'
'Well, last year I went whale-watching. This year I thought I'd try the Anglicans.'

Tim Winton, *The Turning*, 2004

The Humpback, *Megaptera*, shifts its swimming angle using its 'great wings'. These are the long pectoral fins that let it bank underwater like a 30-tonne bird. They do not beat. Energy for the flight comes from the lazy, rolling thrust of tail flukes.

Switching from a horizontal attitude, the whale folds its pectorals in close and shoots upward, propelled by the flukes. The knobby head breaks the ocean's surface, trailing ribbons of white spray that shower like a veil over the rising body. In a quarter of a second most of it has leapt above the swell, leaning backwards precariously. The right fin sweeps behind the body as momentum twists the Humpback onto its side. The left fin flings out, and for an instant the whale looks ready to change nature's laws and flap away. Then gravity takes hold and the inevitable downrush follows. Foam erupts, the left pectoral waves a quick goodbye, and the animal slides below.

When whales rise into the air it defies logic, but they do it all the time. It's thought to be the single most powerful physical act by any animal, equivalent to lifting hundreds of people at once. The breach is the great explosion of energy, the behavioural 'look-at-me', the money shot for watchers, extravagant proof of whales' power. None has more enthusiasm for it than the Humpback.

Some once thought that when Sperm whales breached, they might have been trying to escape attacking fish below, or the whalers themselves. Said Thomas Beale: 'The whale had got a great distance from the ship, when it threw itself completely out of its native element, no doubt endeavouring to escape from its tormenting adversaries by this act.'

Other whales seemed to be amusing themselves, like a Gray in the breakers at Baja California, 'at times making a playful spring with its bending flukes, throwing its body clear of water, coming down with a heavy splash, then making two or three spouts and again settling under . . .'

Right whales readily lift their blunt black shapes to the sky. With other shore watchers at the Head of the Great Australian Bight, I saw one sub-adult gather itself in an underwater swirl and then breach powerfully three times, falling on its belly in making its point. It seems hardly possible that the bigger species would breach. How could a Blue haul that elongated submarine of a body out of its element and return uninjured? But all Humpbacks do—male, female and calf. Sometimes a pair will leap together in a galumphing ballet.

Whale scientists talk about this exuberance cautiously, as if the emotions raised make them nervous. Early theories suggested the animals were shedding skin, or giving external parasites a belting. Some were willing to consider it might just be an expression of high spirits and playfulness. All that energy expenditure though—surely it had to have a purpose.

Perhaps they were considering the world they left behind? 'When a whale breaches in the presence of a nearby boat or a low-flying aircraft,' ran one suggestion, 'its body is often turned so that the eyes are oriented toward the observation vehicle.' Is it a spacing mechanism, an emphatic means of claiming water room? Or does it send messages to others? 'We cannot sort out these potential causes with our preliminary data, but suggest its use in underwater signalling is not unlikely.' And that's where most deductions head.

Breaching is often a social thing. At Silver Bank in the Caribbean, Hal Whitehead watched a festival of leaps. He found a whale more likely to take off within 10 kilometres of other breaching whales. 'At the height of the season such a cluster might have 100 Humpbacks, of which from ten to fifteen might be breaching. Under good conditions they might be expected to hear the sound of a breach over a distance of a few kilometres.'

Humpbacks and other big inshore breeders have an array of skills to make themselves heard above the noisy ocean. A pectoral fin slapped on the water's surface can be as loud as a gunshot. Slammed tail flukes add a bass note. The splash of a breach reverberates nicely.

These can all be messages to other whales. In male rivalries the leap may mean 'I can out-perform you'. In cow–calf pairs it could be 'We're growing strong'. If a whale is disturbed, perhaps a breach says 'Back off'. Or like someone who jumps up and waves in a crowd, it may be just an exclamation. 'Here I am! This is me!'

As Humpback numbers revive, we are becoming familiar with their character. More than any other great whale they swim along the coasts. Natural curiosity draws them in to boats where they might spy-hop, lifting their heads above the water to watch the watchers. Their soaring song is heartwarming. Aerial displays are the wow factor. Worldwide, more than nine million people went whale-watching annually at the turn of the millennium. First among the 83 cetacean species they watched was the Humpback. Increasingly we even know these whales individually.

To the experienced eye, a Humpback's tail flukes are as recognisable as a friend's face. A notch here, a splash of white on black there. Small though it is, the whale's dorsal fin may have a distinctive knob or colour. Maybe the body is pocked with a visible scar. Many a Humpback fluke is etched permanently with the parallel lines of an Orca's raking teeth.

At Stellwagen Bank, off Massachusetts in the North Atlantic, dozens of whales were given names based on their individual markings. Rune had marks like ancient letters inscribed on her dorsal. Lighthouse had just that—a lighthouse shape on one fluke. Identification had clear scientific value as animals were repeatedly seen and records grew. Among the oldest was Salt, a cow with a sprinkle of white on an edge of her otherwise black dorsal, and a record of ten calves over 30 years from the mid-1970s.

In Hervey Bay, Queensland, researchers from the Oceania Foundation unabashedly named their whales. Ropey was first seen trailing an entangling line. Phantom had a mark near his dorsal that looked like the profile of the Ghost Who Walks. Then there was Lotus—he was first known plainly as H2, but mainly as Migaloo, the white Humpback.

'Migaloo' has a ring to it, but the word isn't flattering. Originating in the Mayi-Kutuna language of Leichhardt River in North Queensland, the word 'migloo' made its way into other Aboriginal slang as a derisive term for white people. It's like 'Gubba', the southern indigenous description for government men.

Paul Hodda, a whale researcher from Brisbane, was counting Humpbacks at the peak of their northern migration off Cape Byron on 28 June 1991, when the eighth pod for the day was designated 'H' pod. Then he and his colleagues noticed whale number two in the pod—H2—was an ethereal white. 'A lot of Humpbacks that come past us have some white, but this one did a loop and we could see every bit above the water was totally white,' Hodda said. 'We put out a report, but no one else sighted him that year. Then next year, people realised we weren't on Mullumbimby mushrooms.'

In 1992 there were nine reliable sightings of H2 on migration. The eye-catching colour helped researchers build a re-sight history that detailed a Humpback's individual movements on its Australian winter trek better than any before. The name was chosen soon after by an American researcher, Paul Forestell, in consultation with Queensland Aborigines.

Migaloo was seen most years, often several times, working his way up the New South Wales south coast in June to the Whitsunday group inside the Great Barrier Reef by August, and back down in early October. The 1992 migration was at a stately average speed of around one knot (1.5 kilometers per hour)—slower than most Humpbacks were thought to cover distance.

The reason for the whiteness is yet to be settled. The east Australian stock is significantly lighter than others, but abnormal whites have been recorded in 21 other cetacean species. Some close-up images of Migaloo hint at the telltale pink eye of albinism. DNA work on sloughed skin samples, having already told his gender, would settle this question. Certainly Migaloo appeared to do the things that Humpbacks usually do. He escorted a mother and calf, and was heard singing. He waved his pectorals, and breached.

A Southern Cross University scientist, Dan Burns, who collects Humpback data by boat off northern New South Wales, was disappointed more than once in his attempts to see Migaloo. Late in the 2004 season his luck changed near Lennox Head, just south of Byron Bay.

'We were able to get close enough to see it *was* Migaloo. [That is, close enough to confirm him not by colour, but by fin shape and scarring.]

He surfaced with another Humpback, and then they both went down for a long time. All of a sudden the other Humpback breached, and then 10 seconds later Migaloo breached about 30 metres away.'

'He's really striking. Even when he's under water, you can see him from some distance away. He seems icy blue.' Above the water he was 'quite beautiful'. Burns's photograph froze Migaloo as a toppling alabaster sculpture.

Individual whales usually gain iconic status by being trapped and rescued, like a pod of Gray whales in the Arctic or a Bottlenose whale in the Thames. Migaloo won it by just being his white self. He gathered followers like a movie star on holiday. Sightings appeared in the news and whale-watch operators spruiked the number of times they had seen him. Paparazzi became a little too willing. An underwater photographer had an accidental encounter in which Migaloo brushed beneath him. A luckless trimaran sailor had a hair-raising ride over his broad back.

The nerves were still in David Snell's voice when he described the collision on national radio. 'I just started to see the water change colour, and it just started to go white, glowing white, and it just kept surfacing, and surfaced just about the time that I hit,' Snell said. 'I rode over the top of it, it kept surfacing, lifted the vessel, and consequently ripped off one of my centreboards, and that was lodged in the back of the whale as it continued to go back down again.'

Horrified though Snell was by the accident near Magnetic Island in Queensland, Migaloo appeared to cope. He was tracked by air and showed neither extra fin nor injury. The boat, and Snell, were potentially worse off. Growing protectiveness for whales meant Migaloo had his own law. In Queensland, particularly vulnerable animals could be declared 'special interest whales' and a trigger for this designation was colour variance. Migaloo was the first whale to be listed, in mid-2003, and he was given the same status in following years.

The law demanded a much wider than normal berth be given to him by boats and aircraft, on pain of large fines. The trimaran accident was examined, but Snell was not prosecuted. Instead the state Environment Minister, Dean Wells, thought to satellite tag Migaloo so that an individual watch could be kept. This was the point at which Migaloo's guardians began to talk about the problem of loving a whale to death. Forestell, of Hawaii's Pacific Whale Foundation, said the most amazing whale he had seen in 25 years did not need to be bothered any more.

'Each year the whale has been seen, media intensity has heightened and efforts to capture him on film have increased. This year the attention reached astounding proportions and Migaloo is becoming victimized by his star status . . . It's time to give Migaloo a break. We don't need to stick a satellite tag on him to know where he is. Manage the humans, and leave the whale alone.'

Off Byron Bay, where Paul Hodda and friends first sighted Migaloo, Humpbacks were still being harpooned 30 years earlier. Local whalers hauled carcasses ashore to a small whaling station near the town. A photograph shows a Humpback's abdomen, clearly male, being cut open from tail to head by a man standing atop it in drill trousers and gumboots, and wielding a flensing stick. On a nearby wall sits a young woman in a skirt, her legs primly crossed, taking it all in.

Earlier in the twentieth century Humpbacks were a target of Twofold Bay whalers in southern New South Wales. Along with Rights, they were hunted into the bay by Orcas that learned the value of cooperation with men in boats. At Tangalooma in Queensland and at Norfolk Island, inflated Humpbacks bobbed corpulently at moorings through the 1950s, waiting their turn on the ramps. In an arm of Cook Strait, New Zealand, generations of the Perano family dashed out in longboats, perilously equipped, taking hundreds as they passed by.

None of this was sustainable.

On the coast of Western Australia, shore stations at Point Cloates, Carnarvon and Albany flensed thousands of Humpbacks long after Graham Chittleborough warned of depletion. He once had a fight with the chairman of the Australian Whaling Commission, who threatened to ruin his career because Chittleborough recorded some of these whales' true undersized length. 'This incident should have warned me of the power of industry when it perceives a threat of any kind from science,' he reflected.

Then coastal whaling for Humpbacks ended as if the species had suddenly fallen off the edge of the world.

In the winter of 1962, the whales just didn't come. Some comforted themselves with the illusion that whales had learned to stay clear of the whalers, and were still out there, breaching unseen. Scientists' hunches and hints were finally vindicated in the 1990s. Soviet factory ships had covertly attacked them. After the long-protected Rights were taken, while Blues and Fins were being disguised and Sperm overhunted, Soviets had turned to Humpbacks. Of all the illegal whaling they did, this was the most flagrant attack on any single species.

It seems barely possible today that one country's whalers could illegally kill and process, unexposed, in excess of 25 000 Humpbacks in just two summers. But the Soviet juggernaut did. One fleet alone, *Sovetskaya Ukraina*, took 13 092 Humpbacks between 1959 and 1961. It reported just 760. Here was the 'remorseless havoc' that Herman Melville had foretold a century earlier. Scientists like Chittleborough could do little more than get a Russian shrug at an IWC scientific meeting to confirm their suspicions. No one openly challenged the Cold War enemy.

The recovered records show the Soviets worked mainly in high Antarctic waters at the summer end of the Humpbacks' journey. Stocks that migrated up the coast of Western Australia, eastern Australia, and into the Pacific were viciously hit.

From 1963 the IWC totally protected Humpbacks south of the equator after the sudden, unexplained crash in catches was reported, but the Soviets kept killing them covertly. Five years after the ban, the *Sovetskaya Rossiya* fleet called into Sydney at the end of its season. Locals wondered what the Communists would make of US warships in the harbour on leave from the Vietnam war. Young Russian whalers just smiled for the camera as Captain G.V. Vayner blandly told a reporter the *Rossiya* fleet took its quota of 3321 whales in several different species in the Pacific and Indian Ocean sectors of the Antarctic.

Actually nothing had changed from the days of Solyanik. Vayner was another heroic liar. He had on his ship the yield of an 8009-whale catch, including more than 1000 Sperm from New Zealand waters—and 105 Humpbacks. The last Humpbacks of Oceania harpooned for industrial whaling were probably the eight swallowed by the *Rossiya* machine near New Zealand in March 1968, just before it steamed up to Sydney.

Years of illegal whaling were to pass with no more Humpbacks to kill, until the *Yurii Dolgorukii* fleet found two males and a female to covertly add somewhere south-west of Chile, in January 1972. That ended the catastrophic harrying of Southern Hemisphere Humpbacks. Only a small Tongan indigenous hunt persisted until it was shut down by king's decree in 1978.

The sea is great, and total extermination proved beyond even the Soviet machine. Waving a fin in the lee of an iceberg, blowing off a remote Australian beach, remnant Humpbacks survived.

Before whaling, tens of thousands migrated undisturbed along the coasts of Australia each year. Off the west coast, John Bannister of the West Australian Museum thought whaling might have spared 600. Eastern Australia's stock was much worse off. For more than twenty years after whaling ended, Brisbane radiologist Robert Paterson and his wife Patricia watched from their cottage at Point Lookout on Stradbroke Island, counting migrants. Working back with the aid of the Defence Department's Doug Cato, they figured that fewer than 100 east coast Humpbacks escaped whaling.

This was perilous enough. In the South Pacific, Humpbacks were even more of a memory. The Kiwi patriarch of Right and Humpback research, William Dawbin, had found them easy to locate in the 1950s. He wandered through the islands of the Pacific before setting up at Levaku, the old capital of Fiji, where he saw up to 230 a week. Half a century later, David Paton of Southern Cross University said: 'We saw a maximum of four whales in six weeks.'

Dawbin used to stroll to the waterfront, watch and count. When a chance came, he hopped into a speedboat with a blunderbuss and zoomed out to fire a Discovery mark into a whale. These steel darts were the first whale tags. Retrieved on flensing decks and matched with dates, they were pinpoints of data light for scientists groping in the ocean dark. They also betrayed Soviet malfeasance. A mark that Dawbin fired into a Humpback in Cook Strait was reported by Soviet scientists the next summer as coming out of a Fin whale.

Most Fiji marks were recovered almost due south. But one Humpback carried Dawbin's dart thousands of miles south-west into the polar waters below Western Australia before it was caught. Its message stood like a beacon. Humpbacks did not always stick to the nearest Antarctic waters; they sometimes travelled far and mixed with other stocks. They might also swim north to different wintering waters. Discovery marks from the West Australian stock twice turned up off eastern Australia. A skin biopsy study showed that a young male first seen in the Indian Ocean off Madagascar was swimming off the coast of Gabon in the mid-Atlantic two years later.

Of known animal migrations, the Humpback's is among the greatest. A cow–calf pair photographed cruising north of the equator off Costa Rica in August 2001 popped up in front of a camera again five months and 8425 kilometres later at the Antarctic Peninsula. Humpbacks in this eastern Pacific stock make the longest point-to-point journey recorded for any non-human mammal. They raise the notion that Humpbacks might occasionally cross the Line and keep swimming straight ahead instead of turning around.

There appears not to be much point to this. The cycle of a whale's life would be seriously out of sync. It would arrive at a largely foodless breeding ground deserted by others who were busy eating thousands of arduous kilometres further on at the pole. But as the Fiji mark showed, Humpbacks don't always do the expected. Genetic work gave more evidence of movement between the North and South Pacific, perhaps in cycles linked to glaciation.

Chittleborough and Dawbin unlocked secrets of the Humpback's migration by examining hundreds of whales amid the gore of the flensing decks. Like other baleen whales, the female is bigger. Mature pregnant females lead the way to polar waters and spend most time, around six and a half months, eating krill. They give birth on their return north after an eleven-month gestation. New mothering cows and slower young calves are the last to leave the breeding area and among the earliest to return to its friendly warmth. Males follow on.

The pace of migration varies. Successive technology to the Discovery mark, the satellite tag, has been implanted by American researchers in South Atlantic Humpbacks. Off Brazil, researcher Alex Zerbini said one tagged whale made 3738 kilometres in 45 days to get where it was going, more or less directly. On the African coast, Howard Rosenbaum saw a tagged mother suspend migration as she hung around the South African coast with a calf. Both tracks hinted at the use of subsea cues by Humpbacks. They cruised over oceanic ridges, perhaps using them as waypoints.

Humpbacks also have a habit of running along coastlines. It was Dawbin's belief that their migration routes tracked toward land where they were deflected to move up the coast, making them most visible at the land's seaward projections. In the winter of 1978, when Paul Hodda decided he would like to see a whale, this was where he went to try.

Australian whaling was yet to wind up when a pamphlet about whale protection was thrust into Hodda's hand as he stood in a ticket queue outside a Bob Dylan concert in Brisbane. The flyer was for a local Project Jonah group, who decided it would be good to actually see the creatures they would campaign for. They thought the easternmost point of the mainland, Cape Byron, might be worth trying, and drove down for a mid-winter weekend.

'We sat there all day, and saw one whale in the afternoon. Next day, we saw a couple. Later we mentioned it to people at the National Parks and Wildlife Service and they asked us questions we couldn't answer, such as what species they were. So we decided to go back.'

For two weeks each June–July the volunteers perched atop the 94-metre headland with its wide gaze over the Pacific. Under layers of clothing topped by a Drizabone, with a tarpaulin to pull over their heads, they sat with binoculars while there was light to do so. The group formed the Australian Whale Conservation Society and kept it up for eighteen years. 'When we started a proper survey, from year-to-year you couldn't detect a trend,' Hodda said. 'Some years, the weather would be bad and we couldn't get a good count. But gradually we could tell a recovery was on. There was just a progressive increase.'

Other Antarctic feeders like the Blue were showing little sign of improvement when the Humpback began to bounce back. John Bannister thought the reason was the species' ability to breed at least every two years.

Sometimes they might even be simultaneously lactating and pregnant. There was no sign that the Blue enjoyed such fertility.

Gradually the thrill of a whale sighting, that elating discovery rush, brought more people up to Cape Byron.

'Back then, there was no such thing as commercial whale watching,' Hodda said. 'All kinds of people would come up to us and ask what we were doing. One day in atrocious weather I just went up to have a look-see. Even if you can't count, it can be very atmospheric with whales in the mist. An old gentleman said hello to me on the path and we stopped and chatted. He said: "I suppose you're looking for Humpbacks", so we talked a bit about them. After we'd been talking about fifteen minutes, I said: "I'd better introduce myself". And he did too. He said: "My name is Bill Dawbin".'

By the time Dawbin died in 1998, the animal that his generation of scientists had illuminated was increasing off Australia at a fecund 10 per cent. In 2005 more than 7000 Humpbacks swam up the Australian east coast, and 13 000 along the west coast. Onshore the shift in thinking was just as profound. The more Humpbacks that Australians saw, the more protective they became.

Certainly it was good business, as the booming whale-watching industry showed. In a sure sign of local commercial embrace, whale festivals sprang up at Coffs Harbour, Hervey Bay and Eden. But the Humpback also became strongly symbolic. It was a trophy on a national mantlepiece denuded by native extinctions, proof that biodiversity could repair in a lifetime. To those on the leaper's coastal route, 'the migration' became part of life's seasonal rhythm again. Their formerly whale-less shore had recovered, and the animal tugged at Australian heart strings.

Just how much was visible at a stranding at Cabarita Beach near Tweed Heads in 2006. Wrinkled and slippery, with softly gazing eyes dripping tears, a newborn calf came ashore on a high tide. In the absence of any sign of a cow offshore, the 1-tonne female was stabilised in the shore break. Then overnight she was lifted onto the sand and kept wet. Next day there was a fruitless air search for the cow, and eventually the calf was euthanased by lethal injection. This seemed crazy to Howie Cooke, of the group Surfers for Cetaceans, who spent fourteen increasingly alarmed hours on the rescue attempt.

'Yes, I sang and whispered to that whale all night long to try to ease her dreadful suffering,' Cook said later. 'But now *I* am suffering for not having shouted against the wind, for not having screamed down the walls of obstruction.' Experienced at strandings, he believed the calf was in excellent health and should never have been taken from the sea. Even at night it should have been helped to head out.

'What has happened to our belief in the greatness of whales and their societies, when it is assumed that humans at their convenience are best suited to reunite the calf with her mother, rather than the whales themselves?' All that was needed was to get the calf past the waves as quickly as possible. There it might have been able to swim out and rejoin the migration, 'to be taken in by her family, however extended, and returned to her mum by an aunt or a sister, or even a compassionate lactating mother'.

This implied not only a view of a very highly developed social network in Humpbacks, but also that some people in Australia saw them at least as sentient equals.

'You know when parents gaze at a baby and can't stop?' said rescue volunteer Penelope Sienna, who also spent the night with the calf. 'It was a very similar feeling. I felt she had a question in her eyes: "Why is this happening? Where am I." Total confusion.' As the calf's prospects for survival dimmed, Sienna stayed with the animal until death. 'I kept saying: "I'm sorry. I'm so sorry that this is the only experience of the world you are going to get".'

From the beginning the outlook was bleak. The calf was first noticed listless in the surf around 3.30 pm, but the New South Wales Parks and Wildlife Service area manager, James Law, was not notified for two hours. By then the sun was down, and his staff had knocked off. He called some of them back to the rescue and they made the decision to remove the calf from the water for personal safety. People who resented this did not appreciate the number of rescuers who would have been required to work in shifts stabilising her in the dark, he said.

'People got very passionate,' Law said. 'I had one person ring me and say I was no better than a Japanese whaler, which I found very hurtful.'

In consultation with a vet from the Gold Coast attraction, Sea World, Law concluded the calf should be put down. They decided she had no chance of survival. It was the last day of the school holidays and a large crowd was gathering on the beach. Law worried: 'How would people have viewed that animal being torn apart by sharks in the surf?'

Howie Cooke and his friends might have been dismissed as soft-headed surfers from Byron Bay if they were not proposing the harder decision. They wanted the calf to take its chances at sea, however poor, as soon as she could get there. 'We need to respect the rights of whales and dolphins,' Cook said. 'Let's have faith in the freedom option.'

For most Humpbacks at the start of the twenty-first century, life untrammelled by people was a reality. Stocks were tightly protected and reviving. They prospered in places like Hawaii and New England, as well as the Australian coasts. Off Africa and South America there was less local knowledge of their meanderings, but they were improving as well. The hole that had been blasted in South Pacific Humpback numbers remained exceptionally deep. Only 47 were counted through Cook Strait in 2004's peak migratory fortnight, and a handful in Fiji, though things looked better in Tonga and New Caledonia. Humpbacks have a strong fidelity to their breeding ground. Perhaps there weren't enough Pacific Island whales left to remember where home was. At least the species seemed to be entirely unwanted by whalers—except for one roguish hunt off the Grenadine island of Bequia in the Caribbean.

'Aboriginal Subsistence Whaling', as it is called in the IWC, is the hunt that the coastal whalers of Taiji in Japan were consistently refused permission to join. The inept and legally disputed US Makah Indian hunt used a borrowed quota when they took a Gray whale in 1999. But the category mainly deals with ancient traditional hunts by the Arctic peoples: Chukchi, Inuit and Eskimos. They killed a total of 374 Bowheads, Grays, Fins and Minkes in 2005, mainly using grenade-tipped harpoons. Indigenous whaling also covers the Bequian adventure. Unlike the un-altered Arctic tradition, or even the argued case of the Makah, the history of Humpback whaling on Bequia is younger than *Moby Dick*, and just as much a work of fiction.

The early indigenous people of the Caribbean, the Arawaks and the Caribs, both lived on Bequia but had nothing to do with whaling. Neither did the runaway African slaves, nor the eighteenth-century French colonists, nor most of their British successors. This forgotten vestige of Yankee whaling was begun by a Bequian Scot, Bill Wallace, who brought it to the island from New England in 1876.

Herman Belmar, keeper of Bequian whaling's flame at the IWC, glowed when he described it to me. 'To know it is to feel the importance of whalin' to the average Bequian. When a whale is not even caught, when a whale is sighted, you feel and see the transformation on the island. Work stops. Everybody goes for the hilltops, to see what's happenin'. A whale is caught and then it's an unofficial public holiday. Everybody goes to the whale team, not just to get a piece of whale. It's like a big carnival.'

Belmar constructed an economic history of Bequia that put whaling at its centre. On it grew exports to the Yankees, a boat-building industry and the ability to trade with other islands; even building timber the boats brought back. Then he took a breathless leap to conclude: 'The affluence of our civilization as we see it today on Bequia is hinged directly to whaling.'

Bequia's 5000 locals rely on fly-in tourists and wealthy yachties for the foreign currency that comes to their 18 square kilometres of verdant tropics. Expatriate sun-lovers from Europe and North America have bought into local businesses. Whaling supports very little, but Bequians refuse to discard this piece of the past. 'It's an important cultural identity that we cannot just throw behind the rocks,' Belmar said.

Once a year or so there is a piratical party at a Bequian cove. The word passes and local vendors set up barbecues and sell beer and rum as the triumphant whalers tow in a Humpback to be hacked apart in the red-stained shore wash. Tourists watch this unexpected diversion as the meat is divided widely, and some sold on. This is not the vitally dependent subsistence use of each piece of blubber and sinew found in an Arctic kill. It is a fleshy party, won by whaling methods little advanced since the nineteenth century.

These whalers still unleash a hand-held harpoon from a softly rowed boat. They follow it up with a darting gun. Like the power head that scuba divers used to blast a shark into its death spasms, the gun fires a steel dart into the Humpback with a small gunpowder charge that explodes on a few seconds delay. 'The whaler strikes the whale in the vitals,' Belmar said. That, at least, is the theory.

For decades the chief rogue in this hunt was Athneal Ollivierre, an ancient harpooner who kept killing whales late into his seventies, and was ticked off repeatedly at the IWC for his illegal habit of taking cow-calf pairs. There was a casual cruelty to the earlier whaling. 'Our forebears used to just strike it anywhere, and would often be towed for hours,' Belmar said. 'They would have to cut the rope because they would lose sight of land and the sun went down.' Things are more skilled now. 'Instead of taking five or six hours to die, within twenty minutes they are dead.'

When Ollivierre died, the tradition disappointed anti-whaling nations by surviving, supported by Japanese aid. Belmar said younger, more daring men worked in close to the whale, though under attack the Humpback was feared. 'Trying to keep an open boat afloat in high seas and trying to defend it from a 45-foot (14-metre) whale is quite a task in itself, because the whale does not sit idle and say: "You have struck me with a lance or a harpoon and I'm just going to sit here and die". Quite often the whale comes straight at the boat and tries to put it over, or smash the boat with its fin or tail. It's really a high risk job. I don't think an insurance company would want to insure a whaler.'

He smiled nostalgically, then made a strange comparison. 'It is such a cultural awakenin' each year,' he said. 'It's like the good, big, grizzly comin' out of hibernation.' The Bequian bears won an expanded IWC quota of four whales a year in 2003 and Japan gave them US$89 486 for a new whaling station under an aid program called 'Grassroots for Human Security Projects'. Soon after, Japan announced that the world was about to get a second Humpback kill in the name of science in the Antarctic from late 2007.

Hideki Moronuki, a long-serving whaling bureaucrat with Japan's Fisheries Agency, told me that his country understood the Humpback's place in southern seas. We were sitting in the over-crowded Tokyo office that he shared with a dozen others and piles of paper, while a political sloganeer's loudspeaker echoed through the concrete canyon outside. 'In Australia, the whale watching industry is especially big,' he said. 'So for the tourist, the Humpback is quite important. But I think these two industries, the whale watching and the whale eating, can stand simultaneously.'

We moved on to other issues, but it occurred to me that Moronuki was unlikely ever to have seen Humpbacks, much less known what Australians were prepared to put on their barbecues. He couldn't have heard the gasps of watchers marvelling at a breach. He must not have taken seriously the passion of his polar opposites, the young coastal people who grew up to know Humpbacks as respected equals; researchers who ran the days and years of their lives around the migration; or rescuers emotionally burned by struggles with a single animal. He couldn't. Otherwise he wouldn't have said what he did next.

I asked him to think about the prospect that a Humpback dragged up the stern ramp of *Nisshin Maru* would be identified by a Greenpeace photograph for its colour pattern, or even by DNA captured from a Japanese supermarket meat cabinet. It would be matched with flukes pictured in Cook Strait, a dorsal notch seen off Western Australia, or skin sloughed during a Byron Bay breach. What did he think that Australians and New Zealanders would say about that?

Moronuki laughed as he reached back into schoolbook English. 'I think they will say "our Betty" was killed. Or "our John".'

Or our Migaloo.

15

FISHING FOR COUNTRIES

We are programmed by our inheritance to see other living
things as mainly something to eat, and we care more about our
national tribe than anything else.

James Lovelock, *The Revenge of Gaia*, 2006

Stiff as a board, polished and precise as a Nikon camera, unbending in his
devotion to the cause, Kazuo Shima carried the Rising Sun forward.

'The anti-whaling groups constructed their campaigns like a drama,
with high emotional content to wring money from the public,' Shima said.
'They cast themselves as heroes seeking to protect the fair maiden (whales)
from a villain (Japan). Their campaigns were designed to evoke fear (the
alleged extinction of the world's largest mammals), love and hate.

'To Westerners, the Japanese were the perfect villains. All of the stereotypes of Pacific War propaganda were rolled out to depict Japanese as cruel,
barbaric and inhumane.'

Shima was at the zenith of his long IWC career when he said that. He
had been on the delegation when the moratorium came into force in 1986,
and Japan's commissioner for a remarkable twelve years. Outside the IWC
world, he was little known. Japan's delegation head stood apart from the
dog fights. He seldom appeared in television grabs, at least in the West.
These were left to more telegenic, English-speaking deputies like Masayuki
Komatsu and Joji Morishita. Shima was one of those in the shadows.

Soon to hand over the leadership in 1999, he put his name to an
explanation of why Japan went whaling. This is the conundrum for anti-
whaling Westerners. What's in it for Japan?

'The answer is both simple and complex,' Shima said. 'Pride is a large
part of it. The Japanese have been badly treated: demonized and maligned.'

And if the resource was sustainable, why not use it? 'The principle of sustainable use of renewable marine food resources, the maintenance of our culture and traditions, and the importance of defending truth and reason are too important to be abandoned in the face of an irrational ideology imposed by Western eco-cultists.'

The Japanese pioneered many of the world's distant water fisheries, and as their country prospered, more of other nations' premium fish was sold into their markets. In 2004, the UN Food and Agriculture Organisation calculated US$14.6 billion worth of fish, or 19.4 per cent of the world's total imports, went to Japan with its 1.9 per cent of global population. They like their seafood, and they worry if its control is in someone else's hands.

Japan's whaling policy is run by its Fisheries Agency. For bureaucrats who see whales as just air-breathing fish, this line in the sand—this *principle* of sustainable use—is what they are defending. Shima complained of a 'new taboo'. Westerners had turned whales into a sacred animal, like the Hindu cow, and fish would be next. Morishita reinforced this message more soothingly. He warned readers of the newspaper *Asahi Shimbun*: 'Once that principle of treating wildlife as [a] sustainable resource is compromised, it would be a domino effect in which our right to exploit other fish and animal products would be infringed upon.' What would Japanese consumers have to forgo? High value tuna?

Whaling's symbolic importance to the fishing industry was manifest in the ownership of the fleet. Through years of adverse publicity, the big three fishing companies, Nissui, Maruha and Kyokuyo, kept hold of the whaling company, Kyodo Senpaku Kaisha. Money was spent on building the new chasers, *Yushin Maru* and *Yushin Maru No. 2*, at a cost of more than US$8 million each. The Institute of Cetacean Research's executive director, Mitsuyoshi Murakami, told me that in 2002–03, the ICR took about 5.8 billion yen in income (US$50 million) from the sale of 'by-products of research' and paid roughly 5.1 billion yen (US$44.4 million) to charter the Kyodo Senpaku fleet. The fishing companies' tactics only changed in 2006, when a Greenpeace-led boycott began to threaten some of their US and New Zealand businesses. Kyodo Senpaku was transferred to the ICR in a little explained deal, making the ships essentially the Japanese Government's fleet.

Commerce—the need to keep a whaling iron in the fire, and halt erosion of Japan's global seafood access—partly explained the pursuit of whales. But as Shima said with his pointed rejection of the 'stereotypes of Pacific War propaganda', Japanese nationalists' version of the truth was also at stake among advocates of whaling. He believed the West attacked Japanese whaling because of jealousy at the economic miracle that followed its war defeat. The same miracle that gave the ICR a billion-yen annual subsidy.

Lurking nationalism in Japan, and the way it is dealt with, does make others uncomfortable, even angry. Prime ministerial visits to the Yasukuni Shrine, for example, re-opened old wounds. The Shinto shrine held the names of 2.4 million Japanese war dead, including some of the worst war criminals. Junichiro Koizumi's visits stoked fires in nationalist hearts, and drew protests from neighbours such as China who suffered in what the shrine called 'The Greater East Asian War'. As if a form of words could negate the importance of a prime ministerial deed, the Ministry of Foreign Affairs said: 'He makes the visits as an individual citizen, not in an official capacity.'

In the same spirit, Shima said that because Japan wanted to go whaling it was being smeared and slandered by the West, and then he went a little Churchillian. 'Despite the assaults on our right to maintain our culture and tradition, and our rights under the United Nations Law of the Sea and the International Convention to Regulate Whaling, we shall not give in.'

Japan started to fight back about the time that it was forced to end its objection to the moratorium. 'Its authorities decided to launch a secret exercise to "turn around" several countries that supported the moratorium decision to ensure that a blocking vote (one fourth plus one of voting Members) would be able to prevent any further conservation moves,' said Sidney Holt. In doing so, the Japanese Government took a leaf out of the book written by Holt and others. As David McTaggart had said; 'If you can't beat them, join them . . . and then beat them.'

Sourly for the environmentalists, countries they recruited did switch sides, starting with eastern Caribbean neighbours, St Lucia and St Vincent. Their allegiance changed at the 1986 IWC meeting, two weeks after their prime ministers went on official visits to Tokyo. A year later fisheries grant aid began to flow to both countries, the first trickle in a river of yen still rolling around the world twenty years later.

The blocking vote was first assembled against disorganised anti-whaling countries in Kyoto in 1993. By then it had one of the blandly chilling names bureaucrats think up to conceal their misdeeds. It was a 'Vote Consolidation Operation', run jointly by government and industry circles. As described by the *Yomiuri Shimbun*, it meant actively wooing new supporters. 'Fisheries Agency officials went to places like Pacific Ocean island countries, and countries of the Caribbean this year, and those coun-tries' representatives are now coming to Japan one after another on the invitation of the Overseas Fisheries Co-operation Fund and others.'

Initially finding the Pacific barren ground, Japan did succeed with a group of small nations who had in common their Caribbean location, rejec-tion of former colonial overlords, and poverty. Some also had indifferent records on democracy and the use of aid.

The St Lucian prime minister who first linked with Japan, John Compton, resigned after a US$100 000 foreign aid scandal. St Vincent's leader, 'Sonny' Mitchell, was a local strongman critic of the United States. Dominica's prime minister, Eugenia Charles, had no trouble accepting the gift of 'several hundred million yen' for a fishing complex at the same meet-ing with the Japanese prime minister where she was thanked for voting against the moratorium. Grenada, recovering from US invasion and the toppling of its Marxist regime, was heavily in debt and banned strikes as it started to take yen.

This blocking vote buckled when the tide rolled in for the Southern Ocean Sanctuary in 1994, and even Norway deserted Japan. St Lucia's commissioner left the meeting before the ballot, other Caribbeans abstained, and Kazuo Shima voted 'no' alone. That was the low point. The Caribbeans reappeared in votes for Japan through the mid-1990s when Antigua and Barbuda decided it was time to join. A year afterwards, its first ever Japanese grant aid, 1.28 billion yen (US$14 million) came in

1997. A decade later it had 3.8 billion yen (US$33 million) worth of fisheries projects. To 2005, five Caribbean countries were given around US$200 million in Overseas Development Aid (ODA) grants, most in fisheries aid.

It is unwise to try to tell a Caribbean politician that they have sold their vote, though. Politicians spout florid oratory there and they will come at you with the weight of history.

'I do think that poor countries, poor black countries, are treated differently,' said Clarice Charles, Grenada's education minister, and IWC delegate. 'It is a pity race has to be raised in this modern age', she told reporters. 'But it already brings back the time when we were colonised . . . Years ago we were told what to eat, given salted fish when the sea was abundant with fish. We were made to grow our primary products in the Caribbean and Africa and Asia so that these can be sent to Europe to make secondary products and make them rich, and we bought those products at their prices. And the world commodity market decided the price of nutmeg, the price of cocoa, bananas, sugar. We had no say! And the same nations come to us and say you should not eat whales, you should watch them! And I take great umbrage at that!!'

They speak, too, with the fury of the liberated. Joanne Massiah, a lawyer and senator from Antigua and Barbuda, was the fierce voice of its delegation, the kind of person who was unafraid to lead a 'Break the Silence' street march challenging violence against women after the country's Senate president was beaten and raped in her own home. Massiah's anger at the IWC's 'obs-*cene* polaris-*a-tion*', enriched by her West Indian accent, was a scary thing.

'Year after year, with Caribbean as well as other countries who support the principle of sustainable use, *allegations* continue left and right that we have *sold* our votes, that we are *prostituting* our people for a few fisheries complexes or whatever! We take *grave* exception to those sort of allegations. At the bottom of it all is the *rank* hypocrisy which *permeates* this organisation.'

Sooner or later rhetoric meets reality. No evidence was produced of deliberate interference by anti-whaling governments. Heavy Japanese hands left Vote Consolidation Operation prints on two of the Caribbeans.

In Grenada a diligent government accountant-general sent out a polite query to a former minister and IWC commissioner who, it was alleged, kept for himself payments totalling around £45 000. The man, Michael Baptiste, denied wrongdoing. More revealing than his problem were the words of a 'please explain' letter obtained by the ABC's *Four Corners* program.

> Upon review of our accounts, it has been observed that the contributions from the Government of Japan to the Government of Grenada for the International Whaling Commission were not received . . . for the years 1998 and 1999. However our internal audit revealed that contributions were received for all other years prior to and following 1998 and 1999. Moreover the Japanese have confirmed that it made contributions to the Government of Grenada for the specified periods.

The accountant-general, Patricia Antoine, put in official writing what others whispered. Japanese connections were paying IWC bills.

The other case involved Dominica, whose Environment Minister, Atherton Martin, took a stand over the country's right to decide its own vote. Usually a faithful ally of Japan when the roll was called, Dominica was persuaded by Martin to abstain on a central vote of the 2000 meeting. When it sided with the other Caribbeans instead, Martin quit. In a letter he accused the Japanese of using aid to manipulate his government's vote. He told the BBC: 'They announced that if they couldn't get Dominica to come along with them, they would have to place Dominican projects under review. If that's not an extortion by the Japanese Government, I don't know what is.'

The delegation spokeswoman, Shigeko Misaki, said: 'Japan would not force them to obey Japanese influence.' If only the words of her senior colleagues didn't keep coming back to haunt them. Over time Japanese demands collected like bloopers on a political video, made all the more embarrassing because in its US$9 billion aid program, Japan mostly lived up to its objective of 'cultivating a sound international environment'.

As early as 1987 a Fisheries Agency representative was laying down criteria for grants to Pacific Island countries, which: 'must have a fisheries agreement with Japan and it must take a supportive position to Japan in various international organizations'.

The ambition became more specific as years passed. 'It is necessary to couple effectively the ODA [Overseas Development Aid] and promotion of IWC membership,' said Hiroaki Kameya, Vice Minister for Agriculture, Forestry and Fisheries, in 1999. Later the same year, the vice minister said it again: 'We would like to utilise development aid as a practical means to promote nations to join [the IWC], expanding grant aid towards non-member countries which support Japan's claim'. Kameya said that he had been to Guinea, Namibia and Zimbabwe, in part to 'increase the number of nations working in the IWC and World Trade Organisation'. He thought Morocco and Mauritania were prospects as well.

Given the legislator's candour, it was hardly surprising Masayuki Komatsu felt confident enough to say why his country might take this approach. 'Japan does not have a military power,' he said. 'Unlike US and Australia, you may dispatch your military power to East Timor. That is not the case of Japan. Japan means is simply diplomatic communication and ODAs. So in order to get appreciation of Japan's position . . . that is natural that we must do, result on those two major truths. So I think there is nothing wrong.'

He didn't only defend the use of aid as a lever, however. Komatsu tossed off a colourful sound bite in the same interview that guaranteed a global spread to his words: 'I believe that, you know, Minke whale is, you know, cockroach in the ocean.'

This wasn't the first time he had used the word, but it was snapped up by the ABC's Mark Simkin. Komatsu said it with such delicious contempt. 'Cockroach in the ocean.' He must have felt like a child who pokes a stick into an ant nest and stands back, fascinated by his power to cause a frenzy.

Komatsu was himself not a great whale-eater. The crusader for the cause grimaced as he told me of his distaste for lumps of fried blubber that are one way of eating whale in Japan. 'It's like a Chicken McNugget,' he said. 'I don't eat it. But the younger people in the western part of Japan (do). It's very much astonishing. Once you provide it. They eat it.'

When Simkin pointed out to him that cockroaches were hardly a gourmet delight either, Komatsu had to explain his choice of simile. It was because 'there are too many [and they are] swimming so quick'. Then his explanation became lost in translation.

'A sarcastic analysation is, if you have maybe charming ladies, you aren't worried. If ladies not, you know, charming, you hate it. Or you're going to treat badly. I don't think that this is fair ways.' Was he really saying that if Minkes were thought of as ugly, instead of beautiful, people wouldn't worry about them ? He can't have seen a Right whale.

The sky didn't fall in on Komatsu. New Zealand Prime Minister, Helen Clark, professed herself appalled as she seized on the aid disclosure. 'Japan must surely be embarrassed by today's revelation from one of its own senior officials,' she said. Environment groups were universally outraged. But a Fisheries Agency memo said Komatsu's comments were taken out of context, and Japan moved on. After all, this was the same bureaucrat who told a whaling captain, in front of a video camera, how to deal with Greenpeace. 'When they approach, blow them out of the water.'

Not everyone was a rock star like Komatsu though. For years other Japanese officials travelled around the world like fly-fishermen testing rivers, quietly fishing for countries.

At the height of the Cold War, diplomats used to watch the Soviet hierarchy line up on the Kremlin's podium for the May Day parade, to see who ranked where, who was new, and who had vanished. Japanese officials were hidden by diplomatic etiquette, language barriers and bureaucratic secrecy. But government lists and reports, embassy noticeboards and local press could sketch the recruiters' progress.

Take the good servant of the Japanese Foreign Ministry, Kenro Iino. He was at Shima's side as the delegation spokesman when the IWC commissioner raged at the creation of the Southern Ocean Sanctuary, and remained deputy commissioner for four years. As the Vote Consolidation Operation began, he shifted into other fisheries, coincidentally in key IWC countries like Australia and Denmark. Who would have thought that he would reappear as ambassador to Kiribati, Tuvalu and Nauru, when these micro-nations signed up to the IWC for Japan?

When Iino first stepped into the limelight at IWC meetings, his post back in Tokyo was as the director of the Fishery Division of the Economic Affairs Bureau of the Department of Foreign Affairs. This was a recognised job for a diplomat with a bent for whaling. The man who preceded Iino as director, Shigenobu Kato, became the ambassador accredited to six of Japan's Caribbean allies.

A slight and serious man with wavy hair and spectacles, Iino fitted the archetype of a Japanese diplomat as well as he did his dark suit. Along with the emerging spokesman, Joji Morishita, and the Fisheries Agency official, Hideki Moronuki, Iino made the trip to other international organisations. They flew south to Hobart to bargain over fish catches at the Commission for the Conservation of Antarctic Marine Living Resources. When the prized sashimi fish, Southern Bluefin tuna, was disappearing from waters around Australia, Iino worked from the embassy in Canberra on a treaty between the two countries and New Zealand—a deal in which Masayuki Komatsu played hard ball, and Japan's hidden pillaging of the fishery continued unabated.

Iino was sentimentally a Pacific Japanese. Early in his career he had a posting as second secretary to the Fiji Embassy, which was also the base for island neighbours. He spoke nostalgically of Tonga, a favourite of Japan with its Sumo-sized people and king, Taufa'ahau Tupou IV, who shuttled regularly to Tokyo. In 2002, Iino became His Excellency the Ambassador to Fiji, serving a truly vast patch of Pacific Ocean that radiated north from Fiji to Vanuatu and Tonga, on next to Tuvalu, Kiribati and Nauru, across the equator and up to the Marshall Islands, Micronesia, and Palau. How many hours and days he must have spent gazing out of aircraft windows at the blue below, and its skeins of islands. On some of them, economic strife was matched only by their fear of disappearing under water through climate change. The same sea's EEZs were also their financial hope.

About half of the global supply of tuna was caught in the central and western Pacific, almost totally by foreign fleets—Japan, Taiwan and the United States. Skipjack, Albacore and Bigeye tuna made up 14.4 per cent of Pacific Island exports. In a country like Kiribati with an EEZ almost half the size of the Australian mainland, three quarters of all exports was tuna.

From a billion dollar industry, Kiribati and the other islands had to be content with licence fees around five per cent of returns—that is, when the fish was legally taken. The extent of illegal fishing could only be guessed, and enforcement of EEZs was little more than a brave try. How could Kiribati protect its waters with a single patrol boat?

The same sea, their enemy, pressed in. As waves ate Kiribati seasonal high tides exposed recent graves. Sea walls collapsed and food gardens were flooded. Climate change happened each year and affected people whose standard of living was already impoverished by global measure. Compared to Japan's US$29 400 per capita gross domestic product, and Australia's US$30 700, Kiribati had US$800 in 2004, and the World Bank warned one third of that tiny sum could be lost to rising seas by 2050 if the country didn't adapt. Fisheries licence fees made up most of national income, which meant the country had to be friends with the powerful. Taiwan and China vied as supporters, but leading in aid to Kiribati was Japan, which had given US$104.3 million by 2004.

By running a finger along a map of the cruise of the *Pequod*, you could see that Captain Ahab met his nemesis Moby Dick for the last time in the northernmost waters of Kiribati. In the sailing ship years, adventurers did cruise these seas writing fabulous tales about cannibals while killing around 65 000 whales. As Humpback scientists pointed out, they were now gone from most island shores. Apart from Tonga, there was no history of indigenous whaling, though some, including Kiribati's people, would eat stranded cetaceans.

'We use them as a gift from the gods,' said Kiribati's Alternate Commission at the IWC, Tessie Lambourne. 'We don't have cattle. I myself have eaten whale meat when I was smaller.' She chanced a quick smile. 'It was good.'

Kiribati's moment arrived as anti-whaling nations tried to consolidate the hold on the IWC that they achieved with the Southern Ocean Sanctuary. These countries said that if Southern Hemisphere baleen whale numbers were to recover, they needed protection in the seas where they bred as well as the ocean where they fed. They would wall future commercial whalers out of the oceans, block by giant block—if they could agree how it should happen. Ireland's Michael Canny proposed the grand goal first—to declare the global high seas a sanctuary in return for limited coastal commercial whaling. This meant Japan would have to end all

Antarctic whaling—a very remote possibility. Still WWF thought the idea 'an important attempt to break the deadlock in the IWC', and others flirted with it.

In the Southern Hemisphere, the anti-whaling nations thought differently. Their ambition was to lock away the South Pacific and South Atlantic. *After* these were achieved, the Australian Environment Minister, Robert Hill, said the next goal was the world's oceans.

Considering Japan's dismissal of the Southern Ocean Sanctuary, the new proposals looked like long shots. Perhaps they were born of exasperation as whaling grew despite the moratorium, and seized on by politicians to show that *something* was being done. The Canny plan made no impact beyond internal IWC talks. The South Pacific plan was hated by most of the small island nations it would have encompassed.

In their first response at the South Pacific Forum, they effectively said that they would talk to the Japanese first. A communiqué in 1998 supported 'development' of the sanctuary as it also did 'sustainable use of marine resources'. Forum partners would have to 'fully consult' dialogue partners, that is, Japan.

The new sanctuary first came to a vote in 2000 as the centrepiece of the IWC meeting that Robert Hill hosted in Adelaide. It would have stretched from the Great Australian Bight nearly to Easter Island, and from the Southern Ocean to the Equator. Hill pulled in an 18–11–4 result, far short of a three-quarters majority. He claimed 'strong regional support', but in fact the only Pacific island IWC member, the Solomons, left town on the day of the vote. The South Pacific Sanctuary was looking more like hype than determined whale protection.

Some islands such as Tonga thought better than to enter this sort of tricky contest. 'Too much political decisions to be made,' said the Fisheries Minister, Sione Vailala Matoto. Others like Kiribati—poor, small and endangered—realised that they had one more valuable asset: their sovereignty, their single international vote. And Japan kept on cultivating their friendship.

Kiribati's President, Teburoro Tito, was feted in Tokyo in the accomplished Japanese way. Only later came the arm twist. The leader of the tiny, poor population met the emperor of the world's second largest economy and a line of ministers, visited Hiroshima and then sat down with Prime Minister Yoshiro Mori in 2001. Item two in the official report of the leaders' meeting began: 'Prime Minister conveyed Japan's concerns regarding whaling issues.'

Nobody actually linked whaling with aid. Why would they? The IWC wasn't the only topic at the meeting. The men chatted about a new Pacific fish stocks agreement that worried Japan. Tito said that he would support Japan's permanent membership of the UN Security Council. Only *then* did pledges of money come. Perversely, the disappearing islands depend upon greenhouse polluting diesel power for electricity. A US$10.1 million supply project was agreed for Tarawa atoll, and the coaxing continued.

'We have a very long history,' said the Fisheries Agency's Hideki Moronuki. 'We have established a bilateral agreement on tuna fisheries all of 40 years ago. Whenever we have bilateral talks with Kiribati officials, we asked them to join the IWC. To cooperate with us.'

The Japanese parliamentary secretary for Foreign Affairs, Toshio Kojima, put the case against the South Pacific Sanctuary to island leaders including Tito when he came to Nauru after it held the 2001 Pacific Forum meeting. As Iino arrived in Suva it was clear the sanctuary plan was already in trouble. Australia's claim of 'South Pacific solidarity' was mere spin. The forum noted 'strong reservations of some members', and a 'need for increased scientific knowledge concerning the benefits of a whale sanctuary'.

Each new pro-whaling Pacific member of the IWC made a sanctuary more remote. Palau was the first of Iino's flock to join in 2002, followed by Tuvalu. Marshall Islands came aboard too. In January 2004, Iino presented his credentials on Tarawa in Kiribati. The ambassador was on hand to sign an 'exchange of notes' for the power upgrade's second phase, and by year's end Kiribati was an IWC member. Its Alternate Commissioner, Tessie Lambourne, mildly rejected the Australian media's take on her country. 'Basically the view seems to be that we have been bought by Japan. That is unfair and untrue. We like to be involved in international agreements generally on marine resources.'

Nauru's untidy appearance, late for the 2005 meeting in Ulsan, South Korea, raised deep suspicions. Environmentalist video was shot of its commissioner, Marcus Stephen, talking to a Japanese delegate in the hotel lobby before he reached the meeting room floor. He said the Nauru Cabinet had decided at the last minute to join, and it had taken him and his deputy time to fly the route to South Korea via Japan.

'It's all out of our hands,' he said. 'We arrived only one hour before voting.'

Struggling to restore its financial reputation after years of laundering money for Russian mafia, and with a bankrupt economy unable to sustain its own air link, Nauru was closely watched for evidence of a Japanese pay-off. Australian delegates claimed its IWC fees were paid in cash. Stephen was offended at the insults to his integrity. What emerged from the Solomon Islands was much more convincing: a money trail back to the Japanese whalers.

Previous Solomon Islands commissioners told the ABC *Four Corners* journalist Matthew Carney that their government's IWC fees were paid by the Japanese for a decade. Which Japanese though? Chased down a corridor by Carney, the 2005 Commissioner, Paul Maenu'u, seemed to implicate government. 'We are coming on our bilateral agreement,' he said.

A spokesman for the Institute of Cetacean Research, Glenn Inwood, gave me a tantalisingly different explanation. 'It isn't actually the Japanese Government. It may be other non-government groups that contribute, the way environment groups assist some countries. You would be hard-pressed to find any link with the Japanese Government.' Was another ricepaper wall maintaining its international modesty?

The bribery of foreign officials remained a stain on Japan's reputation long after other developed countries legislated and enforced laws against it. Amazingly, not until April 2006 was a law passed in Japan expressly denying tax deductions for money exchanged for foreign favours. Even then, an OECD Working Group on Bribery said Japanese law enforcement authorities had 'still not made adequate efforts' to investigate and prosecute foreign bribery cases.

In the Solomons a large diversion of Japanese money to individuals was claimed over tuna rights. Tione Bogutu, the permanent secretary of the Solomons Fisheries Department, investigated the disappearance of millions of dollars paid by Japan. 'The fact is that this is money which is due to the

Government of the Solomon Islands as revenue from fisheries,' Bogutu said. 'The money has been diverted elsewhere, and certain officers chose to help themselves.'

Appeals by Australian and New Zealand politicians to Pacific islands gained little ground. Though it was the single largest aid donor in the region, Australia spent most of its money on Papua New Guinea. Nations like Kiribati and Tuvalu also knew Australians as the biggest per capita greenhouse polluter in the world, one that bullied them into weakening their stance on climate change. But what they seemed to dislike more than anything was the way Australians did things.

Kiribati's Tessie Lambourne picked her words cautiously. 'We're grateful that Campbell visited us. But we would also like to take the opportunity to discuss what is important for *us*. We need continuous dialogue with each other.'

Environment Minister Ian Campbell and a media entourage darted across the Pacific by VIP jet to some of these islands before two IWC meetings. In the Solomons, the Australian politician was so forceful with the Prime Minister, Sir Allan Kemakeza, that Campbell told a press conference what his host meant to say.

Kemakeza was being slightly confusing about the Solomons' IWC voting position—a hesitation that was of itself revealing—when Campbell stepped in to say it for him. 'Voting no to the scientific research expansion, and abstaining from the vote on commercial whaling,' Campbell said.

'Yeah, yeah,' Kemakeza said.

It was the kind of diplomacy that gave Australia an unfortunate name in the Pacific. 'Still too much pith helmet,' grunted one New Zealand political adviser I spoke to. It was also ineffective. In the end the Solomons' Commissioner abstained from the scientific whaling vote, backed the resumption of commercial whaling, and under Australian pressure lost his job.

Perceptions of Japan were different. 'Regardless of obvious imbalances in power, Japan has always emphasized respect for sovereignty in dealing with its trade and aid partners,' said analysts from the University of Hawaii's East–West Center. This was 'particularly welcome' in the Pacific when other countries like Australia took 'a more direct managerial approach'.

Japanese interests might pay officials' bills, and countries' IWC fees, they might have a global reputation for bribing foreigners, but Tokyo would never embarrass them by telling them their lines in public.

There *was* a common line though, a mantra of pro-whaling allies. Formed in Japanese whalers' science, it took hold in the Caribbean, spread through the Pacific, and into the next frontier of IWC recruiters in West Africa. It came from a kernel of truth and was spouted from the mouths of the fearful. It was 'whales-eat-fish'.

You could hear it in the frustration of a dealer in Tokyo's Tsukiji fish market. 'It is true that the Southern Bluefin tuna stocks may be depleted around Australia, but that's because of a lack of tuna bait [prey],' the dealer said. 'And the reason there is no bait is because there are too many whales. If only we had been allowed to continue whaling.' In the Caribbean, Grenadan IWC delegate Clarice Charles used it to smear a generic, marauding whale. 'For two years now our fishermen who have invested heavily in large boats, they have been bankrupt because there are no tunas around. Whales eat somethin'. And when they come with the Atlantic current, they eat everything in their path . . . They surely don't just eat sea water.' The newly signed Pacific countries said the reason for joining the IWC was the protection of their tuna. 'We support the conservation of marine resources but for us a priority is our fishery,' said Tessie Lambourne. 'We need independent scientific advice.'

It was true. Whales did eat fish: commercial catches already on the line. Orcas, False Killer whales and Pilot whales hit tuna and Trevalla longlines as they were hauled in in the South Pacific and the Tasman Sea. Sperm whales left only the lips of Patagonian Toothfish hanging on hooks at South Georgia, and frustrated the fishers of Sablefish off Alaska. These whales seemed to learn quickly, and show cunning in their freeloading. Fishers would return to pull a longline and find the same whale waiting toothily at the buoy like a customer seated at a sushi train. It was annoying and cost them money.

This opportunist snacking was not what Japan was talking about. The fear its whalers spread to others was of whales eating down whole fish stocks. The reason for the Tsukiji fish-market seller to worry was not that Japanese demand for Southern Bluefin tuna had chased it to the brink of extinction.

Nor that Japanese fishers had fraudulently taken up to three times more Southern Bluefin than they had declared in an $8 billion deception over twenty years. We should be concerned because whales were eating their prey!

Whales-eat-fish emerged as an argument at the time that Japan was beaten on the Southern Ocean Sanctuary. Kazuo Shima made the astonishing claim at Puerto Vallarta that cetaceans ate 600 million tonnes of fish annually, or more than six times human consumption. It was suddenly nothing less than a life and death issue. 'If the human species is to survive to the future, we shall have to exercise more control over the growth of both human and cetacean populations,' he said.

Greenpeace International's campaigner, John Frizell, just shook his head. 'Japan comes up with one really bizarre idea every year,' he said. This one stuck. It was a reason for lifting the moratorium, and for scientific whaling. It was a claim that all those Caribbean and Pacific islanders could make. When poor, hungry African countries started to come aboard for Japan, whales-eat-fish loomed as an even more frightening thought. It was why nations with no earthly interest in whaling might sit in an IWC meeting only to say 'yes', 'no' or 'abstain'.

There was no doubting the pictures the ICR used in its glossy brochures. Images of whale stomachs opened up in the North Pacific showed Anchovy and Pilchard, Mackerel and Saury packed inside like, well, Sardines. 'Sea Unbalance', one brochure was headed. 'Whales increase, fish decrease.'

In the chase for the truth, the figure to start with was total worldwide food consumption by cetaceans. For the Japanese, the estimate of Tsutomu Tamura subsided from 600 million to 'at least 294–434 million tonnes' for all the species he could calculate. A range of 150–340 million tonnes was acknowledged from the other side by University of British Columbia researchers, Kristin Kaschner and Daniel Pauly.

What mattered about this total was that by far the bulk of this food was not what people eat. It was krill and copepods, those micro-organisms that build baleen whales' immense size. The first lie of the whales-eat-fish argument was the claim that an exponentially greater haul of 'our' fish was disappearing down whales' throats, rather than our own. It wasn't.

Figures on the human wild fishery hovered around 87 million tonnes for the legal catch. Kaschner and Pauly argued that if you took into account catches that were illegal, unregulated or unreported, then the human catch was probably closer to 150 million tonnes. Tamura found known cetaceans ate only slightly more fish than the legal catch. Kaschner and Pauly thought the total somewhat under, and they reached another conclusion.

> Marine mammals consume most of their food where humans do not fish ... At least some of our favourite seafood delicacies, such as tuna, are rarely if ever consumed by marine mammals. Clearly what we have is an attempt at finding a convenient scapegoat for the mismanagement of fisheries, and the reduction of catches caused by excess fishing effort throughout the world.

The overlaps—the fisheries that directly competed with cetaceans for food—were what counted. It had to be acknowledged that, particularly in the North Pacific and North Atlantic, fish targeted by fishermen fell prey to cetaceans as well. Minkes off Norway ate Herring and Sand Lance. The common Japanese table fish, Saury, was eaten by Sei and Minkes in the North Pacific. But in all of those fisheries the greatest predator by far was their oldest: other fish.

Daniel Pauly is one of the world's foremost chroniclers of the fisheries crisis. He said that as global catches began to decline in the 1980s, true losses to ecosystems were masked by a constant drive to take new fish from deeper waters, and by the growth of aquaculture. Wild fishery losses would not halt if more whales were taken. Illegal or uncontrolled fishing, the waste of discarded by-catch, habitat loss by pollution and destructive fishing methods like drift nets and bottom trawling were much more destructive. And why stop at whales? What about the consumption of fish by seals and seabirds, let alone the other fish?

Kaschner and Pauly found Albert Einstein helpful. They remembered the great thinker saying: 'All problems have one simple solution. However, it happens to be completely wrong.'

Missionaries for the whales-eat-fish cause were led by Kazuo Shima, who paradoxically urged rejection of the 'false rumour' that the world's fisheries were depleted. The UN Food and Agriculture Organisation may have observed a fall since the 1950s in wild fisheries' potential, but not Shima.

To him it was a lie that sowed hate against fishermen, and inflamed distrust of fisheries managers and scientists.

Mysteriously, he blamed *The New York Times* and the Associated Press for launching an anti-fisheries campaign. 'They uphold the view that marine mammals are untouchable, and if they want to be consistent, they end up being against any utilization of all marine resources,' said Shima. 'Those of us who uphold the principle of rational use of marine living resources must fight against it by renovating the concept of marine resource management, and correcting the direction of the present global drift.'

Japanese disciples of this doctrine went in search of more converts in Africa. Hideki Moronuki left the paper mountains of the Fisheries Agency behind and toured North Africa. 'I went to Maroc [Morocco], Eritrea, Ethiopia, Kenya. I am the second Japanese to visit Eritrea,' he said proudly. 'Anyway the Japanese Government has given some substantial assistance to Eritrea, and it does not take an interest in the IWC.' Morocco did though, joining in 2001, and more were to follow.

Whales-eat-fish struck a chord in Africa for the pressing reason that people were hungry, and because they were told they could partly blame the whales. The Japan Fisheries Association made it simple. 'Expensive fish is exported to rich countries, while other fish consumed by a large number of marine mammals (dolphins and whales) is detrimental to the African people.' By the way, cetaceans made good food too.

Recruited nations knew as much about whales as they did of penguins. One African scientist I spoke to said he snapped a photograph of a breaching Humpback just offshore from a West African country and showed it to the Prime Minister. 'He just refused to believe it was in his waters.'

'In Africa, the whale now occurs mostly along wild and remote coasts, or offshore,' said the scientist, who was speaking on condition of being unidentified. 'It is not a food source. There are no African pelagic fishers. When there was whaling in the twentieth century, the land-based stations were operated by Norwegians who came out. Whale meat was never fed to local markets. The oil was exported. There was no cultural appreciation for whales and no value for them. Now the Africans say to the Europeans: "Stop telling us what to do". There is no need for kickbacks and bribery on this. They are an open book.'

Unrecognised in a coastal state, whales can only be picture-book imaginings in Timbuktu. Japan's whaling campaign reached this furthest human desert outpost when it recruited the land of Mali.

The Sahara desert encroaches to Mali's north, pressing life out of the country. Against it, distinctive houses and mosques built of mud are statements of a defiant, ancient culture. It is somehow no surprise to learn that a disastrous locust plague ravaged the totally landlocked country in 2002. It is unnerving to read that witchcraft flourishes, and it is plain hair-raising to learn that female genital mutilation still scars an estimated 94 per cent of Malian women.

Mali is very poor. It ranked fourth last of 177 countries in 2004 on a UN Human Development Index which focussed on living a long and healthy life, being educated, and having a decent standard of living. Average life expectancy in Mali was 48, women had seven births, and the GDP per capita was US$994. Fewer than half of its people had access to a sustained water source, one in three was undernourished, and four in five were illiterate. It ranked 99th on Transparency International's global corruption index.

The Niger gives Mali life, and is the closest the country comes to a connection with the sea, two countries away downstream. But at least Mali has a freshwater fishery, unlike Luxembourg, which doesn't even have a river and joined the IWC at the same time. The grand Duchy was among a handful of landlocked European nations recruited by anti-whaling nations to counter Japan. Luxembourg was fourth highest on the same UN index. Average life expectancy was 30 years longer than in Mali, women had a career-juggling 1.7 births, and the per capita GDP was a fat US$62 000. There was no measurable illiteracy, water problem or undernourishment. Famous for its anonymous international banking and tax avoidance, Luxembourg ranked eleventh on the corruption index.

'No one questions when landlocked countries are recruited by the anti-whaling camp,' said the Antiguan, Joanne Massiah, while the Malian IWC deputy commissioner, Héry Coulibaly, sat quietly beside her. 'We are fully independent sovereign states, capable of coming to our own conclusions, relevant to our own economy.'

Mali reached its conclusion based on food. The kind-faced Coulibaly was Director of Fisheries in his country, which produced around 100 000 tonnes of freshwater fish each year from an estimated 73 000 local fishers. In an opening statement to the IWC, Coulibaly said: 'The IWC makes decisions which have effects on developing countries confronted with the problem of undersupply of food. It is in the name of that principle that Mali adheres to the IWC. It is also because we believe that the IWC can contribute to a significant degree to the reduction of poverty, hunger and malnutrition in the world.'

A possible new whale eater. That would warm Kazuo Shima's heart.

Japan's National Research Institute of Far Seas Fisheries cultivated the Africans, and its fishing organisation claimed them as willing converts. The fisheries institute took officials from eight West African countries, including Mali, out on an Atlantic survey where in ten days they saw nineteen groups of cetaceans. Only two were whales, the rest dolphins.

The Japan Fisheries Association claimed that Guinea and Ivory Coast had said: 'If we can rationally use certain abundant whale species which eat so much fish, we can kill two birds with one stone.' None of this was openly contested by anti-whaling countries. It was left to Greenpeace to take officials from Guinea out to the country's own EEZ to document the extensive illegal fishing by Chinese vessels that was robbing the country of its fish stocks.

Essentially Japan was unimpeded in its operation to gain muscle in the IWC. First in the Caribbean, then in the Pacific and Africa, it built a rickety blocking vote to nearly a simple majority. In reaction, anti-whaling countries had to rely for numbers mainly on European states, driving home to Japan's supporters their opponents' colonial past.

The Vote Consolidation Operation shifted into South-East Asia when Cambodia joined. An untiring Shima appeared next in Port Moresby. As President of Japan's Far Seas Purse Seine Fishing Association, he signed a fisheries agreement with Papua New Guinea on Skipjack tuna. He said: 'We have confidence that we can contribute to a lot of development of Papua New Guinea fisheries.'

16

NORMALITY

'Look your worship,' said Sancho Panza, 'what we see there are not giants, but windmills, and what seems to be their arms are the sails that turned by the wind make the millstones go.'
'It is easy to see,' replied Don Quixote, 'that thou art not used to this business of adventures; those are giants, and if thou art afraid, away with thee out of this and betake thyself to prayer while I engage them in fierce and unequal combat.'

Miguel de Cervantes, _Don Quixote_, 1615

'Warning! Warning!' The Japanese voice rang out tinny and urgent in English from the ship's loudspeakers. 'This is the _Nisshin Maru_'s captain. Stop your obstructive actions immediately! Keep away from our ship, or we will have to hose you to fend you off!'

A tape loop of the message honked robotically and ship horns blasted as Sea Shepherd's _Robert Hunter_ swung across the bow of _Nisshin Maru_ trailing a heavy rope. A whaler's video camera lit by a cold yellow sunrise followed the line as it snaked through the water and under the factory ship's hull. A crewman shouted in alarm. Already the open flensing deck was confused and stinking. _Robert Hunter_ had steamed close enough for the black-clad activists of Sea Shepherd to hurl aboard smoke pots and bottles of foul-smelling butyric acid. If the rope snarled its propeller, _Nisshin Maru_ might be crippled enough for the slower _Farley Mowat_ to pull alongside, and it carried a machine to tear a hull. Paul Watson's Ahab-like quest for the whalers was climaxing. But at the start of one of whaling's strangest weeks, he would be robbed of his prize by one of his own Zodiac dinghies.

Two days earlier Watson had posted supporters a gloomy, ruminative poem after fruitlessly scouring the Ross Sea. His little Sea Shepherd

Conservation Society had built a US$2 million campaign, bought a new and faster ship named after his friend, the late Greenpeace founder, and used a helicopter to sweep thousands of miles shuttling between *Robert Hunter* and *Farley Mowat*. On the *Farley* was a heavily braced steel beam, tipped by a 30-centimetre blade that could slide out two metres at deck height, pushed by a hydraulic ram. Watson called it the can opener. When I saw it at a Hobart dock, operated at the press of a button by a thin young man with dreadlocks and a frown, it seemed easily tough enough to slice into a metal hull. Watson's intentions were often hidden somewhere between pyrotechnic theatre and real damaging intent. But among Sea Shepherd's 57 volunteer activists, some looked feral enough to use this weapon.

It fitted the Sea Shepherd legend that powerful forces were arrayed against them. *Farley Mowat* was made a 'pirate' ship, struck off Belize's shipping register. Japanese diplomatic pressure led to *Robert Hunter*, a onetime Scottish fisheries patrol vessel, losing its British flag. The Foreign Office in London said it 'informed' the UK Registrar General of Shipping and Seamen of the Japanese Embassy's request to 'control the *Robert Hunter*'s actions'. Loss of flags made these ships technically liable to boarding and arrest. Watson was tormented by the New Zealand Government, which flew reconnaissance above the whaling fleet, filmed it, then refused to release the position. Even the sky carried an invisible enemy. Watson was certain the whalers bought commercially available satellite surveillance to watch where his ships went, and indeed, this *can* be ordered like a new car. A sales manager from Microsoft Vexcel cheerfully told me: 'Choice of satellites/sensors and how much you are willing to spend for time on the "birds" will dictate your surveillance coverage, re-visit, type of vessel you can reliably detect, etc.' The ICR spokesman, Glenn Inwood, ridiculed the idea that research vessels would need this. 'Sea Shepherd is a comedy of errors,' he said. '[Watson's] problems are better blamed on poor seamanship.'

Escalated protests against the whalers were inevitable when Japan raised its Antarctic kill to a height never before claimed for science. Over the years the Minke hunt increased from 240 to 440, scarcely touching a number thought to stand at around 761 000. But this population became caught in an insoluble IWC scientific dispute. Some believed there could be as few as 268 000 Minkes. With no agreement in sight, Japan nevertheless ratcheted up the kill.

Not only would Minkes be hunted, the whalers would target Fins and, most alarmingly to Australians and New Zealanders, 'their' Humpbacks when the hunt was on at full pace from 2007 to 2008. Up to 935 Minkes, 50 Fins and 50 Humpbacks would be harpooned. Why? The scientific justification for the Second Phase of the Japanese Antarctic Whale Research Program under special permit in the Antarctic (JARPA II) was that Japan had to monitor the Antarctic ecosystem, and work out how many whales to take if there was going to be a commercial kill. In effect, it wanted to take more than 1000 Antarctic whales each year, indefinitely, in order to conserve their species. This was how grotesquely science had been bent.

In the summer of 2005–06, Greenpeace sent two ships south, both of which collided with the whalers. Its *Esperanza* nipped *Nisshin Maru*'s stern for weeks while Watson trailed behind in *Farley Mowat*, only once catching up and panicking the whalers. The next summer a reluctant Greenpeace came to the Southern Ocean late, leaving the running to Sea Shepherd. But as Watson's ships emerged from the Ross Sea and turned west along the ice edge in February 2007, he appeared to face humiliation. Verse 17 of *The Shepherd's Southern Quest* ran: 'We have searched and probed these great vast seas, smashing through the ice/Our two ships have done their best and our crews have given all/ But without support from those who could help/We are simply throwing dice.'

Low on fuel, worrying about finding a port for his flagless ships, Watson threw the dice for very much the last time. Soon after dawn on 9 February 2007 he was back in the game. 'We fooled them with, of all things, "expert seamanship",' he crowed. 'I ran the ships through the ice fields south of the Balleny Islands and came up on them from the other side. We took a pounding, but the satellite cannot track a ship through ice. The ice was our friend.'

Rising steeply from a deep sea floor, the desolate Ballenys were long known as a summer home to whales. Bill Dawbin looked at Japanese catch data from 1953 and saw the East Australian/New Zealand Humpback stock concentrate around these islands as if they were a staging point for the migration. Sea Shepherd's ships popped up in the middle of the fleet and the Japanese scattered. At one point *Nisshin Maru* steamed in apparent confusion directly for *Farley Mowat*, and its can opener, before turning away. *Robert Hunter* caught up with the factory ship and foamed across its bow, the fouling rope trailing, only to see *Nisshin Maru* steam on over it unharmed. Two men in a Zodiac from *Farley Mowat* then tried to heave a net into the propeller. Their dinghy banged *Nisshin Maru's* stern, cracking the dinghy's rigid fibreglass hull.

Karl Neilsen, a commercial diver from Fremantle, Western Australia, and John Gravois, an engineer from Los Angeles, watched in alarm as water poured in and the chase ran over the horizon, leaving them alone in the Antarctic in an open dinghy, with a lowering fog and snow showers. Then they found their VHF radio was out. Soon after, Watson missed them and called in the first of three emergencies that the rescue authority, Maritime New Zealand, would deal with in seven days.

His two ships set up a pattern search, and in a surreal shift, *Nisshin Maru* swung around to help save men who had just tried to disable it, setting aside whaling enmity for the unspoken imperative of survival at sea. Neilsen and Gravois motored a few miles to an iceberg that they tied up against. The wind blew them away from it, and they huddled in the open sea under an emergency blanket, saved from sinking by the Zodiac's inflated tubes. After eight increasingly cold hours, Neilsen heard *Farley Mowat's* horn through the mist, stood up, and was spotted. The *Hunter's* crew watched their radar screen as *Nisshin Maru* turned away and gradually slid off. The ship that Watson (evidently a Star Wars fan) called the 'Cetacean Death Star'—the ultimate killing machine, his Moby Dick—disappeared.

After several more days of searching, Sea Shepherd did manage to find *Kaiko Maru*, the fleet's whale-spotting odd job ship. It was a poor consolation prize; not even carrying a harpoon. But it did allow a rare glimpse of the Japanese whalers. A video of Sea Shepherd's attack was shot by a marine biologist on board the Japanese ship. In turn, a Sea Shepherd camera caught her. Dressed in a fashionable pastel outfit and large sunglasses, she dashed around the open flying bridge of *Kaiko Maru*, describing what was unfolding in front of the camera. With her ship and *Robert Hunter* on course to collide, the brain trust on the Japanese boat was alarmed. 'What's the best thing to do?' she said. 'Shouldn't we announce a warning? Should I pass you the foghorn? Should we do the siren?' The crunch of metal followed, and her camera shook slightly. At that moment a photograph was taken from the *Hunter*. It showed her steady on deck, feet apart, gazing at the other ship. Beside her stood an emotionless Japanese seaman, one of the country's vast army of obedient workers; and an older man, his mouth open in a surprised 'Oh!'. At the controls on the flying bridge, a grim-faced ship's officer in cool hat and glasses half-turned, snarling. *Kaiko Maru* was boxed in against sea ice by Sea Shepherd, its propeller tangled, and its skipper called in to New Zealand the second mayday. Watson radioed an offer of help to the ship, a reciprocation for aid *Nisshin Maru* gave, but there was no reply. *Kaiko Maru* sorted out its own mechanical problems and steamed off.

Watson let it go and turned north for Australia. A few days later *Nisshin Maru* turned up in the Ross Sea, 1000 kilometres away from him. Around 6 am on 15 February the ship's captain phoned the bemused Wellington rescue centre to say the ship was on fire, most of its crew had evacuated, and one was feared dead. The whaling season ended. The late-arriving *Esperanza* stood by *Nisshin Maru* for nine days while the fire in the processing area was extinguished, the death confirmed and repairs made. There was no more whaling, no chance of Greenpeace intervening or of recording the whaling.

Watson contemptuously called Greenpeace's gory videos of scientific whaling 'snuff flix', but in fact they were the revelation of the expanded hunt's first season in 2005–06. As never before, they showed how little death had changed for whales in a century. Whales might be killed instantly with high skill, or endure an agonising demise.

One steely Japanese gunner fired over a Greenpeace dinghy at the instant a fleeing Minke porpoised above the surface. The harpoon was away with the whale halfway out of the water, and the Minke lifeless before it could dive under. In two appalling cases it took around 30 minutes for whales to die. Harpoons glanced off, leaving the animals to flounder unattached as they bled. Chased and harpooned again, they were dragged in to be shot with a rifle. Between these extremes it appeared many others suffered.

Despite greater devotion to scientific whaling than any other country, Japan had allowed only a drip-feed of data on its killing efficiency. Greenpeace's cameras began to fill that gap. Following the chasers for weeks, they recorded a total of 26 harpoonings and handed over video of sixteen for Western scientists to put before the IWC. Of these, twelve cases allowed for an estimate of minimum time to death, and twice it could have been instant. The rest took between ten and 35 minutes to die, some probably from drowning as whales were hauled in closer to the chaser and held up by their harpooned tails.

The Japanese blamed Greenpeace for prolonging these times. 'The point is that Greenpeace knows that if they harass the catcher boats they can get the bloody footage required for their PR campaign,' said Dr Hatanaka, from the ICR. A scientist who was on *Nisshin Maru* claimed to the IWC that in 'undisturbed' situations, Minkes died in an average of two minutes and two seconds. That time doubled if Greenpeace was around. Beyond this comment, he released no data to his IWC peers, and the Japanese would say nothing about times to death for bigger whales.

This highly sensitive first-hand knowledge of whaling only came to light because of environment and wildlife protection groups. No international observers reported openly from Japanese boats. Anti-whaling governments stayed out of the way. They might ramp up the rhetoric at an IWC meeting; outside its walls they looked totally ineffective.

Démarches, or joint protest notes, were lodged repeatedly by anti-whaling diplomats in the years of Japanese whaling's expansion. 'Démarches!' said a furious Sue Arnold, campaigner of Australians for Animals. 'The Fisheries Agency uses them for toilet paper!' After JARPA II was announced the ambassadors of fifteen countries led by Australia called on the Department of Foreign Affairs in Tokyo to say they were 'extremely disappointed'. Six months later the chauffeurs of seventeen countries drove their ambassadors to the same offices so they could express 'strong opposition' to the lethal Antarctic hunt. They were met with a sneer, said Brazil's IWC commissioner, Maria Teresa Mesquita Pessoa. Apart from a little media coverage at home, the ritual was fruitless.

In bilateral talks between leaders, whaling was a barely noticeable irritant. After Japan raised its North Pacific hunt in 2000, the American Secretary of State, Madeleine Albright, found time to tell her counterpart in Tokyo the United States was 'deeply troubled' by its whaling, between longer conversations about the location of air bases and nuclear weapons. With new leaders the message toned down even further. At Camp David, President George W. Bush raised Japanese whaling with Prime Minister Junichiro Koizumi, who 'volunteered cooperation'. An Administration official enthused how this showed 'every issue in which there is disagree-ment is more than swamped by the overall nature of the relationship, and how important the relationship is'.

When Prime Minister John Howard went to the country that he called Australia's best customer, a question from a Japanese journalist about whaling came as a diversion in a press conference preoccupied with the fate of the Mitsubishi plant in Adelaide. 'It has been proven scientifically that the population of Minke has been adequate enough for whaling. How long are you going to oppose?' Howard's response was self-evident. 'There are differences between Australia and Japan on that issue. We won't be changing our position.'

The escalation of the Antarctic hunt led Howard to write to Koizumi saying that as a 'close friend of Australia' it should drop the idea. Koizumi's office confirmed the letter had arrived, but had nothing further to say.

Despite his baby boomer image, Koizumi led a conservative party entrenched in power since World War Two, before an unchallenging media, reporting to a compliant population for whom whaling was barely even a curiosity. It was hard to find a time when Kozumi even commented. Eventually the issue turned up at a joint press conference with Prime Minister Helen Clark on a visit to New Zealand.

The Kiwi leader who was happy to take on Komatsu at a distance con-firmed there was a ritual expression of views. 'I registered that there is an ongoing difference of opinion,' Clark said. 'We have not dwelt on these issues today. They are well rehearsed.'

Koizumi ruminated blandly. 'I believe matters should be discussed on the basis of scientific research,' he said. 'Paying due consideration to the protection of resources and environment. That is Japan's position. Of course that differs from the anti-whaling position. But this difference, I believe, would not impede the good relations between our two countries.'

Clearly whaling ranked far down the list of concerns. According to the cynic's guide to the politics of whaling, this was how everybody wanted it anyway. By confining the vocal fight to the IWC, each side could earn handy political points at home without ever troubling the stock markets.

Electors in Australia knew, for example, that the country was isolated over its response to global warming. The Federal Government always had internal environmental disputes to fight. Hating whaling was easy—it was a nationally unifying, undisputed given. At the same time, Japan imported minerals, beef and seafood in a A$45 billion annual trade that was weighted heavily in Australia's favour. From New Zealand, Japan took aluminium, Kiwi fruit and cheese. Cars and electronics were shipped back to both. There was the whole interwoven annual US$193 billion trade of goods between Japan and the United States. None of this needed to be troubled by a flea like whaling.

The cynics' view was that everyone was satisfied to have the IWC as a stage to play out those well-rehearsed differences, giving anti-whaling countries a chance to rail at the IWC, and for pro-whaling governments to wangle approval of their hunt. There were problems with this notion, not least that the IWC *was* changing, and that many dissatifisied people bent their backs for decades or lifetimes either to stop whaling or keep on doing it.

Australian scientists worked to knock out the legs of scientific whaling arguments. They developed methods to age whales by the DNA of sloughed skin samples, and test their food from collected faeces. The Norwegian vet, Egil Ole Øen, dedicated a career to improving times to death. Relentlessly driven Japanese negotiators, like Joji Morishita, laboured until they physically dropped.

But if the cynics were partly right and no one really wanted to upset the balance of this small Cold War, perhaps that accounted for anti-whaling nations' appeasements over whales. So deeply were the animals corralled inside the IWC that their place in a wider world was forgotten. Scientists, other international organisations, even the courts, found them too volatile.

This showed when the New Zealand Government published a State of the Environment report for its dependency, the Ross Sea region, in 2001. Detailed and lavish, the report found most of the region had been little affected by human activities, and was largely in a pristine state. *Pristine?* As if the largest creature the world has known was never really there. As if the longest Blue whale recorded was not measured at the Ross Ice Shelf.

The report did run a series of graphs illustrating successive crashes in whale catches, and acknowledge that tens of thousands of whales had been taken. It said that commercial whaling would probably resume in the Ross Sea if the moratorium was lifted. But despite New Zealand's willingness to talk loudly in the IWC, this official report by the same government did not include whaling on its list of 'key environmental challenges'. This was the see-no-evil approach that governments took to balancing the politics of the Antarctic.

The same collective hand was held over official eyes when Sue Arnold, the woman who despised démarches, tried to wake the Commission for the Conservation of Antarctic Marine Living Resources (CCAMLR) to whaling. The Antarctic Treaty's marine organisation claims to be world leading because of its 'ecosystem approach' to fisheries. It looks at the effects of fishing on the total marine environment. Industrial whaling took away most of this ecosystem's largest predators, yet CCAMLR does not talk about whaling. Skirting around whales it uses the code words: 'other species'. After JARPA II was announced Arnold came to CCAMLR's annual meeting in Hobart to tilt at this windmill.

She wangled entry to the closed meeting with the only environmental organisation allowed to observe: the Antarctic and Southern Oceans Coalition. She could not address the meeting, but lobbied delegates at breaks, saying JARPA II usurped CCAMLR. Her legal advice said this organisation could investigate JARPA II if any country wanted to set the ball rolling. None did. The official report listed the numbers of whales to be taken, then moved on. The Australian Foreign Minister, Alexander Downer, came to the meeting and said the best way to stop Antarctic whaling was by something called 'diplomatic pressure'. It was more of what Arnold called the 'curious line of least resistance'.

This line was also taken over legal action against Japan. Humane Society International (HSI) tried to bring the whaling company, Kyodo Senpaku Kaisha Ltd, to an Australian court for breaching a Federal whale sanctuary declared in waters off the Australian Antarctic Territory, where whalers took much of their catch. The Federal Government argued against defending its own sanctuary, claiming it could cause a diplomatic breach with Japan. A Federal Court judge, James Allsop, agreed. He thought it would be futile to pursue a whaling company in Tokyo, even though many might think that to slaughter whales was deeply wrong. On appeal, HSI won the right at least to have the case heard and its claims formally weighed.

Wider legal action advocated by the International Fund for Animal Welfare was resisted by anti-whaling governments. IFAW put together impressive legal panels to suggest how Japan could be taken to global courts. The New Zealand jurist Sir Geoffrey Palmer applied his mind to the opinions. Despite being a forthright anti-whaler, he said: 'I'm not persuaded they have legal merit.'

Hideki Moronuki, at his Fisheries Agency desk, taunted Australia over the idea of a lawsuit. 'Yeah, I think it's a good idea,' he laughed. 'Both countries are members of the International Whaling Commission. Not the International Anti-Whaling Commission. So we have to prove our purpose. The International Court of Justice can identify which countries fulfil purpose best. So let's go to ICJ. If Australia should do that, Japan is more than happy.'

These were the words of an emboldened Japan. Arrayed against it were ineffectual joint diplomacy and a refusal by national leaders to take the issue head-on because of their concern for the rich broad relationship. Even discussion of whales was taboo in the organisation that governed their Antarctic stronghold. The courts were impotent or, worse, might help whalers confirm their rights. All that stood in Japan's way were the annoying activists of Greenpeace and Sea Shepherd, and the lack of enough votes to effect change in the IWC. That was next.

With an IWC meeting at its only five-star resort, the St Kitts Government was up to speed on Greenpeace. But its intelligence let it down on Ric O'Barry. St Kitts didn't want *Arctic Sunrise* to dock with its load of Greenpeace troublemakers, and refused permission for the ship to enter the little country's territorial waters. O'Barry quietly came through the airport on a tourist visa and walked onstage.

This American used to capture and train dolphins, including five that were Flipper. His epiphany came with the death of one of them. Ever since, he had campaigned against dolphin maltreatment. As Kittitian politicians made florid West Indian speeches to open the 58th IWC meeting, O'Barry, who had a media pass, stood up at the back of the room. Strapped to his chest was a flat screen showing video footage of Taiji's dolphin drive hunt. He walked up the aisle and planted himself silently in front of the Japanese delegation. They sat immobile, taunted by bloody scenes on a human television. As news cameras swarmed in, large security men hustled O'Barry out. Many people, taken aback by the sudden appearance of a man with something strapped around his chest, caught their breath.

IWC meetings are rich in theatre even without the O'Barrys, and the 2006 session at the Marriott in St Kitts was no exception. After years when the balance of power wobbled, it seemed a simple majority could tip to the whalers. They would gain a grip on decisions of the organisation for the first time since the 1980s.

Japanese desperation for this showed. When it didn't happen in 2005, Akira Nakamae, deputy director of the Fisheries Agency, took the microphone at Ulsan to loathe his foes. 'The anti-whaling people who criticise us with empty, non-persuasive and unbearable emotional language, full of lies, vulgarities, lacking grace—maybe to those it is useless to say anything,' he said. 'However the concept that we advocate, sustainable use of stock upon scientific grounds, has gained increasing importance every year.'

Nakamae shook a verbal fist at the room. 'Some of you seem glad some poor sustainable use countries could not attend this year's meeting. However next year they will all participate. The reversal of history, the turning point, is soon to come.'

This epic warning was followed within months by a strategic shift. After endless meetings discussing the IWC's central technical issue, the Revised Management Scheme, Japan declared it dead. The Dane, Henrik Fischer, had toiled on the RMS hoping to break the deadlock with phased-in commercial whaling in coastal waters. 'Middle-minded' European realists were encouraged when the US backed the plan if all high seas whaling was excluded. But by early 2006 any lingering steam had puffed out of the Fischer train.

'This situation is only benefitting those who like to have a big headline or political applause back home,' said the good policeman of Japanese whaling diplomacy, Joji Morishita. 'There shouldn't be another Never-ending Story.' In St Kitts, he said, Japan would begin 'normalising' this dysfunctional IWC.

Shabby and funky, St Kitts is a federation with neighbouring Nevis in the long island chain that rides the breezes of the Caribbean. The water-front of its main town, Basseterre, was a snapshot of West Indies history, surveyed by Frigate birds, those rakish thieves of other birds' catches.

At one end was the rusted and disused ship loader of a defunct sugar industry. Halfway into town stood the concrete fisheries complex, fronted by a plaque that commemorated this 'token of friendship and cooperation between Japan and Saint Christopher and Nevis, 2003'. Inside the locals bought flaccid parrot fish.

On a tiny traffic island nearby was a monument to 'Caleb Azariah Paul Southwell, National Hero, former Chief Minister and Premier'. His big bronze visage stared sombrely out to sea. A sign explaining him lay broken, and the surrounding white picket fence was smashed, perhaps by one of the big concrete mix trucks that roared past to a dockside building site.

A taxi driver explained the haste to me in a rich Kittitian accent. 'They're buildin' for shappin'. Cruise ships come in. We had the tours, but we didn't have no shappin'. Now we gonna have it.' And most things for sale would be unloaded over the same docks.

Over a hill from Basseterre was Frigate Bay, where the Marriott enclave stood like a castle above the peasants. Outside its walls there was serious crime. Two days before the meeting, a father of two was shot near the resort in an unexplained murder. On the meeting's last day, a 22-kilogram bale of cocaine worth perhaps US$500 000 was found along the beach, 'in the vicinity of Old Jack Tar Cabana'.

Inside the walls, the Marriott was an obese domain of wealthy indulgence with Manhattan prices, swimming lagoons and acres of air-conditioned rooms. Mainly white guests were served by mainly black staff. Bands played schmaltzy Marley—pop-softened reggae. It was hot, windy and off-season; the year's first hurricane had blown through to the north, and thunderstorms crashed past at night.

Close IWC watchers tend to hang out in the hotel lobby on meeting eve. This time the evening buzz at the Marriott was strongly pro-whaling.

An early win for them was the appearance of Mali's smiling Héry Coulibaly. Mali joined late in 2004, but failed to reach Ulsan. It was part of the lost African flock likely to come to St Kitts along with the newest Pacific recruit, the Marshall Islands.

Motivated by Japan's drive for control, the number of IWC members nearly doubled in a decade. On the first day, 65 delegations crammed into the Marriott's Royal Ballroom, surrounded by observers and media. Unlike other international organisations, such as the Antarctic Treaty, the IWC has steadily opened itself to view. The main meeting is entirely visible. There are limits to this generosity. Each NGO may have only one observer and is charged £610 for a seat, although many claim an extra chair for an 'interpreter'. Organisations like Greenpeace and the Japan Whaling Association sail under several names, and pay several times, to get their people through the door.

Like Ric O'Barry, others fly under the radar. I noticed one intense man with a £40 media accreditation who operated video coverage out of a backpack. After realising the Japanese had flashed an image of a dead Fin whale on *Nisshin Maru* across a screen in a Power Point show, I sought him out. It was the first time that any picture had been seen of the endangered giant just added to Japan's list. But despite its news value, none of the dozing television cameras had caught it.

The busy man thought for an instant and said: 'Oh yes! I have it!' I impressed on him—slightly patronisingly in retrospect—its importance and he readily promised to email it to me as soon as he could. It came with a friendly note, signed by Paul, of OrcaLab. My jaw dropped. It was Paul Spong. The man who realised in 1968 that an Orca was teaching him; who spied out the Soviet fleet at Mendocino Ridge for the first protest; and who walked up the stern ramp of a factory ship. Here he was in St Kitts, still bearing witness.

The first test of strength came over the meeting's agenda. For years Japan had wanted to strike off the list subjects it thought irrelevant to core IWC work—like humane killing or the entire work of a conservation committee. With a simple majority it could do that, but its proposal was relatively modest: eliminating debate on small cetaceans. Victory meant Japanese domestic dolphin hunts would be even less scrutinised.

17

VOYAGES

God seems to have made the whale as a proof of his power.

Nineteenth-century handbill

As whaling's warriors flew out of Anchorage to prepare for the next battle, a small, old American spacecraft was trekking further into the cosmos, 15.3 billion kilometres away. After exploring the outer planets, *Voyager I* had left the Solar System behind.

The mission of this highly successful relic of 1970s technology, and its twin, *Voyager II*, was to send back to Earth discoveries about other planets. After that, their trajectories sent them on to infinity. In a gesture of romantic hope, apt for the time they were launched, each carried a record of Earthly life on a gold-sheathed copper phonograph disc. Assembled by the US astronomer Carl Sagan, the Golden Record stored images and sounds to explain its origins to any alien life that might find it. It also made us think about our own trivial and precarious place in the physical universe.

The record's makers etched into the disc a series of natural sounds, including the surf and human laughter. Images were inscribed on it, among them a location map of the Solar System, explanations of continental drift, and of human conception. Before it was sent, most attention was paid to a series of greetings. These were addressed to any life that could decipher human languages—not to mention the diagrammatic instructions for the cartridge and stylus. Some salutations were thoughtful, others banal, and between each ran a few bars of Humpback song.

'So as to leave no hint of provincialism,' Sagan said, 'we mixed these characteristically human greetings with the "Hellos" of the Humpback whale—another intelligent species from the planet Earth sending greetings to the stars.'

The physical dynamism and confiding nature of the Humpback already make it charismatic, and its song adds another dimension entirely. The distinctive, sweeping cry is the first evidence we have of evolving culture in any large, dispersed non-human population on Earth. Culture here does not mean painting art, or holding eating utensils correctly. It means 'information or behaviour acquired from conspecifics through some form of social learning'.

Other animal species may learn in small numbers between themselves, and complex culture among Sperm whales is well studied. But they are not known to spread knowledge socially over great distances, let alone so quickly as to be revolutionary. In a little over two years to 1998, Australian scientists found an entirely new song swept to popularity from the West Australian Humpbacks to the Eastern stock, probably with one or more whales who shifted coasts and brought the hit with them.

Clearly these are animals with enough intelligence to value difference. There are probably other examples of cultural transfer among animals. But Humpback song was the first to be known, and fortunately it is also beautiful.

It has been dissected into graphic sonograms that have hung on walls as art, and been broken up for analysis using our words. Onomatopoeic lists soberly describe the components: moan, whistle, sigh, violin, squeal, gulp, chug, chainsaw, yap, chirp, n-chug, zp, oink, cry, roar, screal, whoomp, growl, ratchet. Assembled instead of dissected, these snatches make a swooping, soaring animal concerto, just the kind of warm and abstract sound that would fit nicely in a message to aliens. It also begs the question of who, to the aliens, would make more sense: the people or the Humpbacks?

As a Humpback singer hangs head down in the ocean, songs are produced internally by air piped along breathing passages and pushed upward through the the skull. Both genders make social sounds, but singing is a male thing, more complex than songbird melody. Shared by each stock, a song is repeated and slowly altered on the winter breeding grounds. Only the nuances differ. It's probably socially important for a male Humpback to keep up with these changes. Female Humpbacks are promiscuous, and songs are displays. Scientists puzzle about whether the males use them to outrank each other, or to directly serenade a cow. Singing generally ceases over the summer, but the Humpbacks remember the songs, and start singing again the following winter where they left off. Lest Humpbacks be thought too benign, it's as well to know that violent physical clashes between males are part of life in their world too.

Not much of this was known when Sagan included the calls of 'another intelligent species' on the Golden Record before the *Voyager* mission launch in 1977. They probably just seemed right at a time when whales were first being celebrated. There was also the grim possibility that this recorded song could be a requiem in space for something wonderful but disappeared.

As Roger Payne taped the actual song that eventually left Earth on the Golden Record, he was concerned the singers might have been exterminated from their greatest domain. 'The number of Humpbacks in the Southern Hemisphere seems dangerously low,' he said. 'Perhaps too low to provide the pool of genetic variability needed to survive the next natural or man-made crisis.'

For these and all other great whales, artificial trouble is very real. Though whaling slowed, in the decades after the *Voyager* launch environmental harm tilted some already precarious whale stocks closer to extinction. Whales were entangled in fishing gear and choked on plastics, struck by ships or poisoned by their anti-fouling paint, deafened or damaged by oceanic noises, and all the time climate change crept closer.

These threats focussed sharply on one teetering Gray whale population of the remote western North Pacific. Extinct in the Atlantic for hundreds of years, the Grays' stronghold was the eastern Pacific where they migrated between the Arctic and Baja California. Along the western Pacific coast, whalers scourged the population such that they were thought gone from there as well. None of the mottled grey and white animals the size of a Humpback had been seen for years.

Somewhere in remote waters shut by the Cold War, a few did survive. They were reported to the outside world in 1983 when marine biologists saw a group of twenty swimming off Sakhalin, a large, sparsely settled island north of Japan. The scientists told the IWC 'this gives at least some hope that the population is not extinct'.

Years of effort in identifying and tracking the Sakhalin Grays yielded a total of exactly 23 reproductively active females in the entire stock in 2005. Around fourteen of a total 92 identified whales were seriously undernourished. In that year alone, another three females drowned in Japanese fishing nets.

Entanglement and plastics threatened reviving whales globally. Plastics were silent killers, only appearing in necropsies of some stranded animals, like the Bryde's whale that washed ashore near Cairns in 2000 with 6 square metres of bags in its stomach. Entanglements became visible dramas as rescuers refined methods of chasing down and freeing whales. With increasing numbers of Humpbacks came more cases of calves drowned in shark-killing nets off Queensland's Gold Coast, and of sub-adults trailing lobster-pot lines off Western Australia, New England or South Africa. The whale by-catch from nets in Japan and Korea was another dimension worse; around 200 Minkes were taken 'accidentally' each year by fishers in these countries, who were allowed to sell the meat for cash.

Entanglement was just a difficult welfare issue for improving coastal stocks. For precarious populations like the Western Pacific Grays, the IWC's scientific committee said much more would mean the end. 'There is a substantial risk of extirpation by 2030. The 2005 level of by-catch is therefore unsustainable, and it is important to avoid further human-caused deaths in this depleted population.'

Unfortunately for the Grays, human impacts on their critical summer feeding grounds grew. One of the world's largest new oil and gas fields was found on Sakhalin's north-east coast. In an initial phase, Exxon Neftegas began seismic exploration in these waters.

The effect on whales of seismic testing of subsea geology by exploding airguns is disputed. At best there is evidence that male Humpbacks will approach a single airgun, perhaps mistaking it for the noise of another's breach. At worst, airgun blasts can fatally injure whales which are too close. The usual response of whales to the multiple airguns of a mineral seismic test is to avoid them, sometimes by many kilometres. Governments often forbid testing in critical seasonal habitat and set extra regulations to separate tests from visible whales.

Scientists at Sakhalin led by the American, Bob Brownell, said the Exxon Neftegas survey shifted the Grays out of a preferred feeding ground to less productive habitat at a time when four of the year's six mothers were already 'skinny' before their migration.

In the project's Phase 2, a consortium of Royal Dutch Shell, Mitsui and Mitsubishi needed to lay 126 kilometres of subsea pipeline from offshore wells that ran partly through the feeding grounds. With this came busy shipping, its poisons and its noise. Toxic anti-fouling chemicals painted on ships' hulls leach into the ocean and seep into marine life. A Dutch study found these chemicals in stranded Sperm whales. The worst, tributyltin oxide, may damage cetacean hearing.

Meanwhile commercial shipping has increased the average ambient noise levels in some seas by about ten decibels in a century. Each extra decibel doubles the volume. It's as if a fog of sound always blankets populated coasts and shipping routes, clouding the hearing that is critical to whales' movement. In a world with fewer whales, the task of locating their kind increases even more for ocean wanderers like the Blues and Fins. As ships run faster and more often, whales' chances of picking out and avoiding vessels decrease, and they are struck and killed. If a population is as small as the Pacific Grays or North Atlantic Rights, the loss of even a few individuals can be profound.

Pulses of military sound add to the fog, or can strike fatally. Naval active sonar 'lights up' the sea beneath the surface to track enemy movement. This sonar can be intense and long-ranging, and does kill whales. The US Natural Resources Defence Council said: 'A range of experts from the IWC Scientific Committee to the US Navy's own commissioned scientists agreed that the evidence linking mass strandings to mid-frequency sonar is convincing and overwhelming.'

The Sakhalin consortium led by Shell decided to put its pipeline plans to an independent panel convened by IUCN that found construction noise, ship strikes, habitat damage and potential exposure to oil and gas pollution were all dangers for Grays. The pipeline was re-routed and inspection systems were introduced as the project signed up energy suppliers in Japan. The total costs of the remote and complex Sakhalin project to the Shell consortium doubled to US$20 billion, but it was still viable in a world where the thirst for hydrocarbons seemed unquenchable.

For Western Pacific Grays, this thirst may prove to be a dominating threat to them, and all of their kind. Global warming is perturbing the oceans, and burning fossil fuels is most likely to blame. Heated oceans raised the average sea level up to 0.2 metres during the twentieth century, according to the Intergovernmental Panel on Climate Change. In the half century to 2000 there was a 40 per cent decline in Arctic sea ice. Around much of Antarctica, the signs were confused. Temperatures were steady and so was snowfall, but isolated evidence of serious upset appeared.

In 1999, scientists counted 274 dead Gray whales of the robust eastern Pacific stock—twice the number of any previous year. Many of the dead whales were emaciated and it was believed that the most likely cause was a decline in their main Arctic prey, amphipods, which in turn fell partial victim to increased water temperatures. 'Skinny Grays' were not just being pushed out of their feeding ground, they may have lost their feed.

For once, whaling helped to find out more. The Australian scientist Bill de la Mare remembered Antarctic whalers in the commercial era had worked into the pack ice edge. Looking back at old records he found that the southern limit of this ice around the continent had sharply retreated over a twenty-year period to the mid 1970s.

In the satellite era, when most sea-ice records started, it was roughly stable, except in the Antarctic Peninsula, where air temperatures rose up to 2.5 degrees in half a century, and in 2002, Larsen B became the largest in a series of floating ice shelves to collapse. Around the peninsula there was a decrease in the region's pack ice, resulting in lost habitat for the microbes that krill lives on. A study found that stocks fell by about 80 per cent in these, some of the world's most productive waters, putting at risk predators like whales. Emphasising the damage, increased harmful ultraviolet light caused by ozone depletion affected microbial sea life. These are dangers that lie ahead on a global scale. The 2007 IPCC report confirmed the polar ice packs will shrink 'under all scenarios'. In some projections, Arctic late summer sea ice will disappear entirely. The increasingly warmed breeding grounds did not look much safer. Warmer waters could intensify cyclones, increase run-off and change the balance of ocean minerals.

The widespread failure to respond strongly enough to climate change has reduced hope that we can dodge the worst of its effects. If the world's best agreed attempt at reining in global warming, the Kyoto protocol, were fully implemented, it would only slow warming by one twentieth of a degree at 2050. The conclusion reached by environmental scientist William Burns was that: 'Many of the potential impacts of climate change, including impacts on cetacean species, may be inevitable.'

On the *Voyager* Golden Record, one of the messages to space came from the plain-spoken Georgia peanut farmer and US President, Jimmy Carter. He described the contents of the record and then offered a humbling thought to its finders: 'We are attempting to survive our time so we may live into yours.'

In few cases have we done as badly at ensuring 'our time' survives as we have with whales. According to the founder of the IWC, Dean Acheson, they were to be wards of the entire world. We are still to agree what caring for them means.

For its part, the Japanese whaling machine would target more whales. Although consumers were beginning to wonder why, the state pushed whale hard, offering it free for school lunches from an annual stockpile that, at nearly 9000 tonnes in 2006, was increasing, though far short of a delicacy like Southern Bluefin tuna.

A species growing at around ten per cent each year, like the Humpback, is an easy proposition for whalers claiming they can take a sustainable yield. Perhaps Japanese consumers deprived of commercially extinct tuna, or hungry people in poor countries, might be persuaded they need to eat sub-sidised whale, rather than be uplifted by knowing they are unharmed.

Internationally, Japan would continue its insistent drive for whaling power. The Prime Minister from 2006, Shinzo Abe, belonged to a 98-strong parliamentary whaling league in the Diet that ritually claimed Japan should quit the IWC, and perhaps one day it would. Meanwhile it could work on IWC 'normalisation', and maintain the deceit of scientific whaling to tighten pressure for renewed commercial whaling, even though in doing this it would look little better than the lying Soviets. It would refuse to provide data if it reflected badly, fail to give a plausible explanation for doubling its take or killing endangered animals, and perpetuate trans-parently false claims that some whales suddenly threatened other species by their very existence. If lies were repeated often enough, perhaps they would be accepted as truth.

Death by harpoon would remain a lottery. Each year hundreds of whales would indisputably be conscious of the weapon after it struck and exploded, and many of those would be inflicted with prolonged, incomprehensible pain. Perhaps Humpbacks' confiding nature might make them easier targets for a sure kill.

Or the opposite might happen. Emboldened by indomitable activists, we would bring the contest to the Japanese and Norse people, and to vulnerable countries that fell under the sway of whalers. We would listen to *their* needs, and carrying tested science, tell the truth about why the long struggle over whales stood in sharp relief as an allegory for our times. With the strength of honesty, control of the IWC would eventually come.

We would say that whalers always did much better at turning away from the suffering they inflicted than they did at admitting it. Whether Bequian carousers, dour Norwegian fishers or highly trained Japanese gunners, it was time they stopped confusing nostalgia and humanity.

We would tell them that a transparent sustainable yield was not something factory whalers ever managed to achieve, and there was no reason to believe this would change. In fact, recurrent fisheries fraud increased the likelihood of deception. We would prove that whaling was no answer to a shortage of seafood; marine conservation was. There was much greater nourishment these inspiring creatures could give our spirits, telling us of capacities far beyond our own, and of the limits to Earth.

In all our unwitting environmental injury to whales, from net entanglement to warming seas, the path to repair is difficult and uncertain. With whaling, the deliberate hurt, all we need to achieve is a change of heart.

A stone farmhouse has stood overlooking Great Oyster Bay on Tasmania's east coast long enough to have known the waters as a noisy breeding ground for Rights and a common way-point for Humpbacks, more than a century ago. Few pass by now, but their memories are strewn around the house, which is decorated largely from the tide-line. In the garden is the greying skull of a small whale with its sculpted cradles for the mysterious sonar. A backbone the size of a footstool slowly disappears under she-oak needles. Long, sun-bleached Right whale ribs rest casually against outbuildings.

In a corner of the white-washed main room is a hand harpoon. The forged iron shaft and head were found on an ocean beach nearby, and given a new wooden handle. The head is wickedly ingenious. When the weapon is plunged through the hard skin and blubber layer, and the whale convulses in shock, a barb jerks the head open so that it turns from an 'I' to a 'T' in the softer flesh beneath, and holds fast.

I picked it up, clicked the head open, let it fall shut, and then returned the harpoon to the shadows, and the honest history of the house.

EPILOGUE

The winter of 2007 featured many sightings of the humpback. The humpback Migaloo's fame grew off Australia's Pacific coast. Whale-watching boat operators raced to find His Whiteness first and crowed when they did. Game fishermen posted a hazy video of his breaches on the Web instead of their leaping marlin. Tracking sightings down the coast, I spoke to a reliable witness who swore she glimpsed him as her jet took off from Sydney airport. As if to telegraph the peril ahead, a char-ter-boat skipper called two other humpbacks swimming with Migaloo "bodyguards."

When the migrating humpback herds turned to the Antarctic in 2007, and to their first threat of a harpoon since 1963, the struggle – intensified. For the United States and Japan, the fifty-humpback quota came into play on the greater chessboard of IWC reform. In Australia, as the celebrity spotting showed, it was personal, and it drove a fundamental shift in gov-ernment policy.

Which would prevail? Another quiet deal to realign the IWC with well-ordered geopolitics? Or was there a real chance to roll back whaling again?

Much was in the hands of Bill Hogarth, a genial Virginian biologist who was the director of fisheries for the U.S. National Oceans and Atmospheric Administration, he led the U.S. delegation when it backed compromise with the whalers, flirting with a return to tightly regulated coastal whaling in 2004. Now as IWC chairman, he coped patiently with Japan's ostenta-tious displeasure in Anchorage. After that, Hogarth kept talking to his vice chair, Minoru Morimoto, about how the humpbacks might figure into things.

Elsewhere the two powers kept whaling off the slate. When the fleet's ceremonial departure from Shimonoseki for the first full season of the – "research" program, JARPA II, coincided with new prime minister Yasuo Fukuda's visit to the White House, the sailing was delayed. No point in spoiling an occasion like that with embarrassment over a lower-order dis-pute like whaling. At the rescheduled farewell in Shimonoseki, expedition leader Hajime Ishikawa made a rousing speech, warning his crews to expect violent environmental terrorists. "We must fight against their hypocrisy and lies," he said.

There would be an extra factor in this equation though. In addition to Sea Shepherd and Greenpeace vessels, for the first time another government's ship would be sent to chase the whalers. The new center-left Australian Labor government had a policy to step up the pressure on Japan. It chose Oceanic Viking, a fisheries patrol ship, to gather video and photographic evidence for a potential international court case. Respectable legal opinions backing action had thumped repeatedly onto politicians' desks. But as one of the authors of these, the Australian National University's professor of international law, Don Rothwell, readily agreed, surveillance carried at least as much political weight.

An official government finger pointing at the whalers' bloody work day after day would be much less acceptable at home in Japan than repulsing scruffy greenies. The new Australian government, moreover, apparently wanted to maximize the embarrassment. "Slaughtering whales is not scientific," said the environment minister, former rock singer Peter Garrett. "It's cruel, it's barbaric, and it's unnecessary."

Within hours of the Australians unveiling their new policy, the U.S. government muscled in. The ambassador in Tokyo, Tom Schieffer, told reporters that he thought there might be an agreement with Japan not to kill humpbacks, at least until after the next IWC meeting. The agreement was the fruit of low-key shuttle diplomacy. A week earlier, Hogarth flew to Japan and asked Morimoto to drop the humpback hunt. The day Canberra made its announcement, December 19, Fisheries Agency of Japan officials were in the U.S. confirming they would shelve the quota. The whales' Australian white knight turned out to be only one piece on the global chessboard after all.

Scheiffer had recently delivered a long and reassuring speech detailing relations between Washington and Tokyo. He spoke about the rise of China and how this might affect the alliance (unsurprisingly, making no reference to whaling at all). But it did illuminate why Hogarth was so busy—and why Schieffer was the one to break the news.

"Back in my home state of Texas, we have an old saying—never trade an old friend for a new friend or you will wind up with no friends," Schieffer said. "When the U.S.-Japan alliance is strong, a calm settles over Asia."

It took two more days for the U.S.-Japan deal on humpbacks to unfold. Before it did, Australia organized yet another diplomatic démarche in which thirty-one countries stated that they "deeply regretted" Japan's entire scientific whaling program. The number did not include the United States, perhaps to preserve Hogarth's sensitivities as IWC chair. Tokyo kept to its habit of treating a démarche like a bad smell among genteel company, making no comment on it at all.

But the foreign minister, Masahiko Koumura, did call a press conference to report on a phone conversation with his counterpart in Canberra, Stephen Smith.

Koumura's version portrayed a generous Japan. He said that Hogarth told him the IWC was not working effectively, and he wanted Japan's help to remedy this. "Mr. Hogarth requested that Japan review its plan to catch humpback whales while such a reform is going on. I explained to Foreign Minister Smith that I had stated that Japan, as vice chair with the IWC, will cooperate with the reform of the IWC."

Then came the ultimatum.

"Also, with regard to the request from Mr. Hogarth concerning humpback whales, Japan has decided to postpone its catch of this species while the IWC is judged to move towards a normalization of its activities. If it is judged that no progress at all is being made towards normalization, then the situation and discussions on the issue would be of a different nature.'

For the first time in a long time, Japanese whalers seemed to have a setback. Some argued that the Humpbacks were set up as pawns to be surrendered . If so, it seemed clumsy. Why would the whalers want all that extra international attention to be transferred to the minkes and fins still facing the harpoon? Pursuit of the fleet was bound to go ahead, yielding many days of unflattering media coverage, and possibly leading to international legal action.

But in making the deal Hogarth understood that, for Japan at least, "normalization" meant a return to commercial whaling. He said, "This move can be seen as a bold step forward in breaking the impasse over whaling that has burdened the IWC for many years."

Elated Australians could look forward to another whale migration unaffected by the harpoon. But the whalers still held the humpbacks hostage.

ACKNOWLEDGEMENTS

This journey began without me realising, and even looking back it is hard to work out when. It could have been the time as a twelve-year-old that I stood on a headland in southern New South Wales and saw my first whale, powering though an ocean swell as if it were a ripple on a pond. Perhaps it was when a family friend gave me a yellowing Sperm whale tooth that I long imagined was a rhinoceros horn.

The way that plants or cooking seep into some people's lives, whales began to colour mine. Things began to collect around me that embroider *Harpoon*. In a market bookstall I found the memoirs of a Soviet whaler. One day a friend appeared outside my writing hut with a beach-washed Right whale's rib bone. For no particular reason, except that it bothered me, I kept a newspaper clipping for twenty years that described the sight of a blizzard whirling across a flensing deck to bring 'red snow'.

I had the good fortune to work as a journalist for Fairfax newspaper editors who understood the importance of pursuing an issue and, as a result, I travelled far. I voyaged twice to eastern Antarctica on Australian re-supply ships, and under the sponsorship of the Department of Foreign Affairs and Trade, went to Japan and Mexico to report on whaling. Japan's Ministry of Foreign Affairs generously invited me to visit, and its government's whaling agencies opened their doors to me repeatedly.

The wizard who tapped me with his wand to begin this book was Richard Walsh, of Allen & Unwin, but there are dozens of people in government, academic, scientific and NGO communities whose work enabled it.

I thank the International Whaling Commission secretariat, including Greg Donovan, Bernard Lynch and Julie Creek, for their always-neutral assistance. In libraries, others who opened doors for me included Andy Smithies and staff at the Australian Antarctic Division, Tony Marshall and staff at the Tasmaniana Library in the State Library of Tasmania, Lucy Johannsohn with the University of Tasmania, staff at the National Library of Australia, and the Institute of Cetacean Research in Tokyo. I praise the increasing trend to open scientific journals to ordinary people, through electronic means such as the Public Library of Science, and the readiness of

260

many scientific authors to respond to requests for their work from someone they had never heard of. Among those internationally who facilitate such help, David Janiger of the Los Angeles Natural History Museum stands out.

Equally free with their hard-won knowledge were Australian scientists including Graham Chittleborough, John Bannister, Bill de la Mare, Peter Gill, Nick Gales, Dan Burns and Rebecca Pirzl. I pay respects to those who over the years threaded their way through the maze of IWC argument with passion, particularly for Australia: Derrick Ovington, Peter Bridgewater, Conall O'Connell and Ian Campbell.

The issue has run long, and many have left it. Even so, some formerly involved made time for me, perhaps none so importantly as Mark Votier, the one-time photo journalist whose inside story is recorded here; and the former whalers of Albany, Gordon Cruickshank, Paddy Hart, Kase van der Gaag and Mick Stubbs. Among the NGOs who freely helped, I thank Nicola Beynon from Humane Society International; Pam Eiser of IUCN; Darren Kindleysides, Mick McIntyre and Vassili Papastavrou from the International Fund for Animal Welfare; John Frizell, Carolin Wenzel, Shane Rattenbury and Keiran Mulvaney of Greenpeace; Paul Watson of the Sea Shepherd Conservation Society; Rune Frovik of High North Alliance and, on behalf of the Institute of Cetacean Research, Glenn Inwood.

Harpoon was brought together with the constant care of Allen & Unwin, including trade publishing director Sue Hines, my book editor Clare Emery, copyeditor Rosanne Fitzgibbon, designer Nada Backovic and illustrator Guy Holt. The evocative species illustrations are the work of Uko Gorter of Kirkland, Washington State.

It is dedicated to Sally Johannsohn, without whose love and encouragement it would not have been written. Her delight in any achievement I made with this book validated my work. My parents, Geoff and Heather Darby, remain guides in my life.

This book recounts troubled international relations, particularly with Japan. I hope *Harpoon* may add a stone to the honest foundation that a lasting bridge between nations needs.

NOTES

Harpoon was commissioned in 2005, but it is based on work that began over a decade earlier. Much of the material in this book came from interviews and press conferences, emails and telephone calls, IWC meetings and lobby exchanges. As a rule, if a matter of fact or quotation is not discoverable in these endnotes, then it has come from my own research or is common knowledge. Any errors are mine.

PROLOGUE

p. xi 'In the north . . . than ten days.' W.A. Watkins, 'Radio tagging of finback whales—Iceland, June–July 1980', *Technical report*, WHOI-81-2, in N. Bose and J. Lien, 'Propulsion of a Fin whale', *Proceedings of the Royal Society 'B'*, vol. 237, 1989, p. 197.

'A 48-tonne . . . of its year.' P.F. Brodie, 'Form, function and energetics of Cetacea: a discussion', in R.J. Harrison, *Functional anatomy of marine mammals*, vol. 3, Academic Press, London, 1977, p. 48.

'Organising this banquet . . . at a time.' J. Goldbogen et al., 'Kinematics of foraging dives and lunge-feeding in Fin whales', *Journal of Experimental Biology*, The Company of Biologists, London, vol. 209, 17 March 2006, p. 1231.

'A Fin's right . . . for the gulp.' C. Madsen and L. Herman, 'Social and ecological correlates of cetacean vision and visual appearance', in L.M. Herman, ed., *Cetacean behavior: mechanism and functions*, Wiley, New York, 1980, p. 115.

p. xii 'In the Japanese . . . recovery of Blues.' Government of Japan, *Plan for the Second Phase of JARPA II—monitoring of the Antarctic ecosystem and development of new management objectives for whale resources*, IWC/SC57/01, and S. Nishiwaki et al., *Cruise Report of the Second Phase of JARPA II in 2005–2006, Feasibility study*, IWC/SC/58/07, International Whaling Commission, Cambridge, 2005/6.

'Overall whale numbers . . . the same food.' S. Childerhouse et al., *Comment on the Government of Japan's Proposal for a Second Phase of Special Permit Whaling in Antarctica (JARPA II)*, IWC/SC/57/022, IWC, Cambridge, 2006.

'The implacable Japanese . . . of scientific whaling.' N. Gales et al., 'Japan's whaling plan under scrutiny', Commentary in *Nature*, vol. 435, 16 June 2005, pp. 883–4.

'In a recent . . . third, grenadeless, harpoon.' The hunters' organisation and Greenland Home Rule Government, *Whale killing methods and associated welfare issues in Greenland*, IWC/58/WKM&AWI 17, IWC, Cambridge, 2006.

'Japan said data . . . not be provided.' *Report of the Workshop on Whale Killing Methods and Associated Welfare Issues*, IWC/58/Rep 7, IWC, Cambridge, 2006.

p. xiv 'Before Japan stopped . . . minutes to die.' S. Ohsumi, 'A Preliminary note on Japanese records on death times for whales killed by whaling harpoon', in *Report of the International Whaling Commission, 27*, IWC, Cambridge, 1977, p. 204; and H. Ishikawa, *Improvement of the time to death in the Japanese Whale Research Program in the Antarctic Sea (JARPA) and Northwestern Pacific Ocean (JARPN and JARPN II)*, IWC/57/WKM&AWI 11, IWC, Cambridge, 2005.

'In the Southern . . . never killed before.' P. Brakes and M. Donoghue, *Killing whales under special permit: the special case of the Fin whale*, IWC/58/WKM&AWI 8, IWC, Cambridge, 2006.

pp.xiv–xv 'It was followed . . . a favoured food.' S. Nishiwaki et al., *Cruise Report of the Second Phase of the Japanese Whale Research Program under Special Permit in the Antarctic (JARPA II) in 2005/2006—Feasibility study*, p. 16.

I RIGHT

CHAPTER 1

p. 2 'Instead he lapsed . . . squalor of man.' B. Chatwin, *In Patagonia*, Simon & Schuster, 1977, p. 128.

p. 5 'Raising his head . . . fit to lowering.' R. Copping, *Journal of reminiscences of Richard Copping, a crewman on Caroline*, April 1833, Archives Office of Tasmania.

p. 6 'It being a . . . being pulled under.' E. Tregurtha, *The Tregurtha Log, relating the adventurous life of Capt. Edward Primrose Tregurtha*, ed. D. Sprod, Blubber Head Press, 1980, p. 105.

p. 7 'The Nuenone Aboriginal . . . in the bay.' C. Pybus, *Community of thieves*, Heinemann Australia, Sydney, 1991, p. 13.

'We have had . . . get supplied with.' W. Bligh, *The Log of HMS Bounty 1787–1789*, Genesis Publications, Guildford, 1975, pp. 288–308.

p. 9 'Had its brothers . . . their oleaginous remains.' J. Jorgensen, *Jorgen Jorgensen's observations on Pacific trade, and sealing and whaling in Australian and New Zealand waters before 1805*, ed. R. Richards, The Paremata Press, Wellington, p. 62.

'a great many . . . the colonists' sleep.' R. Knopwood, *The diary of the Reverend Robert Knopwood, 1803–1838*, ed. M. Nicholls, Tasmanian Historical Research Association, 1977, p. 83.

p. 10 'The midshipman and . . . disappeared at once.' W. Tench, *Sydney's first four years, being a reprint of A narrative of the expedition to Botany Bay, and a Complete account of the settlement at Port Jackson*, Library of Australian History, North Sydney, pp. 175–178.

'I make no . . . not seen yet.' Knopwood, *The diary*, p. 85.

pp. 10–11 'July 1805. Friday . . . Town this day.' Knopwood, *The diary*, pp. 87–90.

p. 11 'She struck at . . . with her fins.' Knopwood, *The diary*, p. 110.

'He struck her . . . stiff with cold.' Knopwood, *The diary*, p. 136.

p. 12 'The lieutenant governor . . . like lamp oil.' L. Robson, *A history of Tasmania, volume I, Van Diemen's Land from the earliest times to 1855*, Oxford University Press, Melbourne, 1983, p. 56.

'On drawing near . . . greediness and rapture.' Tench, *Sydney's first four years*, p. 176.

p. 13 'August 1819, Thurs . . . see the whales.' Knopwood, *The diary*, p. 311.

'Almost all were . . . the nineteenth century.' M. Nash, *The bay whalers: Tasmania's shore-based whaling industry*, Navarine Publishing, Woden, ACT, 2003, *passim*.

p. 14 'The more one . . . place of work.' P. Kostoglou, 'When whaling was a war', in *The archaeology of whaling in Southern Australia and New Zealand*, eds S. Lawrence and M. Staniforth, Brolga Press for the Australasian Society for Historical Archaeology, Curtin, 1998, p. 103.

p. 15 'Whalers are, I . . . clearing the lungs.' J. Boultbee, *The journal of a rambler, the journal of John Boultbee*, ed. J. Starke, Oxford University Press, Melbourne, 1986, pp. 118–21.

'The cerelity with . . . a grand sight.' G. Robinson, *Friendly mission: the Tasmanian journals and papers of George Augustus Robinson*, ed. N. Plomley, Tasmanian Historical Research Association, 1966, p. 71.

p. 16 'Through the superior . . . of inanimate matter.' G. Robinson, *Friendly mission*, p. 71.

'A neatly typed . . . out the toll.' W. Dawbin, 'Right whales caught in waters around South Eastern Australia and New Zealand during the nineteenth and early twentieth centuries', *Report of the International Whaling Commission, Special Issue 10*, IWC, Cambridge, 1986, p. 261.

p. 17 'Monday 31 July . . . cask of beef.' H. Wishart, Log of the *Lady of the Lake*, Crowther Collection, State Library of Tasmania.

p. 18 'Western Australia, killing . . . 1834 to 1847.' J. Bannister, 'Notes on nineteenth century catches of Southern Right whales (*Eubalaena australis*) off the southern coasts of Western Australia', *Report of the IWC, Special Issue 10*, IWC, Cambridge, 1986, p. 255.

'When a good . . . of their treasures.' E. Booth, *Australia: a travelogue through the Down Under part of the British Empire*, vol. 1, Virtue and Co., London, 1874, p. 12.

p. 19 'Black whales enter . . . already greatly diminished.' W. Breton, *Excursions in New South Wales, Western Australia and Van Diemen's Land*, Johnson Reprint Corp., New York, 1970, p. 412.

'My host was . . . the living quarters.' B. Demas, 'Aspects of Tasmania', in H. Rosenman, ed., *Two voyages to the South Seas by J. S-C. Dumont D'Urville, Vol. II: Astrolabe and Zelee 1837–1840*, Melbourne University Press, 1987, p. 508.

CHAPTER 2

p. 21 R. Carson, *Silent spring*, Penguin, Harmondsworth, 1962, p. 257.

'The documentary evidence . . . Bay of Biscay.' A. Aguilar, 'A review of old Basque whaling and its effect on the Right whales of the North Atlantic', *Report of the IWC, Special Issue 10*, IWC, Cambridge, p. 191.

p. 22 'Archaeologists in Canada . . . relative, the Bowhead.' S. Cumbaa, 'Archaeological evidence of the 16th century Basque Right whale fishery in Labrador', *Report of the IWC, Special Issue 10*, p. 187.

'North American colonists . . . migration came inshore.' R. Reeves and E. Mitchell, 'The Long Island, New York, Right whale fishery: 1650–1924', *Report of the IWC, Special Issue 10*, p. 201.

'More prized was . . . the most oil.' H. Omura, 'History of Right whale catches in the waters around Japan', *Report of the IWC, Special Issue 10*, p. 35.

p. 23 'American whalers are . . . took them uncounted.' P.B. Best et al., eds, *Journal of Cetacean Research and Management, Special Issue 2, Right whales: worldwide status*, IWC, Cambridge, 2001, passim.

'In 1998, IWC . . . and a future.' P.B. Best, ed., 'Report of the IWC/MTN Workshop on Assessing the Status of Right Whales Worldwide', in *Journal of Cetacean Research and Management, Special Issue 2, Right whales: worldwide status*, IWC, Cambridge, 2001, pp. 1–60.

p. 24 'The whale holds . . . through the water.' R. Payne, *Among whales*, Scribner, New York, 1995, p. 118.

'Five metres is . . . whales and sharks.' R. Payne, 'Long term behavioral studies of the Southern Right whale (*Eubalaena australis*)', in *Report of the IWC, Special Issue 10*, pp. 161–67.

p. 25 'When approached by . . . a karate stance.' R. Payne, *Among whales*, pp. 105–6.

'Rights emerge as . . . conversation in between.' C. Clark, 'Acoustic communication and behavior of Southern Right whales', in R. Payne, ed., *Communication and behavior of whales*, AAAS Selected Symposium, Westview Press Inc., Boulder, 1983, p. 163.

'One female seen . . . is anatomically possible.' B. Mate et al., 'Observations of a female North Atlantic Right whale (*Eubalaena glacialis*) in simultaneous copulation with two males: supporting evidence for sperm competition', *Aquatic Mammals*, 31(2) 2005, p. 157.

'A colder view . . . reach the female.' R. Connor, 'Male reproductive strategies and social bonds', in J. Mann et al., *Cetacean societies: field studies of whales and dolphins*, The University of Chicago Press, Chicago, 2000, p. 259.

'Competitive mating may . . . energy in pregnancy.' P. Best et al., 'Composition and possible function of social groupings of Southern Right whales in South African waters', in *Behaviour*, 140, no. 11–12, 2003, pp. 1469–94.

'The one-tonne . . . another year later.' S. Burnell, 'Aspects of reproductive biology, movement and site fidelity of Right whales off Australia', in *Journal of Cetacean Research and Management, Special Issue 2*, pp. 89–102.

p. 26 'The audacious James . . . and turned north.' K. Bowden, *Captain James Kelly of Hobart Town*, Melbourne University Press, Parkville, 1964, p. 73.

'An Australian map . . . of 63 degrees.' J. Carpenter, *Map shewing whaling grounds in portion of Southern Hemisphere, 1892*, Crowther Collection, State Library of Tasmania.

'Scottish and Norwegian . . . and Arne Johnsen.' J.N. Tønnessen and A.O. Johnsen, *The history of modern whaling*, C. Hurst and Co., ANU Press, Canberra, 1982, p. 151.

p. 27 'they absquatulated in . . . defaulting bank clerk.' J. Bannister, 'Status of Southern Right whales (*Eubalaena australis*) off Australia', in *Journal of Cetacean Research and Management, Special Issue 2*, p. 105.

'The sightings cruise . . . after 96 days.' J. Bannister et al., 'Right whales off Southern Australia: direct evidence for a link between onshore breeding grounds and offshore probable feeding grounds', SC/48/SH28 in *Report of IWC 57*, Cambridge, 1997, pp. 441–444.

'Its Article 4 . . . is prohibited.' *Convention for the Regulation of Whaling 1931*, signed at Geneva 24 September 1931, entered into force, 16 January 1935.

p. 28 'A scientific paper . . . the world's sight.' D.D. Tormosov et al., 'Soviet catches of Southern Right whales, *Eubalaena australis*, 1951–1971. Biological data and conservation implications', in *Biological Conservation*, 86, 1998, pp. 185–97.

p. 29 'The whale suffered . . . to fall off.' 'Yet another death and near death for the critically endangered Right whales', press release, *New England Aquarium*, Boston, 16 March 2005.

'Amy Knowlton and . . . bore propellor scars.' D.W. Laist et al., 'Collisions between ships and whales', in *Marine Mammal Science*, 17(1) : 35–75, January 2001, p. 36.

II BLUE

CHAPTER 3

p. 34 'At length everything . . . creatress and perfectress.' Lucretius, *On the nature of the universe*, Book II, Line 1149, trans. R. Latham, Penguin, Harmondsworth, 1951, p. 93.

'He pencils it . . . of his research.' P. Gill, 'A Blue whale feeding ground off southern Australia: preliminary findings', Paper SC/52/OS9 presented to the IWC Scientific Committee, IWC, Cambridge, June 2000; P. Gill and M. Morrice, 'Ecology of Blue whales in the Bonney Upwelling Region', Progress report to the Department of Environment and Heritage, Canberra, June, 2004, passim.

NOTES

p. 37 'August 2—at . . . all down-hearted.' H. Swift, Log of the whaling barque *Islander*, 1 January 1881–21 December 1881, Crowther Collection, State Library of Tasmania, Hobart.

p. 38 'He overcame pack . . . in his wake.' F. Schmitt et al., *Thomas Welcome Roys, America's pioneer of modern whaling*, University Press of Virginia, 1980, p. 29.

'It will come . . . centuries to come.' T. Roys, 'The description of whales', The Mariner's Museum, Newport News, Virginia, 1980, pp. 21–22.

'We shot 22 . . . shells all exploded.' T. Roys, quoted in J.N. Tønnessen and A.O. Johnsen, *The history of modern whaling*, C. Hurst & Co., ANU Press, Canberra, 1982, p.16.

p. 39 'Svend Foyn's grenade . . . practical purposes unaltered.' Tønnessen and Johnsen, *The history of modern whaling*, p. 35.

'Commander Foyn's victory . . . superiority of man.' H. Bull, *The cruise of the Antarctic to the South Polar regions*, Edward Arnold, London, 1896, p. 17.

'Sometimes a Blue . . . until it sank.' Tønnessen and Johnsen, *The history of modern whaling*, p. 162.

p. 40 'Streaming north in . . . krill, *Euphausia superba*.' A. Atkinson, et al., 'Long term decline in Antarctic krill stock and increase in salps within the Southern Ocean', *Nature*, 432, 2004, pp. 100–3.

p. 41 'The elements of . . . poetry of whaling.' F. Hurley, *A Blue whale and whaling men on the flensing or cutting up plan at the Grytviken whaling station*, Picture Australia image, nla.pic-an23478495, National Library of Australia, Canberra.

p. 42 'Some including the . . . Shetlands in 1926.' G. Small, *The Blue whale*, Columbia University Press, New York, 1971, p. 32.

'The practical Tønnessen . . . Sea in 1923–24.' Tønnessen and Johnsen, *The history of modern whaling*, pp. 319, 346.

'Quite small noises . . . thoroughly scared whale.' A. Bennett, *Whaling in the Antarctic*, W.M. Blackwood & Sons Ltd., Edinburgh, 1931, pp. 168–69.

'Now a ribbed . . . and pure water.' F. Ommanney, *South latitude*, Longmans, Green & Co., London, 1938, p. 51.

p. 43 'If means can . . . future of whaling.' Bennett, *Whaling in the Antarctic*, p. 164.

'If Norway was . . . in twenty years.' Tønnessen and Johnsen, *The history of modern whaling*, pp. 342–43.

'The bankruptcy of . . . the whale's salvation.' Bennett, *Whaling in the Antarctic*, p. 211.

'These giant argosies . . . *last full cargo*.' A. Villiers, *Whaling in the Frozen South: being the story of the 1923–24 Norwegian whaling expedition to the Antarctic*, Robert McBride & Co., New York, 1925, Introduction.

CHAPTER 4

p. 45 'Only in the . . . the living world.' E. Wilson, *The diversity of life*, Penguin, Harmondsworth, 1992, p. 333.

'The Italians estimated . . . rorquals were recorded.' M. Azzali and J. Kalinowski, 'Spatial and temporal distribution of krill *Euphausia superba* biomass in the Ross Sea (1989–1990 and 1994)', in *Ross Sea ecology*, eds F.M. Faranda, L. Guglielmo and A. Ianora, Springer-Verlag, Berlin, 2000, pp. 436–53.

p. 46 'whales were spouting all around.' R. Huntford, *Shackleton*, Hodder and Stoughton Ltd., London, 1985, p. 204.

'Alan Villiers recounts . . . fat, big Blues.' Villiers, *Whaling in the frozen south*, p. 102.

'Nothing ever daunts . . . which they pass.' Villiers, *Whaling in the frozen south*, p. 124.

p. 47 'Allright Brarmull. Don't . . . to it boys!' H. Brammall, Part of the original Ross Sea whaling diary of Henric Brammall, aged 18, Crowther Collection, State Library of Tasmania, Hobart.

'Slowly the enormous . . . their own bodies.' H. Brammall, 'Whaling under the midnight sun', unpublished manuscript held in the Crowther Collection, State Library of Tasmania, Hobart.

'In a blizzard . . . over the ship.' 'The barbarity of "red snow"', *Mercury*, Hobart, 5 May, 1987, p. 23.

'On his first . . . over bad food.' W. Stewart's diaries extracted in L. Norman, *Haunts of the Blue whale*, OBM Publishing, Hobart, 1978, passim.

p. 48 'He was very . . . the Ross Sea.' H. Brammall, Part of the original Ross Sea whaling diary of Henric Brammall, aged 18.

'The peak of . . . never brought aboard.' Tønnessen and Johnsen, *The history of modern whaling*, p. 386.

pp. 48–49 'The Pacific and . . . for existing licensees.' Pacific and Ross Sea Whaling Company, Sydney, prospectus, 1929, Crowther Collection, State Library of Tasmania, Hobart.

p. 49 'The carbolic in . . . there might be.' C. Wilson, *The History of Unilever*, Cassell & Co. Ltd, London, 1954, p. 130.

'the key was . . . at room temperature.' K. Hunt, 'Raw materials', in *Margarine: an economic, social and scientific history*, ed. J.H. van Stuyvenberg, Liverpool University Press, 1969, *passim*.

p. 51 'Trawling through them . . . in 1939–40.' Tønnessen and Johnsen, *The history of modern whaling*, pp. 318, 319, 183, 313.

'The first serious . . . between major companies.' P. Birnie, *International regulation of whaling*, Oceana Publications, Inc., New York, 1985, vol. 1, pp. 116–18.

p. 52 'In an echo . . . one more time.' A. Kalland and B. Moeran, *Japanese whaling*, Curzon Press, Richmond, UK, 1992, pp. 83–84.

'Many didn't make . . . in February 1943.' Tønnessen and Johnsen, *The history of modern whaling*, pp. 418, 469.

'Unrationed when other . . . did in Japan.' C. Driver, *The British at table*, Chatto & Windus, London, 1983, p. 40 and Patten, M., *Post-war kitchen*, Hamlyn, London, 1988, p. 34.

p. 53 'In McCracken's navy . . . even looking up.' D. McCracken, *Four months on a Jap whaler*, Robert McBride & Co., New York, 1948, p. 3.

p. 54 'The general's decision . . . had good skills.' M. Komatsu and S. Misaki, *The history and science of whales*, The Japan Times, Tokyo, 2004, p. 95.

'The Norwegian analysts . . . meat clearly counted.' Kalland and Moeran, *Japanese whaling*, p. 90.

'MacArthur at the . . . or British viceroy.' P. Calvocoressi, *World politics since 1945*, Longman, London, 1977, p. 78.

'He overrode the . . . still go whaling.' SCAP Memo APO500, 6 August 1946, reproduced in Komatsu and Misaki, *The history and science of whales*, p. 96.

p. 55 'McCracken "somewhat jokingly . . . to count the cost.' McCracken, *Four months on a Jap whaler*, pp. 201–5.

p. 56 'A side of . . . to increase production.' K.J. Coonan, Official Report on the Operations of the Japanese Whaling Factory Ship—SS *Hashidate Maru*, Department of Commerce & Agriculture, Commonwealth Fisheries Office, Sydney, 15 April 1947, pp. 5–6.

p. 57 'saved many people . . . death by starvation.' M. Komatsu and S. Misaki, *Whales and the Japanese*, Institute of Cetacean Research, Tokyo, 2003, p. 66.

CHAPTER 5

p. 58 'A man cannot . . . utmost muscular force.' C. Darwin, *The expression of the emotions in man and animals*, John Murray, London, 1872, p. 72.

p. 59 'The whole purpose . . . sodden, driven slaves.' W. Duranty, 'Red Russia of today ruled by Stalinism, not by Communism', *The New York Times*, 14 June 1931.

'There were 15 . . . equalled our record.' A. Solyanik, *Cruising in the Antarctic*, Foreign Languages Publishing House, Moscow, 1956, p. 74.

p. 60 'wards of the entire world.' Tønnessen and Johnsen, *The history of modern whaling*, p. 532.

p. 61 'Graphs of kills . . . in the bust.' R. Gambell, 'Birds and mammals—Antarctic whales', in W. Bonner and D. Walton, eds, *Key environments: Antarctica*, Pergamon, 1985, p. 235.

'In off hours . . . five-year plan.' Solyanik, *Cruising in the Antarctic*, p. 29.

'The seasonal quota . . . on November 17.' Solyanik, *Cruising in the Antarctic*, p. 29.

p. 62 'Actually in November . . . of the hunt.' V. Zemsky, Y. Mikhalev and A. Berzin, 'Supplementary information about Soviet whaling in the Southern Hemisphere', *Report of IWC 46*, 1996, pp. 131–38.

p. 63 'Ivashin was aided . . . a saleable commodity.' V. Danilov-Danil'yan and A. Yablokov eds, *Soviet Antarctic whaling data 1947–72*, Center for Russian Environmental Policy, Moscow, 1995, p. 5.

'At the same . . . lactating females alike".' I.F. Golovlev, in A. Yablokov and V. Zemsky, eds, *Soviet whaling data 1949–1979*, Center for Russian Environmental Policy, Moscow, 2000, pp. 11–24.

'Naturally, if it . . . would increase greatly.' Solyanik, *Cruising in the Antarctic*, p. 51.

pp. 63–64 'As a rule . . . about our work".' Golovlev, in Yablokov and Zemsky, *Soviet Antarctic whaling data 1949–79*, p. 16.

p. 64 'The IWC-approved . . . were numerical phantoms.' V. Zemsky, Y. Mikhalev and A. Berzin, 'Supplementary information about Soviet whaling', *Report of IWC 46*, 1996, Table 6: 'Slava catches by month and species'.

pp. 64–65 'The reason was . . . a catch ban.' Y. Mikhalev, 'Biological characteristics of Blue whales taken during the first cruises of the whaling fleet *Slava*', IWC SC/51/CAWS/41, 1999.

p. 65 'There with a . . . grounds of "reciprocity".' International Commission on Whaling, *Fourth report of the Commission*, London, 1953, p. 7.

'The *Slava* was . . . equipment were seen.' P.R. Heydon, Memorandum for The Secretary, Department of External Affairs, Canberra, 23 December 1949, Series A1838, File 1514/4, National Archives of Australia, Canberra.

p. 66 'Quaintly, the Australian . . . four other chiefs.' L. McMillan, Memorandum for The Secretary, Department of External Affairs, Canberra, 14 November 1951, Series A1838, File 1514/4, National Archives of Australia, Canberra.

'His contribution to . . . Chile and Peru.' Tønnessen and Johnsen, *The history of modern whaling*, pp. 552–59.

'Famously, he equipped . . . whale tooth footrests.' L.J. Davis. *Onassis and Christina*, Victor Gollancz, London, 1987, pp. 18, 128.

p. 67 'An unheard of . . . twice the average.' Tønnessen and Johnsen, *The history of modern whaling*, p. 592.

'Actually, *Slava*'s report . . . to run out.' Zemsky, Mikhalev and Berzin, 'Supplementary information about Soviet whaling, *Report of IWC 46*, Table 6.

pp. 67–68 'All the whaling . . . against aerial observers.' E. Chernyi, in Yablokov and Zemsky, *Soviet whaling data 1949–1979*, pp. 25–30.

p. 68 'The *Yuri Dolgoruki* . . . Great Australian Bight.' Danilov-Danil'yan and Yablokov, *Soviet Antarctic whaling data 1947–72*, pp. 183–87.

p. 69 'The convention established . . . Tasmanian territorial waters.' C.W. Harders, Memorandum to the Attorney-General, *Soviet whaling vessels in waters near Tasmania*, 21 April 1964, Series A432, Item 1964/3131, National Archives of Australia, Canberra.

p. 70 'I haven't given . . . it's habit-forming.' News of the Day, *The Age*, Melbourne, 27 April 1964.

CHAPTER 6

p. 71 'Pygmies raised on . . . the giants themselves.' M. Lucanus, *The Civil War*, Book 1, II 10 in J. Bartlett, *Familiar quotations*, 15th edition, Little, Brown, 1980.

'The long, low . . . hundreds of kilometres.' C.W. Clark, 'Applications of US Navy underwater hydrophone arrays for scientific research on whales', in M. Annex, *Report of the Scientific Committee*, IWC 45, 1995.

pp. 71–72 'A group of . . . thousandth their size.' R. McCauley et al., *Western Australian exercise area, Blue Whale Project, Final summary report*, Australian Defence, Perth, October 2004, p. 13. Also K.S. Jenner et al., *Evidence of Blue whale feeding in the Perth Canyon*, Centre for Whale Research, Fremantle, 2001.

p. 73 '. . . Japan's fleet expanded . . . the Japanese palate.' Kalland and Moeran, *Japanese whaling*, p. 90.

'Modern whaling ceases . . . and Sei whales.' N.A. Mackintosh, *The stocks of whales*, Fishing News Books, London, 1965, p. 177.

pp. 73–74 'Ichihara argued the . . . near its centre.' T. Ichihara, 'The Pygmy Blue whale, *Balaenoptera musculus brevicauda*, a new subspecies from the Antarctic', in K. Norris, ed., *Whales, dolphins and porpoises*, University of California Press, Berkeley, 1966, pp. 108–9.

p. 74 'The American author . . . immature True Blues.' G. Small, *The Blue whale*, pp. 200–1.

'There is a . . . current sustainable yield.' N. Mackintosh, *The stocks of whales*, p. 202.

pp. 74–75 'The second-ranked . . . a deliberate hunt.' W. Hobart, ed., 'The Fin whale', 'The Sei whale', in *Marine Fisheries Review*, Special Issue 61(1), National Oceanic and Atmospheric Administration, Washington DC, 1999.

p. 75 'According to non-official . . . large scale falsification.' Yablokov and Zemsky, eds, *Soviet whaling data 1949–1979*, p. 7.

'Sidney Holt thinks . . . to Japanese transports.' S. Holt, 'Introductory remarks—preliminary thoughts', in *Investigating the roles of cetaceans in marine ecosystems*, CIESM Workshop Monographs, No. 25, Venice, 2004, p. 24.

'Japan's coastal whaling . . . its own coasts.' T. Kasuya, 'Examination of the reliability of catch statistics in the Japanese coastal Sperm whale fishery', *Journal of Cetacean Research and Management*, 1(1) 1999, pp. 109–22.

'the last true . . . March of 1973.' Zemsky, Mikhalev and Berzin, 'Supplementary information about Soviet whaling', *Report of IWC* 46, 1996, table.

p. 76 'The best estimate . . . No one really knew.' T. Branch et al., 'Evidence for increases in Antarctic Blue whales based on Bayesian modelling', in *Marine Mammal Science*, 20(4): pp. 726–54, October 2004.

'Many sighting cruises . . . eastern Ross Sea.' K. Matsuoka et al., *Distribution and abundance of Humpback, Fin and Blue whales in the Antarctic areas IIIE, IV, V and VI W*, Institute of Cetacean Research, Tokyo, 2005, *passim*.

p. 77 'Their current scarcity . . . illegal Soviet whaling.' Branch et al., *Marine Mammal Science*, 20(4), p. 746.

'In the northern . . . the North Atlantic.' W. Hobart, ed., *Marine Fisheries Review*, Special Issue 61(1), pp. 40–42.

'The Pgymy Blue . . . stock, survive today.' J. Bannister, et al., *The Action Plan for Australian Cetaceans*, Blue whale, Environment Australia, September 1996, p. 231.

III SPERM

CHAPTER 7

p. 80 'Enough is known . . . had only listened.' P. Morgane, 'The whale brain', in J. McIntyre, ed., *Mind in the waters*, Scribner, New York, 1974, p. 93.

p. 82 'The Sperm was . . . any wilful attack.' T. Beale, *The natural history of the Sperm whale*, The Holland Press, London, 1839, pp. 4–5.

p. 83 'Filtered Sperm oil . . . of ballistic missiles.' S. Frost, *Whales and whaling: Report of the Independent Inquiry*, AGPS, Canberra, 1978, p. 288.

'To people with . . . taste most unpleasant.' R. Ellis, *Men and whales*, Robert Hale, London, 1992, p. 406.

p. 84 'The aroma is . . . ambergris still remains.' R.C. Murphy, 'Floating gold', in *Natural History Magazine*, March–April and May–June 1933, <http://www.naturalhistorymag.com/editors_pick/1933_05-06_pick.html> [2 December 2005].

'Around 1.1 million . . . own before whaling.' H. Whitehead, *Sperm whales: social evolution in the ocean*, University of Chicago Press, Chicago, 2003, p. 132.

pp. 84–85 'Saturday December 5 . . . Henry marritt, Ahiou.' Log kept on board the barque *Fortitude* on a whaling voyage 13 January 1843 to 31 December 1848, State Library of Tasmania, Hobart.

p. 86 'These enormous creatures . . . jaw and head.' Beale, *The natural history of the Sperm whale*, p. 135.

'A century later . . . was simple luck.' A.A. Berzin, *The Sperm whale (Kashalot)*, Israel Program for Scientific Translations, Jerusalem, 1972, p. 259.

'Over the 19th . . . a black flag.' G.A. Mawer, *Ahab's trade: the saga of South Seas whaling*, Allen & Unwin, Sydney, 1999, p. 221.

'The *Essex* was . . . survival at sea.' O. Chase, *Narrative of the shipwreck of the whale ship* Essex *in 1819*, Golden Cockerel Press, London, 1935, *passim*. See also N. Philbrick, *In the heart of the sea*, Penguin, Harmondsworth, 2000, *passim*.

p. 87 'As Melville's book . . . the second strike.' C. Sawtell, *The ship* Ann Alexander *of New Bedford, 1805–1851*, Marine Historical Association, Mystic, 1962.

'The whalers might . . . in the 1830s.' Whitehead, *Sperm whales: social evolution in the ocean*, p. 20.

'There have been . . . at this time.' Berzin, *The Sperm whale*, p. 258.

pp. 87–88 'To work as . . . as a weapon.' D. Carrier et al., 'The face that sank the *Essex*: potential function of the spermaceti organ in aggression', *The Journal of Experimental Biology* 205, 2002, pp. 1755–63.

p. 88 'Working their way . . . through the head.' K. Norris and G. Harvey, 'A theory of the function of the spermaceti organ in the Sperm whale *(Physeter catadon)*', in S.R. Galler et al., eds, *Animal orientation and navigation*, NASA Special publication 262, pp. 397–417.

'Sperm whale clicks . . . into the ocean.' Whitehead, *Sperm whales: social evolution in the ocean*, p. 11.

'Bursting out at . . . herds of cows.' B. Mohl, 'Sperm whales clicks: directionality and source levels revisited', *Journal of the Acoustic Society of America*, 107, 2000, pp. 638–48.

pp. 89–90 'A camera mounted . . . immediately after striking.' T. Kubodera and K. Mori, 'First-ever observations of a live giant squid in the wild', *Proceedings of the Royal Society B*, September 2005, pp. 3158–62.

p. 90 'Researchers of the . . . of the Atlantic.' Berzin, *The Sperm whale*, p. 200.

'A nineteenth century . . . 6-metre girth.' F. Bullen, *The cruise of* The Cachalot, Smith, Elder & Co., London, 1899, p. 144; also F. Bullen, *Denizens of the deep*, Fleming H. Revell & Co., New York, 1904, p. 140.

'But acoustic tags . . . sit-and-wait predators.' P. Miller et al., 'Swimming gaits, passive drag and buoyancy of diving Sperm whales', *The Journal of Experimental Biology*, 207, 2004, pp. 1953–67.

'The mode by . . . a curious secret.' Beale, *The natural history of the Sperm whale*, p. 54.

p. 91 'Clan signatures may . . . survival and reproduction.' L.E. Rendell and H. Whitehead, 'Vocal clans in Sperm whales', *Proceedings of the Royal Society B*, 18 October 2002, pp. 5761–67.

CHAPTER 8

p. 95 'For one, I . . . the deadliest ill.' H. Melville, *Moby Dick*, Penguin Classics, New York, 1988, p. 203.

p. 98 ' "Time" has ceased . . . a simultaneous happening.' M. McLuhan and Q. Fiore, *The medium is the massage,* Bantam, New York, 1967, p. 63.

p. 99 'Cousteau harpooned a . . . of the sea.' R. Munson, *Cousteau: The captain and his world*, Robert Hale Ltd, London, 1989, p. 127.

pp. 99–100 'If essentially unrestricted . . . to international folly.' S. McVay, 'The last of the great whales', *Scientific American*, vol. 215, no. 2, 1966, pp. 13–21.

p. 100 'What happens to . . . futility haunts us.' S. McVay, 'Reflections on the management of whaling', in *The whale problem*, W.E. Schevill, ed., Harvard University Press, Cambridge, 1974, p. 370.

'Can he who . . . a higher use.' H.D. Thoreau, 'The Maine Woods', quoted in *The whale problem*, p. 369.

pp. 100–01 'There have been . . . utilization by man.' J.L. McHugh, 'The role and history of the International Whaling Commission', in *The whale problem*, p. 313.

p. 101 'We did what . . . of our efforts.' McHugh, 'The role and history of the International Whaling Commission', in *The whale problem*, p. 313.

p. 102 'This is the . . . how to do.' R. Weyler, *Song of the whale*, Anchor Press/Doubleday, New York, 1986, p. 52.

'At least two . . . thoughts and images.' R. Hunter, *Warriors of the Rainbow*, Holt, Rinehart and Winston, New York, 1979, p. 89.

p. 103 'I don't like . . . and held fast.' D. McTaggart and H. Slinger, *Shadow warrior: the autobiography of Greenpeace International founder David McTaggart*, Orion, London, 2002, p. 50.

'Why haven't we . . . whole earth yet.' T. Wolfe, *The Electric Kool-Aid Acid Test*, Black Swan, Moorebank, 1971, p. 224.

p. 104 'In its way . . . romantic, transcendental glory.' W. Rowland, *The plot to save the world*, Clark, Irwin & Co., Toronto, 1973, p. 124.

'While it was clear . . . on automobile production.' Rowland, *The plot to save the world*, p. 124.

p. 105 'This means that . . . are no more.' Friends of the Earth, *The Stockholm Conference: only one Earth*, London, 1972, p. 30.

'Whale freaks had . . . in the counterculture.' Hunter, *Warriors of the Rainbow*, p. 124.

'I'm not really . . . got the power.' McTaggart and Slinger, *Shadow warrior*, p. 100.

p. 107 'If the very . . . truth, whale massacre.' Hunter, *Warriors of the Rainbow*, p. 212.

'The whale wavered . . . would kill them.' P. Watson, 'An open letter to Norwegians', *Nordlys*, Tromsø, 8 January, 1993.

p. 108 'A sub-committee investigating . . . claim of violation.' A.G. Bollen, 'Chairman's report of the twenty-eighth Meeting', *Twenty-seventh report of the Commission*, IWC, Cambridge, 1977, p. 27.

CHAPTER 9

p. 109 'Sometimes you say . . . them being true.' B. Dylan, *Chronicles*, volume one, Simon & Schuster, New York, 2004, p. 220.

p. 112 'The skipper and . . . whale's right rear.' *Albany Advertiser*, 6 September 1977.

p. 113 'The only thing . . . run, was violence.' Hunter, *Warriors of the Rainbow*, p. 397.

p. 114 'Didn't he think . . . of all proportion.' C. Hindaugh, *It wasn't meant to be easy*, Lothian Publishing, Port Melbourne, 1986, p. 175.

'In Albany in . . . could be expanded.' *Albany Advertiser*, 6 December 1999.

p. 115 'It is instructive . . . justify their use.' P. Singer, 'A submission to the Australian Government's Inquiry into Whales and Whaling', reprinted in *Habitat* 6:3, Australian Conservation Foundation, Hawthorn, June 1978, pp. 8–9.

pp. 115–16 'Our conclusion then . . . degree of intelligence.' S. Frost, *Whales and whaling: Report of the Independent Inquiry*, AGPS, Canberra, 1978, pp. 181–203.

p. 116 'When ASDIC is . . . on the surface.' S. Ohsumi, 'Criticism of Japanese fishing effort for Sperm whales in the North Pacific', Report of the IWC, *Special Issue 2, Sperm Whales*, Cambridge, 1980, p. 26.

'The highest intelligence . . . absolute brain size.' J. Hooper, *Omni Interview*, January 1983, Penthouse Media Group, New York.

'something that later scientists discount.' See L. Watson, *Whales of the world*, Hutchison & Co., London, 1985, p. 48; Whitehead, *Sperm whales: social evolution in the ocean*, pp. 357–58.

p. 117 'what some people . . . of exceptional intelligence.' S. Holt, 'Whale management policy', in *Twenty-seventh annual report of the IWC Scientific Committee*, Cambridge, 1977, p. 135.

'The Sperm whale . . . other higher primates.' J-P. Fortom-Gouin and S. Holt, 'Reasons for recommending zero female catch limits for Sperm whales', Report of the IWC, *Special Issue 2, Sperm whales*, p. 26.

'a mind anatomically . . . in the Waters.' J. McIntyre, *Mind in the waters*, Yolla Bolly Press and Project Jonah, Sausalito, 1974, p. 83.

'If whales are . . . it is murder.' Weyler, *Song of the whale*, p. 203.

p. 118 'Some members felt . . . of killing animals.' A.G. Bollen, 'Chairman's report of the thirtieth annual meeting', *Thirty-first report of the International Whaling Commission*, IWC, Cambridge, 1981, p. 25.

''University of California . . . we are here.' Weyler, *Song of the whale*, pp. 222–24.

p. 119 'Like it or . . . have thought possible.' J.N. Tønnessen and A.O. Johnsen, *The history of modern whaling*, C. Hurst & Co., ANU Press, Canberra, 1982, p. 675.

p. 119–20 'A 1200-tonne . . . doubt future supplies.' *Albany Advertiser*, 8 November 1977.

p. 121 'A British wildlife . . . Freetown, Sierra Leone.' N. Carter and A. Thornton, *Pirate whaling 1985, and a history of the subversion of international whaling regulations*, Environmental Investigation Agency, London, 1985, p. 5.

'The engineer bravely . . . the Japanese market.' C. Stevens, 'In remembrance of Nick Carter', *Animal Welfare Institute Quarterly*, Summer 2000, vol. 49, no. 3.

p. 122 '"Sierra, Sierra," Watson . . . to end today.' P. Watson, *Ocean warrior*, Allen & Unwin, Sydney NSW, 1994, p. 5.

'We traded a . . . from the *Sierra*.' P. Watson interviewed in *Bite Back* magazine <www.directaction.info/library_watson.htm> [5 January 2006].

p. 123 'These operations have . . . Japanese whaling colonies.' Carter and Thornton, *Pirate whaling 1985*, p. 12.

'It's an age-old . . . then beat them.' McTaggart and Slinger, *Shadow warrior*, p. 158.

p. 124 'Holt knew Lyall . . . to Paul Spong.' Y. Umezaki, *Kujira to Inbou* (whales and plots), ABC Shuppan, 1986, translated from the Japanese at <http://luna.pos.to/whale/gen_ume_kaeri.html> [8 January 2006].

'This is a *great* day', Weyler, *Song of the whale*, p. 219.

'My government is . . . grant to Seychelles.' 'Blackmail! Japan's last desperate tactic', *South China Morning Post*, in D. Day, *The whale war*, Routledge and Kegan Paul, London, 1987, pp. 103–4.

p. 126 'They settled into . . . them, and how.' McTaggart and Slinger, *Shadow warrior*, p. 157.

'It claimed there . . . over minimum size.' T. Miyashita and S. Ohsumi, 'Estimation of the population size of the Sperm whale in the Southern Hemisphere using sightings data', *Report of the thirty-third meeting*, IWC, Cambridge, 1981, pp. 805–7.

'This is an . . . like private properties.' Y. Umezaki, *Kujira to Inbou.*

p. 127 'This is a . . . of the Commission.' Statement by FAO Observer, *Report of thirty-fourth annual meeting*, IWC, Cambridge, 1983.

p. 128 'The Japanese Whaling . . . "leave the conference".' *The Australian*, 27 July 1982.

IV MINKE

CHAPTER 10

p. 132 'The history of . . . of the whale.' F. Ommanney, *Lost leviathan*, Hutchison & Co., London, 1971, p. 69.

pp. 132–33 'The lecturer at . . . who helped him.' G. Pritchard, 'On the discovery of a fossil whale', in *The Victorian Naturalist*, 4 January 1939. The Field Naturalists Club of Victoria, Blackburn, pp. 151–57.

p. 133 '*Mammalodon colliveri* is . . . and other mysticetes.' E. Fordyce, 'Evolution and zoogeography of cetaceans in Australia', in M. Archer and G. Clayton, eds, *Vertebrate zoogeography and evolution in Australasia*, Hesperian Press, Marrickville, 1984, pp. 929–42.

'The richness of . . . another fossil skull.' E. Fitzgerald, 'A bizarre new toothed mysticete (*Cetacea*) from Australia and the early evolution of baleen whales', *Proceedings of the Royal Society B*, 15 August 2006, p. 3664.

p. 134 'The shape of . . . relative: the hippopotamus.' P. Gingerich et al., 2001, 'Origin of whales from early artiodactyls: hands and feet of Eocene protocetidae from Pakistan', *Science*, 293, 2001, pp. 2239–42.

'The origin of . . . the eastern Tethys.' S. Bajpal and P. Gingerich, 'A new Eocene archaeocete (*Mammalia, Cetacea*) from India and the time of origin of whales', in *Proc. Natl. Acad. Sci. USA*, vol. 95, December 1998, pp. 15464–68.

'At Wadi-Al-Hitan . . . of the valley.' 'Wadi Al-Hitan' (Whale Valley) (Egypt), *IUCN World Heritage Evaluation Report*, IUCN, Gland, May 2005, p. 14.

p. 135 'mechanism of considerable . . . of living whales,' R. Kellogg, 'The history of whales— their adaptation to life in the water', in *The Quarterly Review of Biology*, vol. III, 1928, p. 41.

'They were lastingly . . . million years ago.' P.D. Gingerich, 'Cetacea', in K. Rose and J. Archibald, eds., *Placental mammals: origin, timing and relationships of the major extant clades*, John Hopkins University Press, Baltimore, 2005, p. 245.

'Ewan Fordyce believes . . . 30 million years.' E. Fordyce, 'Whale evolution and Oligocene Southern Ocean environments', in *Paleogeography, Paleoclimatology, Paleaoecology*, Elsevier, Amsterdam, 1980, p. 330.

pp. 135–36 'Fossil skulls tell . . . swimming and diving.' E. Fordyce and L. Barnes, 'The evolutionary history of whales and dolphins', in *Annual Review of Earth Planetary Science*, 22, 1994, p. 445.

p. 136 'Palaeontologists last century . . . found the IWC.' Kellogg, 'The history of whales—their adaptation to life in the water', p. 40.

'Ice ages, sea . . . which is us.' S. Palumbi, in 'The secret lives of whales', media release for AAAS meeting, 19 February 2005, <www.eurekalert.org/pub_releases/2005-02/s-tsl020805.php> [2 March 2006].

p. 137 'Historical records claimed . . . the historic count.' J. Roman and S. Palumbi, 'Whales before whaling in the North Atlantic', in *Science*, vol. 301, 25 July 2003, p. 508.

'Better records were . . . and 360 644 Blues.' P. Clapham and C.S. Baker, *How many whales were killed in the 20th century?* IWC Scientific Committee paper SC/53/014, IWC, Cambridge, 2001.

'The globe-straddling . . . the world's oceans.' H. Whitehead, 'Estimates of the current global population size and historical trajectory for Sperm whales', in *Marine Ecology Progress Series*, vol. 242, 25 October 2002, pp. 295–304.

pp. 137–38 'December 23. In . . . to our larder.' H.J. Bull 'The cruise of the *Antarctic* to the South Polar regions', *Journal of the American Geographical Society of New York*, vol. 28, no. 4 (1896), pp. 434–35.

p. 139 'Records of their . . . squealing behind it.' J. Ford, G. Ellis et al., 'Killer whale attacks on Minke whales: prey capture and antipredator tactics', in *Marine Mammal Science*, vol. 21, no. 4, October 2005, pp. 603–18.

p. 140 'Other scientists proposed . . . set at 5000.' *Twenty-fourth report of the Commission*, IWC, London, 1974.

'The two remaining . . . total of 7713.' J.N. Tønnessen and A.O. Johnsen, *The history of modern whaling*, C. Hurst & Co., London, 1982, p. 641.

p. 141 'Peru fell over . . . dropped its objection.' N. Carter and A. Thornton, *Pirate whaling 1985, and a history of the subversion of international whaling regulations*, Environmental Investigation Agency, London, 1985, p. 28.

p. 142 'In response the . . . excess Minke meat.' R. Reagan, *Message to the Congress reporting on the whaling activities of the Soviet Union*, 31 May 1985, The public papers of President Ronald W. Reagan, Ronald Reagan Presidential Library, University of Texas.

CHAPTER 11

p. 143 'All our science . . . the head cook.' A Huxley, *Brave new world*, The Easton Press, Norwalk, 1987, p. 207.

NOTES

'As Komatsu tells . . . foreigner—the gaijin.' I. Kitagawa, 'Whaling advocate not blubbering over name-calling', in *The Daily Yomiuri*, <www.yomiuri.co.jp/newse/20040717wo62.htm> [20 July 2004].

p. 144 'A prodigious 81 000 . . . half that figure.' 'Global catch by country', Commission for the Conservation of Southern Bluefin Tuna, Canberra, <www.ccsbt.org/docs/pdf/data/CatchByOYF.txt> [24 March 2006].

'Yet that year . . . a tiny fraction.' *Annual statistics on fishery and aquaculture production 2004*, and *Annual report on the developments in the fisheries 2004*, Statistics and Information Department, Ministry of Agriculture, Forestry and Fisheries, Tokyo.

p. 145 'The way the . . . whaling and fishing.' M. Komatsu and S. Misaki, *Whales and the Japanese*, The Institute of Cetacean Research, Tokyo, 2003, p. 90.

'They won there . . . Japan Whaling Association.' US Supreme Court, *Japan Whaling Assn v. American Cetacean Soc.*, 478 US 221 (1986), <www.justia.us/us/478/221/case.html> [24 March 2006].

p. 146 'Of sixteen special . . . reached the commission.' *Eighth report of the Commission*, IWC, London, 1957, p. 26.

p. 147 'Japan dreamed up . . . and suckling whales.' *Sixteenth report of the Commission*, IWC, London, 1966, p. 9.

'IWC commissioners couldn't . . . the Scientific Committee.' *Fourteenth report of the Commission*, IWC, London, 1964, p. 8; *Fifteenth report of the Commission*, IWC, London, 1965, p. 20.

'The government will . . . Minister, Moriyoshi Sato.' M. Sato, quoted in Whale and Dolphin Conservation Society whaling history, <www.wdcs.org/dan/publishing.nsf/allweb> [26 March 2006].

pp. 148–49 'When I use . . . master—that's all.' R. Gasson, ed., *The illustrated Lewis Carroll*, Jupiter, London, 1978, p. 168.

p. 149 'Our ignorance about . . . of commercial whaling.' F. Nagasaki, 'The case for scientific whaling', *Nature* 344, 15 March 1990, p. 189.

'Some Japanese researchers . . . thousands of whales.' W. de la Mare, 'Problems of scientific whaling', *Nature* 345, 28 June 1990, p. 771.

'Governments' treatment of . . . bandwagon' against it.' *Chairman's report of the forty-third meeting*, IWC, Cambridge, 1991.

p. 151 'A Japanese account . . . act" by Greenpeace.' T. Kojima, 'The Japanese research whaling', from *Whaling issues and Japan's whale research*, ICR, 1993, <http://luna.pos.to/whale/icr_wjwr_jrw.html> [14 April 2006].

p. 152 'I half expected . . . doves fly past.' K. Mulvaney, *The whaling season*, Island Press, Washington DC, 2003, p. 39.

p. 154 'The acting Japanese . . . shown 'more restraint'.' R. Peake, 'Protest to Japan over slaughter of whales', in *The Age*, Melbourne, 14 February 1992.

p. 159 'I was shocked . . . was being ignored.' I. Kitagawa 'Whaling advocate not blubbering over name-calling' in *The Daily Yomiuri*.

p. 160 'A few weeks . . . continuing its research.' *Chairman's report of the forty-fifth annual meeting*, IWC, Cambridge, 1993.

'Against the electric . . . original harpoon wound.' C. Puplick, *Report of the National Task Force on Whaling*, Department of Environment and Heritage, Canberra, 1997, p. 39.

p. 161 'Pressure intensified until . . . within 30 seconds.' *Chairman's report of the forty-eighth annual meeting*, IWC, Cambridge, 1996.

At the House . . . minds,' Banks said.' T. Banks, *House of Commons Hansard*, London, 20 December 1995, column 1467–68.

CHAPTER 12

p. 163 'Butterfly: "they say . . . is in that" ', G. Puccini, *Madama Butterfly*, act one, G. Ricord and Co., London, 1907.

'No one has the . . . stop eating it.' M. Komatsu and S. Misaki, *The truth behind the whaling dispute*, ICR, Tokyo, 2001, p. 41.

'Sentiments run deep . . . being treated unfairly.' R. March, *Reading the Japanese mind*, Kodansha International, New York, 1996, p. 42.

p. 164 'It is almost . . . from all others.' K. Van Wolferen, *The enigma of Japanese power*, Papermac, 1990, p. 9.

pp. 165–66 'A couple of . . . it from cameras.' Sea Shepherd, *Taiji dolphin campaign*, <www.seashepherd.org/taiji.s.html> [8 April 2006].

p. 166 'A MORI poll . . . once a month.' *Majority of Japanese public does not support whaling or consume whale meat*, <www.mori.com/polls/1999/whaling.shtml> [8 April 2006].

'A Gallup poll . . . for "sustainable whaling".' Nippon Research Center Ltd., *Opinion poll on scientific whaling, internet survey: summary report*, 15 June 2006, Tokyo, Commissioned by Greenpeace Japan.

p. 167 'The Commission does . . . advice it receives.' *Chairman's report of the forty-second annual meeting*, IWC, Cambridge, 1991, p. 26.

p. 168 'What is the . . . with such contempt?' P. Hammond, Letter to Dr R. Gambell, Secretary, IWC, 26 May 1993, posted at: <www.highnorth.no/Library/Management_Regimes/IWC/le-fr-th.htm> [10 April 2006].

'Unfortunately many governments . . . appease these organizations.' M. Komatsu and S. Misaki, *The truth behind the whaling dispute*, ICR, Tokyo, 2001, p. 27.

p. 169 'Bill and Sidney . . . short time frame.' D. McTaggart and H. Slinger, *Shadow warrior*, Orion, London, 2002, p. 227.

p. 170 'It is a . . . and irregular manner.' Komatsu and Misaki, *The truth behind the whaling dispute*, p. 79.

p. 171 'The Japanese umbrella . . . decisions for them.' 'What is Janic', <www.janic.org/en/whatisjanic.htm> [24 April 2006].

p. 173 'In reality this . . . are in place.' M.A. Zacharias, et al., *Incorporating the science of marine reserves into IWC Sanctuaries: the Southern Ocean Sanctuary*, SC/56/SOS5, IWC, Cambridge, 2004.

'If you have . . . and you're discredited.' 'Sir Peter Scott: a lifetime of natural history', in *Greenpeace Examiner*, <www.archive.greenpeace.org/gopher/campaigns/magazine/pre1991/gpexam5.txt> [14 May 2006].

CHAPTER 13

p. 175 'What aligns wolf . . . and kill animals.' B. Lopez, *Of wolves and men*, Scribner, 1978, p. 88.

p. 176 'Like sheep or children.' M. McClure, *For the death of 100 whales*, 1955, <www.thing.net/~grist/l&d/mcclure/mcclurea.htm> [30 June 2006].

'I'm not one . . . this is disgusting.' McTaggart and Slinger, *Shadow warrior*, p. 145.

p. 177 'The culture of . . . the European Union.' B.T. Hodges, 'The cracking facade of the International Whaling Commission', in *Journal of Environmental Law and Litigation*, University of Oregon, no. 295, 2000.

p. 178 'gather in flocks . . . for the purpose.' *The king's mirror*, <www.mediumaevum.com/75years/mirror/sec1.html#XII> [30 June 2006].

'In the gruelling . . . transform into whales.' San Francisco Museum of Modern Art, exhibit notes, *Matthew Barney—drawing restraint*, film synopsis, June 2006, p. 8.

p. 179 'A draft contract . . . the North Atlantic.' Carter and Thornton, *Pirate whaling 1985*, p. 20.

'My men delivered . . . they were reeling.' P. Watson, *Ocean warrior*, Allen & Unwin, Sydney, 1994, p. 151.

p. 180 'Against IWC resolutions . . . driving the market.' R. Reeve, *Icelandic pirate whaling 1991*, Environmental Investigation Agency, London.

p. 181 'Hunting and killing . . . of civilised countries.' R. Kelly, 'Kelly condemns whale killers', *media release*, Minister for The Arts, Sport, The Environment and Territories, 30 June 1992.

'That is rank . . . our paths cross.' T. Banks, UK Hansard, 22 May 1996, column 236.

'When did the . . . dominates the issue.' G. Bruntland, quoted in C. Ingebritsen, 'The politics of whaling in Norway and Iceland', *Scandinavian Review*, Winter 1997–98.

p. 182 'I decided to . . . they killed us.' P. Watson, *The battle of the Lofotens*, <www.seashepherd.org> [3 July 2006].

pp. 182–83 'Even though Mr . . . was not justified.' 'Coast guard would have sunk Watson's ship', *Dagbladet*, Oslo, 7 July 1994.

p. 183 'The movie's worldwide . . . around $US153 million.' Box Office Mojo, <www.boxofficemojo.com/movies/?id=freewilly.htm> [2 July 2006].

p. 185 'There came a . . . have a harbour.' J. McPhee, *The control of nature*, Pimlico Books, London, 1989, p. 37.

p. 187 'The kill was . . . to export it.' 'Norway: whaling season starts', *High North News* 04/05/1999, <www.highnorth.no/news/nedit.asp?which=216 [2 July 2006].

'Whale trade pressure . . . go commercial whaling.' S. Altherr, *Iceland's whaling comeback*, WDCS, HSUS, Pro Wildlife 2003, p. 6.

p. 188 'As whales are . . . sustainable fisheries policy.' H. Asgrimsson, *Address on foreign affairs*, Althing, 26 March 2002, Icelandic Ministry of Foreign Affairs, p. 227.

'Well how many . . . get on track.' D. Kagan, *Keiko swims from Iceland to Norway*, CNN, 4 September 2002.

pp. 189–90 'A Canadian anthropologist . . . mirror of nature.' A.Brydon, 'The predicament of nature: Keiko the whale and the cultural politics of whaling in Iceland', *Anthropological Quarterly*, vol. 79, no. 2, Spring 2006, pp. 225–60.

V HUMPBACK

CHAPTER 14

p. 194 'You've started going . . . try the Anglicans.' T. Winton, *The turning*, Pan Macmillan, Sydney, 2005, p. 302.

'It's thought to be . . . people at once.' H. Whitehead, 'Why whales leap', *Scientific American*, 252, March 1985, p. 70.

pp. 194–95 'The whale had . . . by this act.' T. Beale, *The natural history of the Sperm whale*, Holland Press, London, 1835, p. 50.

p. 195 'at times making . . . again settling under.' C. Scammon, *Marine mammals of the north-western coast of North America*, Dover, New York, re-published 1968, p. 25.

'When a whale . . . the observation vehicle.' C.J. Madsen and L.M. Herman, 'Functions of vision in cetacean life', in L.M. Herman, ed., *Cetacean behaviour: mechanisms and functions*, Wiley, New York, 1980, p. 53.

'We cannot sort . . . is not unlikely.' K.S. Norris et al., 'Lagoon entrance and other aggregations of Gray whales', in R. Payne, ed., *Communication and behaviour of whales*, Westview Press, Boulder, 1983, p. 285.

'At the height . . . a few kilometres.' H. Whitehead, 'Why whales leap', p. 74.

p. 196 'Worldwide, more than . . . was the Humpback.' E. Hoyt, *Whale watching 2001*, International Fund for Animal Welfare, Yarmouth, 2001, p. 152.

pp. 196–97 '"Migaloo" has a . . . for government men.' F. Ludowyk, ed., *Ozwords*, Australian National Dictionary Centre, Canberra, 2001.

p. 197 'Migaloo was seen . . . in early October.' P. Forestell et al., 'Observations of a hypopigmented Humpback whale, *Megaptera novaeangliae*, off east coast Australia: 1991–2000', *Memoirs of the Queensland Museum*, 47 (2), Brisbane, p. 444.

'The reason for . . . other cetacean species.' D. Fertl et al., 'First record of an albino Bottlenose Dolphin (*Tursiops truncatus*) in the Gulf of Mexico, with a review of anomalously white cetaceans', *Marine Mammal Science*, vol. 15, no. 1, January 1999.

p. 198 'I just started . . . back down again.' D. Snell on 'The World Today', 19 August 2003, ABC Radio transcript <www.migaloowhale.org/snell.html> [4 April 2005].

'In Queensland, particularly . . . was colour variance.' *Nature Conservation (whales and dolphins) Conservation Plan 1997*, Office of the Queensland Parliamentary Counsel, Brisbane.

p. 199 'Each year the . . . the whale alone.' P. Forestell, 'A plea for a whale', <www.migaloowhale.org/forestell.html> [6 April 2005].

pp. 199–200 'This incident should . . . kind from science.' G. Chittleborough, *Shouldn't our grandchildren know?*, Fremantle Arts Centre Press, 1992, p. 44.

p. 200 'One fleet alone . . . reported just 760.' V. Danilov-Danil'yan and A.Yablokov, eds., *Soviet Antarctic whaling data 1947–1972*, Center for Russian Environment Policy, Moscow, 1996, pp. 57–60.

'Young Russian whalers . . . of the Antarctic.' '1200 Russian sailors here on R and R', *The Sydney Morning Herald*, 21 May 1968, p. 1.

pp. 200–01 'Actually nothing had . . . up to Sydney.' Danilov-Danil'yan and Yablokov, eds., *Soviet Antarctic whaling data 1947–1972*, p. 271.

p. 201 'For more than . . . Humpbacks escaped whaling.' R. Paterson et al., 'The status of Humpback whales, *Megaptera novaeangliae*, off east Australia thirty years after whaling', *Biological Conservation*, vol. 70, no. 2, 1994, pp.135–42.

p. 202 'A skin biopsy . . . two years later.' C. Pomilla and H. Rosenbaum, 'Against the current: an inter-oceanic whale migration event', *Biology Letters*, 1–4, 22 December 2005, p. 476.

'Of known animal . . . of turning around.' K. Rasmussen et al., Biology Letters, published online, April 2007 <www.journals.royalsoc.uc.uk> [20 April 2007].

'Genetic work showed . . . linked to glaciation.' L. Medrano-Gonzalez et al., 'Trans-oceanic population genetic structures of Humpback whales in the North and South Pacific', in Memoirs of the Queensland Museum, 47(2), 2001, p. 465.

p. 203 'The pace of . . . them as waypoints.' IWC Intersessional workshop on Southern Hemisphere Humpback whales, Hobart, 4–7 April 2006.

p. 205 'Yes, I sang . . . compassionate lactating mother.' H. Cooke, 'Death of a baby whale', media release, Surfers for Cetaceans, 21 July 2006.

p. 208 'The Bequian bears . . . Human Security Projects.' 'Japan assists in the restoration of the whaling station in Bequia', statement by the Embassy of Japan in Trinidad and Tobago, 24 June 2005, <www.tt.emb-japan.go.jp/st-vincent-the-grenadines/whaling-station-bequia.htm> [23 July 2006].

CHAPTER 15

p. 210 'We are programmed . . . than anything else.' J. Lovelock, The revenge of Gaia, Allen Lane, London, 2006, p. 4.

'The anti-whaling . . . barbaric and inhumane.' K. Shima, 'Japan and whaling', in Social Science Japan, Information Center for Social Science Research on Japan, University of Tokyo, Issue 16, August 1999, p. 5.

pp. 210–11 'The answer is . . . Western eco-cultists.' Shima, 'Japan and whaling', p. 6.

p. 211 'In 2004, the . . . of global population.' 'The international fish trade and world fisheries', fact sheet, UN Food and Agriculture Organisation, May 2006, <www.fao.org/newsroom/common/ecg/1000301/en/enfactsheet2.pdf > [30 July 2006].

'Shima complained of . . . would be next.' K. Shima, 'The domestic system', speech at <www1m.mesh.ne.jp/nora/japanese/cmnt/s-shima.html> [4 August 2006].

'Once that principle . . . be infringed upon.' T. Kanamitsu, 'Japanese whaling policy leads many observers to wonder what motivates the Japanese to continue hunting whales at the risk of antagonizing Western countries', in Asahi Shimbun, 29 November 2002.

p. 212 'The same miracle . . . yen annual subsidy.' A. Ishii and A. Okubo, 'An alternative explanation of Japan's whaling diplomacy in the post-moratorium era', Journal of International Wildlife Law and Policy, IO, 2007, pp. 55–87.

'He makes the . . . an official capacity.' 'Basic position of the Government of Japan regarding Prime Minister Koizumi's visits to Yasukuni Shrine', Ministry of Foreign Affairs, Tokyo, October 2005, <wwww.mofa.go.jp/policy/postwar/yasukuni/position.html> [29 July 2006].

'Despite the assaults . . . not give in.' Shima, 'Japan and whaling', p. 6.

'Its authorities decided . . . further conservation moves.' S. Holt, 'Propaganda and pretext', in Marine Pollution Bulletin, 52, Elsevier, p. 364.

p. 213 'Their allegiance changed . . . visits to Tokyo.' Greenpeace, 'Vote-buying—Japan's strategy to secure a return to large-scale whaling', Greenpeace Briefing, 1 December 2001.

'Fisheries Agency officials . . . Fund and others.' *Yomiuri Shimbun*, 13 April 1993, quoted in IFAW, *Japan's strategy to control the world's living marine resources*, 1996, unpaginated.

'The St Lucian . . . to take yen.' J. Rogozinski, *A brief history of the Caribbean*, Plume, New York, 2000, pp. 347–66; and L. Busby, *Japan's 'Vote Consolidation Operation' at the International Whaling Commission*, Third Millennium Foundation, Paciano, Italy, June 2006, p. 30.

pp. 213–14 'The Caribbeans reappeared . . . in fisheries aid.' Busby, *Japan's 'Vote Consolidation Operation' at the International Whaling Commission*, Annex 3.

p. 215 'Upon review of . . . the specified periods.' 'The whale wars, whaling letter', *Four Corners*, ABC, 2005, <www.abc.net.au/4corners/content/2005/whale_letter.htm> [August 2006].

'They announced that . . . know what is.' A. Martin to R. Piggott, 'Buying votes from Dominica', BBC Newsnight, 20 October 2000.

'cultivating a sound international environment.' A. Gillespie, *Vote-buying in international fora*, ASMS, Waedenswil, 3 December 2001, p. 11.

'must have a . . . various international organizations.' Overseas Fisheries Co-operation Foundation Conference Report: Symposium on South Pacific Fisheries Development (Tokyo), in Gillespie, *Vote-buying in International Fora*, p. 7.

p. 216 'It is necessary . . . of IWC membership.' *Suisan Keizai Shimbun*, 24 June 1999, in 'Buying a return to commercial whaling', Greenpeace briefing, April 2002.

'We would like . . . World Trade Organisation.' P. Brown, 'Japan admits using aid to build pro-whaling vote', in *The Guardian*, London, 11 November 1999.

'Japan does not . . . in the ocean.' M. Simkin, AM, ABC Radio, Sydney, 18 July 1999, <www.abc.net.au/am/stories/s331281.htm> [4 August 2006].

p. 217 'Japan must surely . . . own senior officials.' H. Clark, 'NZ appalled at Japanese admission on whaling tactics', media release, Prime Minister of New Zealand, 18 July 2001.

'When they approach . . . of the water.' J. Brooke, 'An environmentalist who loves to eat whales', *The New York Times*, 19 October 2002.

p. 218 'The man who . . . Japan's Caribbean Allies.' 'About the Embassy of Japan Trinidad and Tobago', <www.tt.emb-japan.go.jp/about.htm> [4 August 2006].

'When the prized . . . fishery continued unabated.' A. Darby, 'Revealed: Japan's $2 billion tuna fraud', *The Sydney Morning Herald*, 12 August 2006.

'About half of . . . the United States.' G. Finin and T. Wesley-Smith, *A new era for Japan and the Pacific Islands: the Tokyo summit*, Analysis from the East-West Center, Honolulu, no. 32, September 1997, p. 4.

'In a country . . . exports was tuna.' R. Alexander, 'Japan and the Pacific Island countries', in S. Levine and A. Pawles, eds, *Contemporary challenges in the Pacific*, University of French Polynesia, Tahiti, 2001, *passim*.

p. 219 'Compared to Japan's . . . country didn't adapt.' World Bank, 'International coalition tackles impacts of climate change in Kiribati', media release, Sydney, 18 July 2005.

'Taiwan and China . . . million by 2004.' 'Outline and Evaluation, Visit to Japan of His Excellency Mr Teburoro Tito, Chairman of the Pacific Islands Forum', Ministry of Foreign Affairs, Japan, 23 February 2004.

'By running a . . . waters of Kiribati.' 'Map of the cruise of the *Pequod*', in H. Melville, *Moby Dick or The Whale*, Penguin Classics, New York, pp. 655–56.

'In the sailing . . . around 65 000 whales.' S. Childerhouse, in 'Whale sanctuaries', *Report of the Scientific Committee*, IWC, Cambridge, 2000.

p. 220 'an important attempt . . . in the IWC,' WWF, 'Statement on proposals under discussion in the International Whaling Commission', December 1997, p. 2.

'*After* these were . . . the world's oceans.' R. Hill, 'Major research boost as Australia set to host international whales conference', media release, Minister for the Environment, 5 July 1998.

'A communiqué in . . . that is, Japan.' 'Forum Communiqué', Twenty-ninth South Pacific Forum, Pohnpei, Federated States of Micronesia, August 1998.

'Too much political . . . to be made.' 'Tonga: Whaling getting too politicised, says Fisheries Secretary', Radio New Zealand, 18 April 2006.

p. 221 'Prime Minister conveyed . . . regarding whaling issues.' 'Visit to Japan of His Excellency Mr Teburoro Tito, the Chairman of the Pacific Islands Forum (Outline and Evaluation)', Ministry of Foreign Affairs, Japan, 23 February 2001, <www.mofa.go.jp/region/asia-paci/kiribati/pifcv0102/outline.html> [23 July 2006].

'The forum noted . . . a whale sanctuary.' 'Forum Communiqué', Thirty-third South Pacific Forum, Suva, Fiji, August 2002.

p. 222 'Previous Solomon Islands . . . agreement," he said.' M. Carney, 'The whale wars', *Four Corners*, ABC, Sydney, 18 July 2005.

'The bribery of . . . foreign bribery cases.' OECD, 'Japan: Phase 2bis. Report on the application of the Convention on Combating Bribery of Foreign Public Officials in International Business Transactions', OECD Directorate for Financial and Enterprise Affairs, 15 June 2006.

pp. 222–23 'The fact is . . . to help themselves.' Carney, 'The whale wars', *Four Corners*, ABC.

p. 223 'Nations like Kiribati . . . on climate change.' T. Flannery, *The weather makers*, Text, Melbourne, 2005, pp. 287–88.

'Perceptions of Japan . . . direct managerial approach.' Finin and Wesley-Smith, *A new era for Japan and the Pacific Islands: the Tokyo summit*, p. 6.

p. 224 'It is true . . . to continue whaling.' P. McCutcheon, *The World Today*, 2 November 1999, <www.abc.net.au/worldtoday/stories/s63672.htm> [23 July 2006].

'It was true . . . cost them money.' M. Donoghue et al., 'Report of the Workshop on Interactions between Cetaceans and Longline Fisheries', New England Aquarium Aquatic Forum Series Report 03–1, May 2003.

pp. 224–25 'Nor that Japanese . . . over twenty years.' A. Darby, 'Japan cuts its catch as cost of scam soars', *The Sydney Morning Herald*, 12 August 2006.

p. 225 'For the Japanese . . . he could calculate.' T. Tamura, 'Regional assessment of prey consumption and competition by marine cetaceans in the world', The Institute of Cetacean Research, Tokyo, 2006.

'A range of . . . and Daniel Pauly.' K. Kaschner and D. Pauly, 'Competition between marine mammals and fisheries. Food for thought', Humane Society International, May 2004, p. 10.

p. 226 'Marine mammals consume . . . throughout the world.' Kaschner and Pauly, 'Competition between marine mammals and fisheries. Food for thought', p. 3.

p. 227 'They uphold the . . . present global drift.' K. Shima, 'Whaling and the rational use of marine living resources', in *Whaling controversy and the rational utilization of marine resources*, Institute of Cetacean Research, Tokyo, 2002, p. 28.

'Expensive fish is . . . the African people.' 'Voices of African countries on the whaling issue', in *Isaribi—fishing fire*, Japan Fisheries Association, no. 49, March 2006, p. 1.

p. 228 'It is unnerving . . . that witchcraft flourishes.' S. Kante, 'Mali's human sacrifice: myth or reality?' *BBC News World edition*, 20 September 2004, 08.24 GMT.

'and it is . . . of Malian women.' Amnesty International, *Female genital mutilation in Africa, information by country*, <http://web.amnesty.org/library/pdf/ACT770142004ENGLISH/$File/ACT7701404.pdf> [14 February 2007].

'Mali is very . . . five were illiterate.' United Nations Development Program, *Human Development Reports*, Mali, <http://hdr.undp.org/statistics/data/countries.cfmc?c=MLI> [10 June 2006].

'It ranked 99th . . . global corruption index.' Transparency International, *Corruption Perceptions Index 2006*, <http://www.transparency.org> [6 December 2006].

'Luxembourg was fourth . . . problem or undernourishment.' United Nations Development Program, *Human Development Reports*, Luxembourg.

p. 229 'Japan's National Research . . . the rest dolphins.' H. Kato and T. Miyashita, 'Japan progress report on Cetacean research, May 2004 to April 2005', *IWC SC/57/ProgRep.Japan*, IWC, Cambridge, 2005.

'The Japan Fisheries . . . with one stone.' Japanese Fisheries Association, 'Voices of African countries on the whaling issue', in *Isaribi—fishing fire*, no. 49, p. 2.

'It was left . . . of its fish stocks.' Greenpeace International, *Pirate Fishing/Atlantic weblog*, Amsterdam, <weblog.greenpeace.org/oceandefenders/archive/pirate_fishing_africa> [8 September 2006].

'We have confidence . . . New Guinea fisheries.' 'Agreement allows Japan to fish PNG waters', *Papua New Guinea Post Courier*, Port Moresby, 3 May 2006.

CHAPTER 16

p. 230 'Look, your worship . . . and unequal combat.' M. Cervantes, *Don Quixote*, Cassell & Co., London, 1953, p. 63.

p. 232 'Rising steeply from . . . for the migration.' W. Dawbin, 'The migrations of Humpback whales which pass the New Zealand coast', in *Transactions of the Royal Society of New Zealand*, vol. 84, part 1, October 1956, pp. 147–96.

p. 234 'Following the chasers . . . their harpooned tails.' R. Leaper et al., *An independent review of the efficacy of killing methods of Antarctic Minke whales*, IWC/58/WKM&AWI 23, and *Report of The Workshop On Whale Killing Methods And Associated Welfare Issues*, IWC/58/Rep 7, IWC, Cambridge, 2006, pp. 12–13.

p. 235 'The point is . . . their PR campaign.' H. Hatanaka, 'Activists try to stop non-lethal research', media release, Institute for Cetacean Research, 12 January 2006.

'In bilateral talks . . . and nuclear weapons.' US Department of State, 'Joint press availability with Secretary of State Madeleine K. Albright and Japanese Foreign Minister Yohei Kono', Tokyo, 30 July 2000.

pp. 235–36 'At Camp David . . . the relationship is.' Office of the Press Secretary, The White House, 'Background briefing by senior Administration officials on the President's meeting with the Prime Minister of Japan', Washington, 30 June 2001.

p. 236 'It has been . . . changing our position.' Prime Minister's Press Office, 'Transcript of the Prime Minister The Hon. John Howard MP press conference', Hotel Okura, Tokyo, 3 August 2001.

'I registered that . . . our two countries.' Ministry of Foreign Affairs, Tokyo, 'Opening statements by Prime Minister Junichiro Koizumi and Prime Minister Helen Clark of New Zealand at the joint press conference', 2 May 2002.

pp. 237–38 'This showed when . . . of the Antarctic.' E. Waterhouse, ed., *Ross Sea Region 2001: A State of the Environment Report*, New Zealand Antarctic Institute, Christchurch, 2001.

p. 238 'It was more . . . of least resistance.' S. Arnold, 'Japanese whaling in Antarctica targets our Humpbacks', *The Canberra Times*, 16 November 2005.

'He thought it . . . was deeply wrong.' J. Allsop, *Humane Society International Inc. v. Kyodo Senpaku Kaisha Ltd*, Federal Court of Australia, NSD 1519 of 2004, Sydney, 27 May 2005.

p. 240 'The anti-whaling . . . soon to come.' A. Nakamae, item 10.2 (3), Scientific permits, proposed resolutions, *verbatim record*, IWC 57, IWC, Cambridge, 2005.

pp. 240–41 '"Middle-minded" European . . . whaling was excluded.' United States, *Response to the Chair's Proposal for a Way Forward on the RMS*, IWC/NO4/RMSWG4, IWC, Cambridge, November 2004.

p. 243 'Belize's godparent, the . . . was covering costs.' N. Hasell, 'The unexpected face of fight to save whales', *The Times*, London, 23 April 2007.

p. 244 'The way that . . . a historical thing'. Institute of Cetacean Research, Day three transcript, report of press conference from IWC 58, St Kitts and Nevis, <www.e- kujira.or.jp/iwc/ iwcmeeting.html> [24 August 2006].

'They promised that . . . of inconclusive negotiations.' Governments of Antigua & Barbuda et al., 'Towards normalization of the International Whaling Commission', Statement, February 2006.

pp. 244–45 'Dozens of "sustainable . . . for more money.' 'PM pleads for more help from Japan on OCES', *Antigua Sun*, 31 May 2006.

p. 246 'But distance is . . . counter-whaling countries.' Day four transcript, report of press conference from IWC 58, St Kitts and Nevis, ICR, 2006.

CHAPTER 17

p. 247 'God seems to . . . of his power.' R. Burton, *The life and death of whales*, André Deutsch, London, 1973, p. 1.

'So as to . . . to the stars.' C. Sagan, *Murmurs of Earth*, Random House, New York, 1978, p. 27.

p. 248 'It means "information . . . of social learning".' L. Rendell and H. Whitehead, 'Culture in whales and dolphins', *Behavioural and Brain Sciences*, vol. 24, Cambridge University Press, 2001, p. 312.

'In a little . . . hit with them.' M. Noad et al., 'Cultural revolution in whale songs', *Nature*, vol. 408, 30 November 2000, p. 537.

'Onomatopoeic list soberly . . . whoomp, growl, ratchet.' D. Cato, 'Songs of Humpback whales: the Australian perspective', and A. Mednis, 'An acoustic analysis of the 1988 song of the Humpback whale, *Megaptera novaeangliae*, off Eastern Australia', *Memoirs of the Queensland Museum*, vol. 30, 1990–91, Brisbane, pp. 277–90, and pp. 323–32.

p. 249 'The number of . . . man-made crisis.' R. Payne and S. McVay, 'Songs of Humpback whales', in *Science*, vol. 173, no. 3997, 13 August 1971, p. 585.

'The scientists told . . . is not extinct'. S. Blokhin et al., 'On the Korean-Okhotsk population of Gray whales', *Report of the IWC 1984*, quoted in D. Russell, *Eye of the whale*, Simon & Schuster, New York, 2001. p. 430.

p. 250 'Years of effort . . . Japanese fishing nets.' *Report of the Scientific Committee*, IWC, Cambridge, 13 June 2006, p. 43.

'Plastics were silent . . . in its stomach.' M. Short, 'A submission to the Senate Inquiry into the Plastic Bags (Minimisation of Usage) Eradication Fund Bill 2002', Australian Parliament, Canberra, 2002.

'around 200 Minkes . . . meat for cash.' C. Baker, *A protected area of Korea's coastal whales*, workshop announcement, University of Auckland, School of Biological Sciences, 2005.

'There is a . . . this depleted population.' *Report of the Scientific Committee*, IWC/58/Rep 1, IWC, Cambridge, 13 June 2006, p. 43.

'At best there . . . of another's breach.' R. McCauley et al., 'Marine seismic surveys—a study of environmental implications', in *APPEA Journal*, Canberra, 2000, p. 692.

'At worst, airgun . . . are too close.' M. Jasny, 'Sounding the depths II, the rising toll of sonar, shipping and industrial ocean noise on marine life', Natural Resources Defence Council, November 2005, p. 30.

pp. 250–51 'Scientists at Sakhalin . . . before their migration.' R. Brownell et al., 'Sakhalin Gray whales—concerns regarding the 2001 Exxon Neftegas seismic surveys', Letter to V.Y. Ilyashenko, Ministry of Natural Rescorces, Moscow, 1 September 2001.

p. 251 'Toxic anti-fouling . . . damage cetacean hearing.' F. Ariese et al., 'Butylin and phenylton-compounds in liver and blubber of *Physeter macrocephalus* stranded in the Netherlands and Denmark', *IVM report W98-04*, Free University, Amsterdam; and L. Song et al., 'On membrane motor activity and chloride flux in the outer hair cell: lessons learned from the environmental toxin, Tributyltin', *Biophysical Journal*, 88: 2350–62 (2005).

'Meanwhile commercial shipping . . . doubles the volume.' P. Tyack, ed., 'Research Program to Evaluate Effects of Manmade Noise on Marine Mammals in the Ligurian Sea', ACCOBAMS, Istanbul, 24 October 2003, p. 3.

'If a population . . . can be profound.' D. Laist et al., 'Collisions between ships and whales', *Marine Mammal Science*, 17(1), Society for Marine Mammalogy, 2001, p. 58.

'A range of . . . convincing and overwhelming.' Jasny, *Sounding the depths II*, p. v.

'The Sakhalin consortium . . . dangers for Grays.' 'Sakhalin whale reporturges prudence', news release, *Report of the Independent Scientific Review Panel*, IUCN, Gland, Switzerland, 16 February 2005.

pp. 251–52 'Global warming is . . . serious upset appeared.' 'Summary for policymakers', *A Report of Working Group 1 of the Intergovernmental Panel on Climate Change*, IPCC Geneva, 2001, p. 4.

p. 252 'In 1999, scientists . . . increased water temperatures.' B. Le Boeuf et al., 'High Gray whale mortality and low recruitment in 1999: potential causes and implications', *Journal of Cetacean Research and Management*, 2(2): 85–99, 2000.

'For once, whaling . . . the mid 1970s.' W. de la Mare, 'Abrupt mid twentieth century decline in Antarctic sea ice extent from whaling records', in *Nature*, vol. 389, 4 September 1997, p. 57.

'In the satellite . . . predators like whales.' A. Atkinson et al., 'Long term decline in Antarctic krill stock and increase in salps within the Southern Ocean, *Nature*, vol. 432, 3 November 2004, p. 100.

'These are dangers . . . will disappear entirely.' 'Climate change 2007: The physical science basis', *Summary for policymakers*, IPCC, Geneva, 5 February 2007.

p. 253 'The conclusion reached . . . may be inevitable.' W.C.G. Burns, 'From the harpoon to the heat: climate change and the International Whaling Commission in the 21st century', *Georgetown International Environmental Law Review*, Washington, Winter 2001, p. 8.

'For its part . . . Southern Bluefin tuna.' 'Japan pushed whaling as consumers' appetite fades,' E. Lies, Reuters, 11 February 2007; and 'Fishing industry statistics', Ministry of Agriculture, Fisheries and Forestry, Japan, 2006, <www.maff.gp.jp/www/info/bunrui/bun06.html> [7 February, 2007].

'The Prime Minister . . . day it would', D. McNeill, 'Resentments sustain a moribund meat trade.' *The Japan Times*, 11 February 2007.

EPILOGUE

p. 256 'He led the U.S. . . . whaling in 2004.' Associated Press 'U.S. Explains Commercial Whaling Position,' *Washington Post*, 22 July 2004.

'At the rescheduled . . . violent environmental terrorists.' H. Tabuchi, Associated Press, *Washington Post*, 19 November 2007.

p. 257 'Slaughtering whales is not scientific . . . it's unnecessary.' P. Garrett, Joint Press Conference with Foreign Minister Stephen Smith, Parliament House, Canberra. <http://www.foreignminister.gov.au/transcripts/2007/071219-ds.htm>

'Out of the . . . next IWC meeting.' Reuters "Japan seen halting humpback whale hunt," Tokyo, 19 December 2007. <http://uk.reuters.com/article/worldNews/idUKT17714420071219>

p. 258 'Back in my . . . settles over Asia.' Ambassador Schieffer Addresses Japan National Press Club. 24 October 2007. <http://tokyo.usembassy.gov/e/p/tp–20071024–76.html>

'He said Hogarth . . . a different nature.' Press Conference by Minister for Foreign Affairs Masahiko Koumura, Friday, 21 December 2007, 6:35 p.m. <http://www.mofa.go.jp/announce/fm_press/2007/12/1221-2.html>

p. 259 'This move can . . . burdened the IWC for many years.' Japan Agrees to Suspend its Hunt of Humpback Whales," NOAA media statement, 21 December 2007. <http://www.noaanews.gov/stories2007/20071221_humpback.html>

INDEX

INDEX